STORIES OF ADOLESCENCE, COUNSELLING AND ENGLISH STATE SCHOOLS

Spanning from the end of the Second World War to the present day, this book discusses theories of adolescent development and case studies of child-centredness from novels, television and film to interrogate English secondary state schools' approaches to the 'good' development of their students.

The author weaves discussion of the development of schools-based counselling, beginning in the 1960s, to critically engage with the English state school approach to supporting the mental health of adolescents. This book teases out what is embedded in the idea of 'child-centredness' and how the child-centred teacher or counsellor is variously cast as the rotten core or virtuous centre of the English state secondary school. Chapters engage with political debates against various historical backdrops, such as contemporary discussion around the role of social media and technology in children's mental health. Readers will be encouraged to reflect on the ever-changing perspectives surrounding student development, child-centredness and mental health within education and how this may influence their own practice.

A humorous yet informative exploration of child-centredness within the intersection of education and therapy, this book is essential reading for school counsellors, therapists working with children and young people, secondary school teachers, pastoral staff and policy makers within education and mental health.

Angela Keane is a BACP-accredited counsellor and psychotherapist who works with adults and adolescents. She has been involved in state secondary schools as a governor, counsellor, parent and pupil. Earlier in her career she was a lecturer in English Literature at a number of universities.

STORIES OF ADOLESCENCE, COUNSELLING AND ENGLISH STATE SCHOOLS

From *To Sir, with Love* to *Waterloo Road*

Angela Keane

Routledge
Taylor & Francis Group
LONDON AND NEW YORK

Designed cover image: Getty Images

First published 2026
by Routledge
4 Park Square, Milton Park, Abingdon, Oxon OX14 4RN

and by Routledge
605 Third Avenue, New York, NY 10158

Routledge is an imprint of the Taylor & Francis Group, an informa business

British Library Cataloguing-in-Publication Data
A catalogue record for this book is available from the British Library

ISBN: 9781041201168 (hbk)
ISBN: 9781041201151 (pbk)
ISBN: 9781003715122 (ebk)

DOI: 10.4324/9781003715122

Typeset in Times New Roman
by codeMantra

In memory of Mary Keane, mam to six of us and unsung heroine in each of our school stories.

CONTENTS

ACKNOWLEDGEMENTS

This book started as a question on social media: what stories about English state schools have you seen or read? The responses set me off on this 'journey' from the 1950s to the present. Thank you to Helene Herrington for Jilly Cooper's *Wicked!*, John McLeod for Beryl Gilroy's *Black Teacher*, Joanna Midgley for Zoe Heller's *Notes on a Scandal* and Laura Tisdall for the secondary modern stories. Along the way, I've collected the school stories of friends, family, clients and colleagues which have taken me through the gates, into the playgrounds and classrooms of many English state secondary schools. Some are represented directly here in short narratives: thanks to Viven Jones and Valerie Cheetham for the story of their father, John Cheetham; to Pat Smith and Bridget Fitzpatrick for the story of their husband and dad, John Smith; to Patrick Keane, Eileen Larkin and Susan Elston, my siblings who shared their own stories. Thanks to my nieces, Rebecca Metcalfe, Jacquelyn Pearse, Emily Keane and Helena Keane, who brought to life in vivid detail St Martin's in Billingham, the school we all attended between the 1980s and the 2010s. For the memories of my late niece Kathryn Keane, who was also a pupil at St Martin's in the 1990s, thanks to her dad, Patrick and cousins, Rebecca and Jacquelyn. Thanks to my parents Martin and Mary Keane who endured their own school stories but ensured their six children had better times. My three children, Sadie Jones, Alfie Jones and Iris Jones, generously allowed me to share their experience of education during the COVID pandemic. Their experiences at high school are also weaved into the later stages of this book.

As a school governor and school counsellor I have had the privilege to talk to many staff and high school students, whose perspectives have challenged and reinforced my own views on English state education. David Pilkington and Andy Park spoke to me at length about their long careers in schools and brought education policy and politics to life. Conversations with other teachers, especially Christian

Harris, Helene and Stuart Herrington, Juliette Serle and former teachers turned therapists Jan Artingsall and Amanda Phillips have taught me about the pressures and the joys of the job. Clients have given me an understanding of what school feels like when life is difficult, when school is a sideshow not the main event of getting through the day. Thank you for your trust in me. Thanks to my supervisors Jan Artingsall and Dianne Radford for their attention and care for me and my clients and their interest in this project. To my counselling colleagues and friends Billie Andrews and Donna Sullivan, thank you for sharing the highs and lows of our niche profession!

To my lovely editor Lauren Redhead, who has supported this book since I sent her an unsolicited proposal, thank you. You have been upbeat, direct and enthusiastic. To the editorial team at Routledge, thank you for weeding out the errors and inconsistencies. Thanks to everyone who read chapters as I was pulling them together: Susan Elston, Bridget Fitzpatrick, Christian Harris, Vivien Jones, Eddie Jones, Sadie Jones, Alfie Jones, Iris Jones, Patrick Keane, Emily Keane, Helena Keane, Eileen Larkin, Andy Park and Dave Pilkington.

To the school storytellers, thank you for keeping our teenagers and our education system in the national conversation. It is the novelists, film directors, TV producers, documentary producers, writers and performers who capture the parts of school life that policymakers pay attention to.

Finally, endless gratitude to the little tribe who have tolerated me talking about education policy, watching endless reruns of *Waterloo Road* and only really paying attention when they're telling me about school life: our wonderful children Sadie, Alfie and Iris Jones. My pride in you has nothing to do with your GCSE results (though well done on those) but so much to do with the fabulous people you've grown to be. To my partner Eddie Jones, alumni of Ponteland County High School; had we shared a school playground, I'd have walked round it with you to avoid those awkward lunchtimes. With love to you and thanks for, well, everything.

Foundations

INTRODUCTION

Adolescence in the state school story

Beginnings

> In September 1977, aged 11 years and 11 months, decked out in grey skirt and jumper, blue and gold tie, I got off the bus at St Martin's Roman Catholic Comprehensive School in Billingham. There was no gate, just a path through an expanse of playing fields yielding to a collection of 1960s glass, aluminium and concrete boxes which had formerly been home to a boys' secondary modern.
>
> There had been no introduction, no 'transitional activities' to soften the landing or to explain the task ahead. Where was my guide? I turned the mission into survival, became the indispensable helper to my far more desirable friends (or so they seemed to me). I avoided the terrors of PE and collected O-levels like they were magic beans. In the subsequent five years I had managed not to displease the Catholic Church (the opportunity did not arise) and to please my English and History teachers. After my last exam (Chemistry, Grade C) I got back on the bus in grey skirt, the privileged navy jumper of the third, fourth and fifth year, and blue and gold tie. I was now aged 16 years and 8 months, with a body that seemed to me far inferior to the straightforward one I had arrived with. I had 'gone through' puberty and arrived in adolescence with the guidance of a Catholic Morality syllabus (Grade A) and two Biologies (General and Human, C and B). No map, no mission.

In February 1978, the caretaker Mr Garfield opens the gates to Grange Hill High School, a brick building with waxed corridors which has the look of a former grammar school. Benny Green tentatively walks through the gates, not dressed in school uniform and clutching a trademark football. Alan and David call for Tucker,

DOI: 10.4324/9781003715122-2

and Mrs Jenkins neatens her son's tie before he scarpers to the bus stop with his sidekicks. In her kitchen Trisha Yates mourns having to swap her tights and heels for white socks and sensible soles. Justin Bennett is chauffeured in his dad's car, while Judy Preston is chaperoned by her mum. Justin and Judy, it seems, are not where they expected to be on the first day of secondary school and are suffering the indignity of educational downward mobility. By the end of his fifth year, Tucker, adorned in leather jacket, still with Alan as his loyal friend, and Trisha, sporting the coolest fringe of 1982, have accrued heroic status. Their final task is to oversee a satirical end-of-term revue, a world upside down skit to mark their passage to adult life, which shows they are comfortable with peers and more powerful than the teachers.

My school story and Tucker and Trisha's share the structure of a comprehensive school and a time period, as the country lurched from a Labour administration which had overseen strikes and power cuts to the shock of Thatcherism. It was the transition from post-war optimism that saw investment in state education and the building of the broader 'welfare state' to a period in which self-reliance and market forces were in the ascendant.

While I was preoccupied with blending in, not getting into trouble and having the right shoes, my television peers at Grange Hill played out fights for democracy and social justice while negotiating friendship, accelerated physical, emotional and neurological growth and PE lessons with Mr Baxter. We were all 'doing' adolescence.

Attachments

I cast off the tie and jumper once I left St Martin's, but I have kept a tribal attachment to the place and to comprehensive schools in general, a fellow feeling when someone I meet reveals they went to 'a comp'. This didn't happen very often when I worked as an academic, which probably heightened my idealisation and sense of belonging to a place with which I actually had an ambivalent relationship. There were some less than optimal aspects of my secondary education. Comprehensives and the broader English state system are a mixed bag and have not served all their pupils, nor their teachers, well. The latest round of A-level results in August 2025 shows big regional discrepancies, with the northeast of England where I was 'schooled' faring least well. The annual kerfuffle about GCSE and A-level results, illustrated with images of happy, jumping girls, kickstarts the scramble to close the gap in attainment between inland cities and coastal towns, north and south, the affluent and the deprived. The examination system as it is, of course, means that around a third will never be a happy jumper; the gap can never close, it can only be rearranged.

Our three children 'did well' in our local comprehensive school, each of them excelling in subjects they have gone on to specialise in, including subjects which not all state schools offer to GCSE. We are a well-resourced family and were able to supplement the 'core offer' with additional sports and arts classes and use a language that got us heard when there were problems, as inevitably there are when teenagers collide with a system designed on averages not particulars.

In the hope of using my voice for children other than my own, I have taken my 'sharp-elbowed' status into school governance and extended my private counselling practice, where I work with adolescents and adults, to include occasional stints as a school counsellor. Again, these experiences, which begin with my commitment to the idea of state education, often leave me less certain of the reality as it is. Governance reveals a system that does not serve enough children in it. It also gives those who, like me, are not tasked with teaching an insight into the extraordinary demands of the job of running a school.

As a counsellor I have met some wonderful teenagers from a range of backgrounds, for whom 'school' reflects their sense of inadequacy, and who defend against that mirror by acting out, turning inward or avoiding it altogether. For many others, school is where they want and need to be, equipped as they are cognitively and emotionally for the complexity of the environment. Most of us, I suspect, were and are somewhere in between these poles. Counselling adolescents in school is often just about being a reliable, stable adult who can bear silence, does not expect young clients to express emotion directly or in perfectly formed sentences and can tolerate the unpredictability of a school day. For most adolescents, school storms arrive and attuned adults, including but not only counsellors, can offer a steadying hand while they pass. For others, storms are followed by tsunamis, adults lose their grip and teenagers are swept away from school entirely. The rising numbers of permanent exclusions in state primary and secondary schools suggest those steadying hands are needed more and offered less readily.

School counselling

Part of my motivation to write this book was to find out more about the history of school counsellors and I discovered that counsellors have never fully arrived in English secondary schools. They have never been embraced as fully funded or fully integrated members of school staff, unlike in Wales where counselling provision has been statutory since 2013. They have existed 'in principle' since 1965 when school counsellor training courses were launched for teachers with at least five years' experience. English school counselling emerged in the mid-1960s, not from the esoteric margins of psychoanalytic theory but from the same context as comprehensive schooling. As part of the provisions of the emerging welfare state, the 1944 Education Act launched technical, secondary modern and grammar schools to educate children of different 'aptitudes', based on a belief in children's innate and largely unchanging intelligence and potential. Comprehensive schools were the answer to the questions these schools raised. Eschewing selection at age 11, comprehensives were founded on the developmental belief that children had the potential to develop and the political belief that society needed to unravel the knot between social class and educational opportunity. School counsellors were introduced to navigate individual children through this complex system.

As an occasional school counsellor, I have often felt more like a principle than a reality. I have lurked in 'confidential' places, waiting to see if my teenage client will make it out of Maths to spend 45 minutes with me. Unlike a classroom teacher, I have time and space to pay attention to what they're saying (or sometimes not saying at all), what they might mean, what's hard and what will help to make it easier. Experience and training in the 'norms' of adolescent development help me to distinguish the recurrent but nonetheless painful refrains (around academic achievement, friendship, rapid and intense shifts in mood, changes in family dynamics) from more intransigent difficulties that threaten their safety. Often, our relationship ends abruptly or never really starts, overtaken by the urgency of school demands or a crisis in the client's life that requires some other form of intervention. I have learned to approach every beginning as a potential ending.

I am sitting in a windowless room, waiting for Year 9 pupil Emmy. She has been referred to me by the safeguarding team who are aware that she has lost a lot of weight in a short amount of time. She has been cutting her arms, she has a difficult relationship with her mum and she may be at risk of being sent out of the country against her will to live with extended family. After three sessions, she's starting to relax in my company. This time, Emmy doesn't arrive. The safeguarding team explain that a jewelled penknife was found in her school bag the day before (it was searched following a verbal threat from Emmy to another girl) and she was excluded that day. I didn't find out what happened next to Emmy. She had been referred to me as a vulnerable child, subject to concern and empathy; she was withdrawn as a potential perpetrator of violence. Safeguarding policy could only write her character in binary form.

What is adolescence?

The subjects of counselling at secondary level are the wonderful, mercurial people we know as 'adolescents'. Derived from the Latin 'adolescere' (to grow into maturity), the term adolescence first appeared in English written form in the Middle Ages. The boundary between childhood and adolescence seems consistently to start with the physiological onset of puberty, though in some cultures and contexts it is marked by a ritualised event. Its ending, the transition between adolescence and adulthood, is much more mobile across time, place and context. Literary historian Sally Shuttleworth, in a book which examines a period in the nineteenth century when the 'inner workings of the child became for the first time an explicit object of study', notes that the idea of childhood at this time was 'elastic' enough to encompass adolescence and that adolescence itself continued into the twenties

(Shuttleworth, 2010, p.2). The childhoods in question were middle and upper class, from households where increased levels of education meant prolonged separation from the adult demands of work or domesticity. Working-class childhood ended with the start of labouring or reproductive capacity and was identified more with the ability of the body than with the mind. In a sense, then, as defined by emerging developmental psychology of this period and the literature which shared its fear of and fascination with the child mind, adolescence was itself an exclusively middle- and upper-class phenomenon, as those were the subjects whose inner worlds were available for scrutiny.

The American psychologist and professor of pedagogy G. Stanley Hall is credited with the invention of the modern 'myth' of adolescence, as Patricia Meyer Spacks referred to it in her study of literary representations of adolescent characters (Spacks, 1981). In an enormous study which considers adolescence in a vast range of contexts, Hall shifts between admiration for the potential of 'the adolescent' and the denigration of their pathological instability of emotion, their risk taking and self-absorption (Hall, 1904). Hall's study is less class-bound than those of British nineteenth-century observers. Although Hall is critical of the adolescents of his time and place (early twentieth-century America), he also captures the begrudging respect and admiration for adolescent energy and rebelliousness that appears more strongly in twentieth-century representations of 'youth'. If earlier representations had rewarded youthful submission to adult authority and social conformity, Spacks demonstrates that the twentieth century began to mythologise the adolescent's drive for self-fulfilment and 'anti-social' behaviour, even as it complained about and feared it.

Both Shuttleworth and Spacks illustrate that adolescence is less a scientifically observable biological period, than a shifting, variable projection, to be looked back upon wistfully, reined in or reviled. It is, as John and Virginia Demos saw it, an idea masquerading as a fact (Demos, 1969, p.632). Such work makes a case that particular ideas about adolescence were developed both in psychological and medical discourse and in literary texts, particularly memoir and the coming-of-age novel (the bildungsroman). From Samuel Richardson's *Pamela* to Muriel Sparks' *The Prime of Miss Jean Brodie*, from moralising conduct guides to the psychological observations of Erik Erikson, explorations of adolescence hold together tensions between generations, between internal and external experience, group authority and individual vulnerability.

The psychological invention of working-class adolescence

In part, this book explores representations of adolescence from the 1950s in England, a point at which psychological interest in the young (from infants to the young in their mid-twenties) intensified. These subjects were no longer exclusively middle or upper class. The attention for psychologists and psychiatrists had extended, during the Second World War, to evacuees, orphans and the patients of the child guidance clinics (the forerunner of Child and Adolescent Mental Health Services (CAMHS)). The evacuees, the orphans or the patients were treated as vulnerable subjects of special concern for mental health professionals. But the potential to explore or pronounce upon the inner and outer worlds of many adolescents was also presenting itself in the assembly halls, corridors and classrooms of post-war state secondary schools. The extension of the educational franchise from 1944 meant that more children, of all social backgrounds, were in school for longer. If we accept that adolescence loosely denotes a period after physical childhood and before the onset of adult economic and social responsibility, then more adolescents, including working-class adolescents, were created by the 1944 Education Act. The explicit purpose of post-war schooling was to offer knowledge and skills to those who would rebuild the nation, but the side effect of being in school meant that more adolescents were available for the scrutiny, consternation and fascination of adult observers. Attention could now be given to the minds of working-class adolescents, subject to the same wistful and pathologising projections as their middle- and upper-class peers, in education policy, pedagogy and developmental psychology, which informed and reflected the secondary school classroom.

The growth of 'mass media', cinema, television, comic strips and popular fiction provided a new diversity of representation, for and of working-class adolescents. Secondary school becomes a setting for fiction which plays out the fears and fantasies about the losses of war and the hopes for the future and projects those losses and hopes onto the minds and bodies of the adolescents within the classroom.

In the secondary modern novels of the 1950s, by writers like Edward Blishen, Michael Croft and E.R. Braithwaite, there is traffic of adolescent boys, and occasionally girls, between school, the child guidance clinic and the juvenile court. This cohort of 'troubled' youths is a counterpoint to the young men educated in grammar schools, many of whom have served in the recent war, who teach them. Some of these teachers are represented in terms reminiscent of Richard Hoggart's description of 'the uprooted and anxious' boys like him who gained scholarships to grammar schools before the war (Hoggart, 1958). Hoggart's scholarship boys are at odds with their working-class home life, more comfortable in the women's world of their mothers than the men's world of their fathers and brothers; they are anxious to 'do well' (p.296). According to Hoggart, the currency with which the scholarship boy has bought himself a place in the grammar school is his 'brains' and his school masters were the cashiers in 'the new world of brain-currency' (p.296). Uneasy with his own father, the scholarship boy makes a 'father figure of his form-master' (p.297). As teachers in the secondary modern novels, such young men offer themselves as father figures but struggle with charges who are indifferent to the currency of brains.

The wayward youth, who rejects the promise of the new education offered to him in the secondary modern, and the anxious, feminised boy, over-invested in the grammar school who grows into the modern teacher, are two variants of the working-class adolescents in the post-war education landscape. The young of the working class are now represented as more than bodies, but their minds are not seen to be settled. This mental dis-ease is sometimes represented empathically; at others it comes from an authorial discomfort with the potential proximity of working- and middle-class adolescents in secondary education. This unease turns to something more visceral in some quarters when, with the advent of the comprehensive school in the 1960s, the potential proximity between 'all kinds' of adolescents of different provenance becomes a widespread possibility. This discomfort is not just from those who would prefer academic selection to be preserved. It is also there in stories and commentary of the political left, which fears that something will be lost when the working-class adolescent aspires to the life of their middle-class peers.

Historian Carolyn Steedman captures this tension in her autobiographical social history, *Landscape for a Good Woman*, where she revises Hoggart's typology of the working-class northern childhood (Steedman, 1986). Her mother was one of many who 'waited and wanted', who desired the spoils of consumerism, a desire which is invisible to social history and inimical to a left-wing narrative which privileges solidarity over the self, community over the individual, as though they cannot be held together. As the historian Sally Alexander writes in an essay about the impact of psychotherapy on the developing welfare state (including state schools) in mid-twentieth-century Britain, 'history learns from psychoanalysis and then forgets what it learned, as if the unconscious – the deep and hidden parts of our selves – mental lives of ordinary people are inaccessible or difficult to bear in mind when writing historical narrative' (Alexander and Taylor, 2012, p.149). History from and of the inside is not, it seems, historical to some and the contradictory interior lives of working-class people are not convenient to some strands of social history.

Steedman's narrative puts working-class women into a story that has been dominated by stories of men. In the earlier sections of this book, the story I tell is also of men, male teachers, psychotherapists and the predominantly male adolescent characters in the school stories. Stories of women and girls appear more in later chapters. The early chapters tell the dominant story of the male therapists in whose image I was trained (Bowlby, Winnicott, Rogers) and the male novelists, dramatists and screenwriters who recalled their time as teachers from the 1950s to the 1980s. Others have focused on the women from the earlier period, who shaped mid-twentieth-century British psychotherapy and those who taught and were taught in twentieth-century state secondary schools (Oram, 1996; Wolf and Antonis, 2023). Perhaps I have fallen into the trap of telling the story of class before the story of sex and gender, but I hope I have woven these stories together in ways which recognise that there are others still to tell.

In stories about secondary moderns, grammars, comprehensives and their current variants, academies, the emerging desires of working-class adolescents (for friendship, belonging, entertainment, futures better than the present) are pitched against the official purpose of the school and the education system (knowledge, skills, future employability). Our formal discourse about schools addresses desire only to pathologise it. Desire is what distracts from success, at least as far as that is measured in educational outcomes.

Telling the story

Schools are saturated in ideas about child development and human relationships, ideas which are drawn from psychology and psychotherapy. What is pedagogy but a means of engaging the internal world of those being 'educated'? Other than in the most utilitarian forms, such ideas are pushed to the margins of educational discourse at secondary level. The status of school counsellors illustrates this.

School counselling arrived out of the context in which children would no longer be 'selected' for a route through their secondary education, and when comprehensive schools would usher them towards their adolescence. Counsellors were proposed initially as guides through large organisations for those potentially ill-equipped to navigate them. While counsellors are not leading characters in the stories I explore in this book (though there are some notable appearances), it is *their* way of being, their interest in the internal world of the adolescent, that connects us, the readers and viewers, to the narratives. In the stories I have read and watched, I found some wonderful, some awful, but all interesting stories and insights into our popular culture's version of English state schools since the 1944 Education Act. In education policy, adolescence is shaped according to the assumptions of an incumbent government about what makes a good society (usually as a reaction against the last set of assumptions). Leaving ages, curricula and inspection criteria reveal the ending for which schools are to prepare their adolescent charges. Novels, films, TV series and documentaries about schools delight us (or at least me) because they reveal the forlorn rationality of such policy. They capture adolescents catatonic with boredom or uncontainable in their energy and adults whose most important skill is improvisation. Happy endings are rare and are certainly not signalled by an O-level or GCSE certificate. The drama lies elsewhere, in the gaps in the timetable.

Inclusive school structures, curricula and people who attend to the inner worlds of adolescents in schools have at various points been vilified for sacrificing knowledge and creating victims of the young. In the 1970s, the academic journal *The Critical Survey* serialised the Black Papers, pamphlets which railed against the dominance of so-called 'progressive' pedagogical ideas in schooling and represented it as a villainous combination of left-wing ideology and psychological nonsense (Cox and Dyson, 1969–77). In the early 2000s, critics balked at the so-called 'therapeutic turn' in education, what they saw as the 'dangerous' shift from the dissemination of knowledge in the classroom (teaching) to an emphasis on relationships and facilitation (learning) (Ecclestone and Hayes, 2008, 2019). Baroness Spielman has recently made similar remarks about an over-investment in emotional difficulty by schools since the pandemic (Eccles and Lintern, 2025). Not only would scholarship be undermined by such approaches, but adolescents would also be rendered helpless and anxious.

When Michael Gove became Education Secretary in 2010, his proposed reforms to the system seemed to be founded on a similar critique. Teaching from the front, assessment by examination and knowledge-filled curricula were back in favour. Schools would be motivated to succeed by a competitive marketplace of schools (academies) and stirred by the distant rumble of grammar school reintroduction, a 'promise' which is intoned like a traditionalist chorus. The villain of his story was 'the Blob', the left-wing education establishment of teachers, unions and local authorities who swallowed aspiration and excellence (Garner, 2014).

Doing the best for our children

The over-arching shape of the story I tell here is of the centring then the decentring of adolescence in English state education. It is, as many stories, a tale of three parts. It begins with post-war optimism in the power of the state to improve the lives of more and more children through schooling; at first, after the 1944 Education Act, through increased access to grammar schools and the establishment of secondary moderns and, briefly, technical schools, and eventually through non-selective, comprehensive schooling, all with the oversight of local education authorities, inspectors and trainers. A shadow falls in the late 1970s and 1980s, when increasing government distrust in local education authorities and in the outcomes and approaches of comprehensive schools led to the centralisation of many features of state education. This culminated in the arrival of the national curriculum and standard assessment tests after the 1988 Education Reform Act. In the 1990s, the establishment of the Office for Standards in Education (Ofsted) increased schools' 'accountability'. In the ongoing third act, state schools have been subject to the contradictory forces of centralisation and the idea of freedom through the education market. Despite moments where 'every child' mattered, the human relationship with the child/adolescent has been marginalised in favour of 'outcomes', which are the entry point to...what?

I have limited my attention to stories of English state schools, even though this means excluding stories like *Derry Girls*, *Gregory's Girl* and *In My Skin*. Scotland and Northern Ireland have separate education systems, and schools in Wales are required by statute to provide school-based counselling, unlike in England where there is no such obligation and the number of counsellors employed to work in English state secondaries is vague.

This book also tells a story of the ambivalent status that state schools have in English culture. Most people who were educated in England since the Second World War were taught in a state school. Unlike the NHS which, despite its current crisis in image and performance, has been largely a source of national pride, 'the education service' (a term which has been tried out but has never stuck) has never been held in such esteem. One reason for this, perhaps, is that we were all teenagers when we were 'consumers' of secondary education and adolescence rarely gives rise to celebrations of adult authority, the discipline of learning stuff and regurgitating it in a sports hall. Our memories of and relationship with state schools are refracted through that stage of our lives. This ambivalence is not just rooted in our personal histories, however. English cultural wariness about state schools is also tied up with our class system. To 'do the best' for our children is to work hard, save up (or use one's inherited wealth) and rescue them from descent into the local comprehensive by sending them to private school. There they will aspire, rise up or maintain the family's social status quo. There are children with additional needs for whom state provision is not enough or appropriate but that is not what is signalled in that much used phrase, 'doing our best' (Millar, 2018). Class sizes, facilities and rightness for a child's temperament or talents (honed through intensive tutoring) are the usual rationalisations for opting out of state provision. I have never heard anyone say out loud that they are opting for private education for their children because they do not want them to mix with children who are less affluent than them, who live in a less gentrified part of town or who may not have useful connections when they are older. But I do remember a parent of children at my local primary school who wondered aloud what his 11-year-old son would 'learn' from his then best friend if they carried on to the same state secondary school. He didn't take the risk of finding out.

Contemporary English fiction, the kind that is a conduit for middle-class taste and concerns, uses the state secondary school as shorthand for the socially other. In Meg Mason's much celebrated 2021 novel about 'a woman's struggle with mental health', the narrator Martha offers a description of her twin sister's educational fate, brought upon her by the financial impoverishment of their bohemian parents. Her sister Ingrid, who failed to get a scholarship at the private school, was enrolled in a 'free' high school which, Ingrid told people, 'offered female students two kinds of uniform … the normal one and the maternity one' (Mason, 2021, p.28). Parodic though Martha's casual denigration of state school students may be, there is an implied complicity with a readership who would wryly understand Ingrid's social misfortune. There are many such examples of fictional descriptions of state-educated children. What starts as a satirical jibe at the state school system turns into the othering of the 'class' of students educated there. Sebastian Faulks' novel, *A Week in December* (Faulks, 2009), for instance, celebrates the success and aspirational pluck of a London Tube driver with the auspicious name Jenni Fortune. She is set apart from her fellow workers as she likes to read a book alone at lunchtime. Jenni had also been set apart from her peers in a state school where reading had not been encouraged as 'the teachers had been too concerned with crowd control and the non-discriminatory management of the children to have much time for education as such' (Faulks, 2009, p.70).

The slippage between 'the system' – the public sector preoccupation with 'management', with equality and equity – and the badly behaved state school 'crowd' is casual yet deliberate. It is not that novelists have a responsibility simply to celebrate those educated at state schools, but there are class-based assumptions in these tropes that inform our broader cultural attitudes to state schools and (some) of the adolescents who attend them.

Types, plots and journeys

From the secondary modern stories of the 1950s to the academy tales of recent years, there are recurrent features that make up an English state school story. Outside the school gates, we meet an ingenue teacher with a drive to change lives. They first must win over the traditionalist overlords of the staff room and often the school caretaker, who is the gatekeeper of ancient school lore. Assistance comes from an attractive colleague or a sympathetic arts teacher while obstacles (sometimes literal obstacles like chairs and tables) are hurled across classrooms. Faceless bureaucrats, interfering governors and feckless or sharp-elbowed parents test the commitment of our heroic pedagogue, before they rise through the ranks to senior leadership or crash back through the school gate, burnt out, to take refuge in the private sector. The students are popular and gobby, geeky and bullied, sporty and powerful; all are seeking friendship, recognition and safety and a rare few have eyes on academic qualifications.

The recurrence of character 'types', narrative tropes and plot devices is the subject of the long history of narrative theory and debate about the 'purpose' and apparent 'universality' of features of storytelling. In the early twentieth century, the Russian folklorist Vladimir Propp (motivated in part by a desire to elevate the status of popular storytelling) identified the recurrent character types found in the folk or fairy tale (Propp, 1968). These include the hero, the villain, the donor (the magical agent who initiates the plot), the helper (who aids the hero), the princess, the dispatcher (who sends the hero to restore equilibrium) and the false hero. The Bulgarian intellectual Tzvetan Todorov characterised the recurrent pattern of events in stories as a five-part structure: the opening equilibrium (normality); the disruption; the recognition of disruption; the repair; the new equilibrium (Todorov, 1977). French anthropologist Claude Levi-Strauss distinguished between the syntagmatic structure (the sequence, the surface level of the story) and the paradigmatic structure (the pattern or the latent meaning of the story) (Levi-Strauss, 2001).

The mid-twentieth-century psychoanalyst Carl Jung explored the motifs (recurrent symbols) in religious stories, legends, myths and fairy tales. He found in them 'psychological' significance, but in a communal not a personal sense, famously described in his work on the 'collective unconscious' (Jung, 1991). For Jung, the personal unconscious is conscious material that has been forgotten or repressed by the individual; the collective unconscious has never been conscious experience. It is made up of 'hereditary' archetypes, 'definite forms in the psyche which seem to be present always and everywhere' (p.42) and found in story motifs. In 1949, Joseph Campbell was inspired in part by Jung to identify the 'universal' features of heroism, in mythology across cultures and history (Campbell, 1949). The features of the 'hero's journey' – the 'call to adventure', crossing the threshold to the unknown, the trials of the adventure, transformation and the return – have been adopted in narrative therapy, where the client is invited to engage with their challenges as aspects of a story and to reimagine or reframe them (White and Epston, 1990).

Several narrative theorists have taken Jung's and Campbell's ideas and run with them, including Christopher Booker, whose encyclopaedic 2004 study *Seven Basic Plots: Why We Tell Stories* finds that across time and space, archetypal plots recur and seem to exist because of our collective need for wholeness and resolution (Booker, 2004). Underpinning all seven plots (overcoming the monster, rags to riches, the quest, voyage and return, comedy, tragedy and rebirth) is a Jungian process of change in the protagonist (the persona) who must first confront then assimilate the dark qualities of the antagonist (the shadow). The outcome of all seven plots and their variants is a form of psychological completion.

Screenwriter John Yorke is sceptical of works like Booker's which attempt an overarching account of the structure and purpose of stories from a Jungian perspective. Yorke's *Into the Woods: How Stories Work and Why We Tell Them* focuses more on film and television and finds the purpose of storytelling to be multiple: to appease the human need for order, to satisfy the human tendency to look for causal links, to fulfil the need for opposites to exist and be reconciled, to connect us empathically to other humans and to bring our internal selves into line with the external world (Yorke, 2013).

These approaches to storytelling – its forms, structures, patterns and repeating echoes – have been instructive in my approach to 'the state school story', to understand their recurrent and diverse features and to consider their broader purpose. By 'purpose' I don't simply mean 'intention'; I mean what questions do they pose and answer, what need in us individually and in our culture do they satisfy?

Booker's typology of the 'rags to riches' and 'voyage and return' plots is discernible in the school story. The rags to riches plot is, in Booker's account, about rites of passage (innocence to experience, transformation through maturity or encountering and overcoming 'shadow' forces). Any story with adolescents at its centre will have elements of this plot, but as many school stories also follow the fortunes of inexperienced teachers who eventually earn their state school stripes, the rags to riches plot is often echoed in the progress of the adult protagonist. The 'voyage and return' plot is summarised as one in which a protagonist ventures away from the safety of home to encounter new places and people, only to return transformed (or not). Again, this is a plot that underpins the school story: the school is sometimes the safe home, sometimes the dark 'other place' and more often both. These 'journeys' are also internal, as characters develop, like Campbell's hero, or, as John Yorke has pointed out, stay resolutely unchanged, especially in the long-standing multiple series dramas.

When I was growing up, the school stories I enjoyed were about girls in private boarding schools, like Enid Blyton's *Malory Towers* and St Elmo's of *Bunty*'s *The Four Marys*. These places seemed so mythical they could just as plausibly have been populated by woodland creatures. I don't remember being bothered by the lack of representation of 'girls like me' (I don't think I classified myself as any particular type of girl). These were escapist fantasies, not a mirror to my experience. When Tucker Jenkins and Trisha Yates arrived in my living room in February 1978, I remember that *Grange Hill* became appointment television for me, but I wasn't conscious of feeling 'represented'. Trisha was no more like me than was St Elmo's Mary Radleigh ('Raddy'). However, she existed in a fictional environment that was based on schools like mine. As I'll suggest in a later chapter, *Grange Hill* is not an unqualified celebration of comprehensive schooling in the late 1970s. Its aim was to tell a story about the kinds of schools that most children went to from the point of view of children. *Grange Hill* reproduced the appeal of the boarding school tales in which children take centre stage and adults have walk-on parts, but with fewer midnight crumpets and more lunchtime protests.

Developing character

To the extent that characters in these stories develop, their development owes its shape to psychology and psychotherapy as well as to the history of fiction. Since Freud, developmental theory has found diverse ways to explain the internal changes we experience across our lifespan. As I will explore in Chapter 1, the theories themselves echo the recurring 'plots' of myth and story as they each propose an 'agent of change' (perhaps an internal 'libido', maternal attachment, family dynamics, the ecosystem of self, society and environment).

In schools, 'child development' is formally left behind after the primary stage or diverted to the watch of the school's additional extras, like counsellors or nurses, when something is 'going wrong'. Early years' practitioners measure a range of developmental milestones which are cast aside at the secondary stage in favour of 'learning behaviours' or just 'behaviour behaviours'. When schools invoke 'character', they use terms like resilience, grit and self-regulation, which all imply a child with an internal set of 'character skills' rather than a child developing in relation to others and their environment, including the teacher and the school.

'The school' (the building, the community of staff and students, the geographical location) is both a setting and a developmental marker, making the school story a social variant of the bildungsroman. Development in school stories is communal and individual. Long-term television dramas like *Grange Hill* and *Waterloo Road* depict many cohorts of pupils and staff and their plots cyclically revolve around 'issues' of teenage life, staff politics and school organisation. Novels and one-off dramas tend to sketch a shorter timescale but try to balance the 'human interest' of following a limited number of characters against the backdrop of a large system. The secondary modern school stories of the 1950s, for instance, are focalised through young, male teacher narrators and follow their 'development' from rookie to accomplished pedagogue. Later narratives, like Barry Hines's *The Blinder* (Hines, 1969) and *A Kestrel for a Knave* (Hines, 1999) or Alan Bleasdale's *Scully* (1984), focus on the lives of the pupils while staff are background extras in their dramas.

Development and social realism

The stories I explore in this book (from the 1950s to the present) are largely 'realist': the form of storytelling that became dominant from the nineteenth century to represent 'life as it is really lived' (Lay, 2002, p.5). Raymond Williams defined the realist text as secular (as opposed to mystical), grounded in the contemporary place and time in which it was produced, representing marginalised groups (principally the working class) and largely influenced by the political intent of the artist (Williams, 1974). There are, in fact, many forms of realism (Hallam and Marshment, 2000). *Social* realism is a particular form, associated with a rejection of 'mainstream' social norms and forms of representation and highlighting moments of social conflict. Predominantly associated with film, television drama and documentary, the production values of social realist texts are matched to their political intent with the use of local and untrained actors (as in Ken Loach's adaptation of Hines's book, *Kes* (Loach, 1969)). The social realist film uses actual locations rather than sets, and techniques that foreground 'authenticity' over 'artifice', quotidian detail over melodrama.

Social realist stories foreground class conflict and the human cost of political decisions and rarely resolve the difficulties that befall their characters. The same problems crop up cyclically, sometimes over decades in serial dramas, and happy endings are fleeting. Such is life, they seem to say. They are less 'rags to riches' than 'rags to riches to rags again'.

State schools, particularly secondary moderns and comprehensives, were claimed as 'social realist places' in stories from the 1960s to the late 1990s. The stories are embedded in particular times and places and often wrestle with or at least allude to contemporary shifts in education policy. The schools are conjured as working-class spaces (and celebrated or disparaged as such), even though the cohorts of most state schools are, and always have been, socially and economically mixed. They are not written as socially or individually transformative spaces: an opening credit of a caretaker scrubbing graffiti off school hoarding signals limits to opportunity and aspiration before he's even put his chamois down. Most of the stories try not to locate social limitation *in* individual students nor necessarily in the ambitions and intentions of their teachers but in 'the school system' which reproduces broader social inequalities. They are often portrayed as places of activity but not of change and rarely of progress.

Social realist conventions and values include resistance of social norms, collectivism versus individualism, sociological truth versus their psychological truth (Lay, 2002). Individual psychology, domesticity, family and other aspects of cultural identity are subordinate to or in the service of the depiction of social conflict and the telling of 'real working-class experience'. Critical arguments have turned on whether narratives which focus on desire for individual escape from, for instance, the post-industrial town (as in the 'New Wave' films of the 1950s and 1960s) are as 'real' as those which dramatise collective solidarity (such as in the television dramas produced and directed by Tony Garnett and Ken Loach in the 1960s and 1970s). As critics Hallam and Marshment have illustrated, the split between the personal and the political, the individual and the collective, the sociological and the psychological in social realism does not bear up to scrutiny (Hallam and Marshment, 2000). Even the stories which most steadfastly champion political collectivity do so through the depiction of personal relationships and by engaging the emotions as well as the understanding of the viewer. This is illustrated again in Loach's *Kes*, in which a critique of a school system which offers little to many of its pupils sits behind the story of Billy's final days at school and his potential emotional escape through his relationship with his kestrel.

The assumption that state school stories *should* be told according to the conventions of social realism was revealed recently in a review of Netflix's *Sex Education* when a perplexed critic from *The Independent* criticised the first season for not evoking 'a distinctive time and place' (Power, 2019). Set in the ambiguously located Moordale High and Cavendish Sixth Form College (it was filmed in Wales, but the characters have a variety of English accents), the drama looks more to an American or Australian high school tradition of sports jocks and quiz team geeks than to its English predecessors. It is an understatement to say that it foregrounds 'identity' over issues of class. It is, according to its creator Laurie Nunn, 'aspirational' in its narrative arc in a way that is distinctly un-English, a 'utopia' rather than a realist representation of an English state school (Nicholson, 2020). As *Sex Education* illustrates, state school stories from the turn of the twenty-first century onwards have a looser relationship with social realism.

Education for all

Tensions between the representation of the individual and the collective in social realism are also endemic in the idea of the state school. Since 1944, education policy has tried to address the problem of 'education for all' with a range of approaches laid out in white papers and subsequent legislation: selective schools and nonselective schools, with an academic or vocational emphasis; local or centralised accountability and inspection regimes; 'free' or prescribed curricula; ever-changing assessment methods for different 'aptitudes'; an emphasis on learning and an emphasis on teaching. The degree of political trust in the teaching profession can be charted with the frequency and prescriptive detail of each intervention.

This history has been captured and dramatised from the 1950s secondary modern stories (*Roaring Boys* (Blishen, 1977), *Spare the Rod* (Croft, 1954), *To Sir, With Love* (Braithwaite, 2005)) to the academy stories of the 2010s (*Waterloo Road* and *Ackley Bridge*). Many school stories are written by former teachers whose familiarity with the nuances of policy and practice lends them the 'authenticity' prized in social realism. The authentic elements of fiction are inevitably bedded in formal convention just as documentaries about 'real' schools, like Channel 4's *Educating* series, rely on tropes drawn from the tradition of the fictional school story. The broader cultural conversation about state schooling – in politics and the media – is littered with tropes familiar from the fiction.

Because I was born in 1965 and am (only just) part of what we have learned to call Generation X, I engage with stories in analogue form, as I did in my childhood and adolescence of the 1970s. Novels in physical form, chapter by chapter, television series and comic strips in weekly instalments, film at the cinema. Even though I can now stream everything all at once, I still think chronologically and in a linear fashion. The generations who have recently left or are moving through secondary school (Z and Alpha) have a different relationship with storytelling, comfortable with simultaneous content, multiple media platforms and networks of communication. This simultaneity is shaping their sense of self, other, belonging and place (including their relationship with school) in ways that are beyond my understanding and the scope of this book. Just to say, however, that if those of us brought up in the analogue world simply pathologise the world of the 'digital natives', we miss new forms of storytelling, subjectivity and society that are emerging while we're looking for the remote control.

Psychologising social history and historicising psychology

Sex Education puts a therapist, albeit a 16-year-old ventriloquising his sex therapist mother's wisdom to his peers, at the centre of its narrative. Therapists, certainly sex therapists, do not 'belong' in the social realist story just as 'psychology' does not seem to belong in social history. Most of the stories I have explored cast counsellors, therapists and psychologists as marginal, comical or vaguely mystical figures. The secondary modern stories refer to new 'crank' psychological theory embraced by the least effective teachers. *Carry on Teacher* (1959) is devoted to the chaos generated by the visit of a self-regarding child psychiatrist, Alistair Grigg, played by Leslie Phillips in full smooth, upper-class pomp. At the same time, the stories dramatise teacher-student relationships and family dynamics in terms drawn directly from contemporary psychology and the work of psychotherapists like Donald Winnicott. The 'social realist' classic *Kes* – determinedly about the real life of a child from a pit village – is imbued with Romantic ideas about the natural child and their freedom to learn, popularised by the American teacher and humanist therapist Carl Rogers and looking back to Rousseau and British Romanticism, which idealised childhood subjectivity.

As Mathew Thomson argued in his book *Psychological Subjects*, the post-war period saw the 'grass roots' pragmatic adoption of psychological theory in mainstream schools (Thomson, 2006). While psychoanalysis, derived from Freudian theory, was sidelined as too elitist, sexualised and potentially dangerous to have an explicit part in school life (though of course its ideas are there at a subliminal level), more humanistic approaches to the development of 'whole children' have been very much part of the mainstream school and its stories since the 1940s. When school counsellors first arrived in a specialised capacity after university training courses were launched in 1965, they were tasked with navigating adolescents through large and complex schools, extended leaving ages and fears of delinquency which were, in some quarters, attributed to the longer period that teenagers were 'held' in school. They were also permitted to enter their inner worlds, to the discomfort of some who held and still hold the view that schooling is exclusively for the acquisition of knowledge about and skills for use in the external world.

Counsellors have come and gone from English mainstream state schools, depending on funds and fashions. Currently 'the whole child' is drowning in attainment targets and, despite the popular awareness of the impact of adverse childhood experiences (ACES) on child development and the saturation of our culture with the language of trauma and anxiety, psychological behaviourism is the order of the day as a way of managing distress in schools. Being a benign but attuned adult presence in a school seems like a radical act of subversion.

The following chapters explore how we got here, tracing the history of school counselling in state schools and the theories on which the developing practice was based. This history is woven into chapters which explore state school stories (in fiction and nonfiction) and bring together the social and psychological histories of the English 'comp' and its classmates, the secondary modern, the grammar and the academy. Social realism has given way to more 'aspirational' and utopian narratives in which identity is more significant than class and individual psychology is more compelling than social critique.

In practice, is the idea of the adolescent in education policy so different now from those imagined in the 1950s, when 11-year-olds were selected for vocational or academic routes through the educational maze? In the last 80 years, how much have ideas changed about who state secondary school children are, what barriers they face and what opens growth and opportunity? While the terms of the conversation about the vulnerability or resilience of adolescent mental health and the role of state schools in its 'maintenance' have changed, this book illustrates that it's been a long-standing and fractious argument.

Structure and themes

This book starts with a moment in my own secondary school story. Subsequent chapters include the school stories of family, friends, colleagues and clients across the decades, though I have used pseudonyms for the real schools they attended or worked in. Alongside these anecdotes are my readings of educational policy, developmental theory, school counselling texts and works of fiction. In my work as a therapist, the family is usually privileged as the system of origin, of relational patterns, attachment systems, bonds and ruptures. We make family maps and intergenerational webs to make sense of present predicaments. The school system may be secondary in the story of our individual development, but as I found in the conversations that inform this book, its impact is just as strongly felt. Our school stories don't just 'place' us socially, they also shape both us and the society in which we try to coexist.

In this introduction I have summarised features of narrative theory to find some common, foundational features of 'the state school story' and consider the more particular relationship between the state school story and social realism. Storytelling is a means of human connection. Like school counsellors, tellers of the school story find the human in the system and help us to find our way through it.

This next chapter adds to this foundation and outlines a selection of theories of adolescent development and their influence on school counselling. It tells a story of the shift from post-war human interrelatedness in Bowlby, Winnicott and Rogers to recent, almost 'transhuman' developmental process between adolescent and technology. This shift is presented apocalyptically in Jonathan Haidt's *The Anxious Generation: How the Great Rewiring of Childhood Is Causing an Epidemic of Mental Illness* (Haidt, 2024) and with more optimistic agency in books like Nicole Vignola's *Rewire: Break the Cycle, Alter Your Thoughts and Create Lasting Change* (Vignola, 2024). The chapter goes on to provide a summary of the development of school counselling in English state schools and the significance of its representation in popular culture.

The rest of the book is structured in three chronological parts. The structure echoes the 'developmental' story of the first chapter, in that it gradually broadens its focus from theories about infancy, to childhood, adolescence, family systems, 'ecological systems' and finally to a more atomised sense of development with a focus on the impact of trauma on identity. Each chapter engages with a therapeutic term (like holding, shame, trauma) some of which have become so familiar that they have lost the impact of their original usage. By reading the school stories through these therapeutic concepts I hope to recapture their value and suggest ways of thinking about our relationships with the adolescents in our lives, including our own adolescent 'parts', which go beyond their chronological ages or Key Stage.

Part One, 'Rebuilding', is organised around post-war education policy that shaped English secondary state schooling and ideas about adolescence and adolescent development. These ideas were part of a fairly optimistic, 'humanist' response to post-war recovery. Chapter 2, the first chapter in this section, considers the work of Donald Winnicott and John Bowlby on motherhood and maternal deprivation, the influence of which is evident in popular culture of the post-war period. Novels and films from the 1950s about children in secondary modern schools, including E.R. Braithwaite's novel from 1959, *To Sir, With Love* (Braithwaite, 2005), feature pupils who lack 'good enough' mothers or parental attachments. Aligned with emerging educational policy and pedagogy, which were adapted to the greater numbers of working-class adolescents in education for a longer time, the stories make a case for pupils to be engaged with material relevant to their own lives not to be taught abstract concepts. These stories carve out a role for the pastoral teacher who prefigures the school counsellor.

Chapter 3 addresses the Newsom Report of 1963, which reviewed the status and outcomes of secondary modern schools. It was the first government report to recommend the introduction of school counsellors to state secondary schools. While the arrival of the first training courses for school counsellors in England in the 1960s was no doubt prompted by the Newsom Report, the rising acceptance of school counselling was influenced by the work of Carl Rogers. Rogerian ideas inform stories in the 1960s which celebrate adolescent spontaneity and authenticity and denigrate an education system which stymies 'natural' development. This is apparent in Barry Hines's *A Kestrel for a Knave* (Hines, 1969), adapted for the film *Kes* (1969) by Ken Loach, and in Edward Blishen's second novel about Stonewall Street Secondary Modern, *This Right Soft Lot* (Blishen, 1969).

Part Two, 'Backlash', explores state school stories of the 1970s and 1980s, especially those which chart the arrival of and resistance to the comprehensive school and its cultural associations. Chapter 4 argues that the 1960s' child-centred promotion of learning over teaching and of democracy over hierarchy in school structure provoked the ire of commentators on the political left and right, most vociferously in the special issues of *The Critical Survey* known as 'the Black Papers' from 1969 to 1977 (Cox and Dyson, 1969–77). In this period, local authority funded training courses for school counsellors were phased out before they had an opportunity to make an impact. The comprehensive school came to be associated with low educational standards and purposeless, 'delinquent' adolescence, of the kind characterised in Erik Erikson's *Identity and the Life Cycle* (Erikson, 1980). Stories including Willy Russell's play *Our Day Out* (Russell, 2002) and Phil Redmond's long-running serial *Grange Hill* (1978–2008) are ambivalent about the comprehensive ideal and give voice to the radical critique of comprehensives. *Grange Hill* itself, however, was held up by the Conservative government and right-wing press as an example of the dangers of progressive or child-centred education.

Chapter 5, the second in this section, proposes that education policy under Margaret Thatcher began the shift away from local education authority control and, hypothetically, gave more authority to families (or a particular version of the family), introducing a marketplace and 'choice' into the educational arena. Fictional adolescents from this period, like Sue Townsend's Adrian Mole (Townsend, 2017), Alan Bleasdale's Francis Scully (*Scully*, 1984) and *Grange Hill*'s Zammo and Danny Kendall, do not live in families who are able to 'shop around'. These are families under pressure, who make more sense in terms drawn from Murray Bowen's *Family Therapy in Clinical Practice* (Bowen, 1978) (about strained family systems) than in celebrations of economic individualism. School counselling, which, briefly, had been promised for all, was by now associated with fringe progressivism. Financial constraints on schools ensured that counsellors would not be the staple of mainstream schools that had been imagined in the 1960s.

The last chapter in this section, Chapter 6, takes us to the 1990s. By this decade, post-war optimism about social welfare and an education system that would bring equal opportunity had been decimated by the politics of self-reliance and by voices which, rightly, drew attention to the problems of humanism's 'universalising' tendency. Not all children had fared equally under the post-war consensus. The latter period of the Conservative administration saw extensive education reform, and, from teachers' point of view, more stress in 'the system'. Urie Bronfenbrenner's *The Ecology of Human Development* (Bronfenbrenner, 1979) provides a helpful frame to challenge the Thatcherite belief in the individual and the family over society. It centred the child in their own biology and personality, their families, their communities and their historical moment, over time and space. Two school stories on either side of the Conservative and New Labour administration from the late 1990s represent the school as a zone in that ecology. Jimmy McGovern's *Hearts and Minds* (1995) is about the collapse of hope of a newly qualified teacher in Liverpool and Lucy Gannon's *Hope and Glory* (1999–2000) focuses on an aspirational 'New Labour' super head. These two television dramas are like a call and response to the collapse of the post-war way of thinking about schools and its consequences for the teaching profession.

The backdrop for Part Three, 'Fragmentation', is the New Labour 'third way' of the later 1990s and early 2000s, the merger of the public and private sectors to reenergise and bring back wealth to British society. In education, this saw the rise of academy schools, which was accelerated under the Coalition government and the last Conservative administration. The 'progressive/traditionalist' binary that sets the tone for earlier debates about what is 'best for our children' gives way to a more fractured and individualised model of state education. Amongst other reasons, a broader cultural and political interest in people's emotional lives meant that school counselling came back into fashion in the early 2000s (though it was still not mandated in English schools and was now organised by charities and private providers).

Chapter 7, the first in this section, considers New Labour's 'Every Child Matters' policy of the early 2000s. This safeguarding policy was a blueprint for schools to be both 'holding' environments, offering protection and support (including through counselling) and shaming environments, through increased surveillance of staff and adolescents. While counselling texts emphasise the potential for the integrated therapist to hold the school community together, school stories emphasise the experience of shame in the school system. Zoe Heller's *Notes on a Scandal* (Heller, 2004) is about the shaming of Sheba Hart, a teacher who engages in sexual activity with an underage pupil. Alan Bennett's play *The History Boys* (Bennett, 2004) looks back to the late 1980s and a group of grammar school sixth formers in Sheffield who are being hot housed for Oxbridge entrance. Though 'about' the tension between knowledge and skills in education, the play is shot through with the sexual shame of Hector, the boys' General Studies teacher. Jilly Cooper's *Wicked!* (2006) is a satire on 'safeguarding' culture in education and a celebration of the aspirational, and in some ways boundaryless, head, Janna Curtis, and the real life 'super head', Marie Stubbs, whose story inspired Cooper's novel (Stubbs, 2003).

Chapter 8, on splits and mergers in the school system, proposes that the school counsellor can reconcile the splits in schools between students and staff, within the staff room and between the inner and outer worlds of staff and students. Extending the metaphor, it explores the split from local authority control of schools that was at the heart of the academies and free schools programme from the late 1990s. Stories like *Waterloo Road* (2006–15; 2021–), *Ackley Bridge* (2017–22) and the *Educating*...series (2011–20, 2025) show schools navigating the threat of academisation, merger with other schools, the internal splits within the school populations and between the 'inner' and 'outer' worlds of students and staff. In such stories, the academy school is written with a new set of tropes about the merging of public and private at several levels.

Chapter 10, the concluding chapter in Part Three, addresses the tension between the emphasis on resilience in contemporary education discourse and the understanding of cultural and institutional trauma in the history of secondary education. While dismissed as individualistic 'identity politics', the claiming of sexed, gendered and racialised identities emerges from resistance to historical trauma. The chapter provides an insight into the psychological process of individuation and ideas of trauma-informed and trauma-responsive organisations. It explores the representation of traumatised identities in stories from the early 2020s, including *Blue Jean*, *Sex Education*, *Heartstopper*, *Adolescence*, *Rocks* and *Waterloo Road.*

In an Afterword, I focus on the history of school inclusion and the backlash to each wave of 'expansion' that has been explored in this book. Its context is the COVID-19 pandemic, the promises that were made of a system reset and the failure of those changes to materialise. In fact, we are amid another push back on attitudes towards adolescent mental health.

This book is not a guide to adolescent development, nor does it propose particular ways of working with adolescents in secondary schools. It does, however, encourage teachers, counsellors, parents or anyone interested in state secondary education to reflect on their own school story. How does your school experience show up in the present? What are your assumptions about the purpose of secondary education? Are you a guide, facilitator or rescuer? Or, deep down, are you too cool for school, still playing out an unfinished adolescent process but now you're the one running the place? Read on.

References

Ackley Bridge (2017–2022) Channel 4.

Alexander, S. and Taylor, B. (eds.) (2012) *History and Psyche: Culture, Psychoanalysis, and the Past*, Basingstoke: Palgrave Macmillan.

Bennett, A. (2004) *The History Boys*, London: Faber and Faber

Blishen, E. (1969) *This Right Soft Lot*, London: Thames and Hudson.

Blishen, E. (1977) *Roaring Boys: A Schoolmaster's Agony*, London: Thames and Hudson.

Booker, C. (2004) *The Seven Plots: Why We Tell Stories*, London: Continuum.

Bowen, M. (1978) *Family Therapy in Clinical Practice*, New York: Jason Aranson.

Braithwaite, E.R. (2005) *To Sir, With Love*, London: Vintage.

Bronfenbrenner, U. (1979) *The Ecology of Human Development: Experiments by Nature and Design*, Cambridge, MA: Harvard University Press.

Campbell, J. (1949) *The Hero with a Thousand Faces*, New York: Pantheon Books.

Carry on Teacher (1959) [Film], Thomas, dir., Beaconsfield: Beaconsfield Productions.

Cooper, J. (2006) *Wicked!* London: Corgi.

Cox, C.D. and Dyson, A.E. (eds.). (1969–1977) *The Critical Survey*, London: Critical Quarterly Society.

Croft, M. (1954) *Spare the Rod*, London: Longmans, Green and Co.

Demos, J. and Demos, V. (1969) 'Adolescence in historical perspective', *Journal of Marriage and Family*, 31(4), pp. 632–8.

Eccles, L. and Lintern, S. (2025) 'You're not therapists, schools told in warning of "negative spiral"', *The Sunday Times*, September 28.

Ecclestone, K. and Hayes, D. (2008; 2019) *The Dangerous Rise of Therapeutic Education*, New York: Routledge.

Educating... (2011–2020; 2025–) [TV Series] Channel 4.

Erikson, E. (1980) *Identity and the Life Cycle*, London: W.W. Norton & Co.

Faulk, S. (2009) *A Week in December*, London: Hutchinson.

Garner, R. (2014) 'What is "the Blob" and why is Michael Gove comparing his enemies to an unbeatable sci-fi mound of goo which once battled Steve McQueen', *The Independent*, February 7.

Grange Hill (1978–2008) [TV Series], BBC.

Haidt, J. (2024) *The Anxious Generation: How the Great Rewiring of Childhood is Causing an Epidemic of Mental Illness*, Harmondsworth: Penguin.

Hall, G.S. (1904) *Adolescence: Its Psychology and its Relations to Physiology, Anthropology, Sociology, Crime, Religion and Education*, 2 vols, New York: Appleton.

Hallam, J. and Marshment, M. (2000) *Realism and Popular Cinema*, Manchester: Manchester University Press.

Hearts and Minds (1995) [TV Series] Channel 4.

Heller, Z. (2004) *Notes on a Scandal*, London: Penguin.

Hines, B. (1969) The *Blinder*, Harmondsworth: Penguin.

Hines, B. (1999) *A Kestrel for a Knave*, London: Penguin.

Hoggart, R. (1958) *The Uses of Literacy*, Harmondsworth: Penguin.

Hope and Glory (1999–2000) [TV Series], BBC.

Jung, C. (1991) *The Archetypes and the Collective Unconscious*, London: Routledge.

Kes (1969), [Film], Loach, dir., London: Kestrel Films.

Lay, S. (2002) *British Social Realism: From Documentary to Brit-Grit*, London: Wallflower Press.

Levi-Strauss, C. (2001) *Myth and Meaning*, London: Routledge.

Mason, M. (2021) *Sorrow and Bliss*, London: Weidenfeld & Nicholson.

Millar, F. (2018) *The Best for My Child: Did the Schools Market Deliver?* Woodbridge: John Catt Educational Ltd.

Nicholson, R. (2020) '*Sex Education* creator Laurie Nunn: "You can't have sex scenes flowery!"', *The Guardian*, 7 April.

Oram, A. (1996) *Women Teachers and Feminist Politics 1900-1939,* Manchester and New York: Manchester University Press.

Power, W. (2019) '*Sex Education* review: Gillian Anderson's Netflix comedy is eager to please but tonally confused', *The Independent*, 11 January.

Propp, V. (1968) *Morphology of the Folktale*, Austin: University of Texas Press.

Russell, W. (2002) *Our Day Out, Willy Russell Plays: 1*, London: Methuen.

Scully (1984), [TV Series], Channel 4.

Sex Education (2019–23), [TV Series], Channel 4.Shuttleworth, S. (2010) *The Mind of the Child: Child Development in Literature, Science, and Medicine, 1840–1900*, Oxford: Oxford University Press.

Spacks, P.M. (1981) *The Adolescent Idea: Myths of Youth and the Adult Imagination*, New York: Basic Books.

Steedman, C. (1986) *A Landscape for a Good Woman: A Story of Two Lives*, London: Virago.
Stubbs, M. (2003) *Ahead of the Class*, London: John Murray.
Thomson, M. (2006) *Psychological Subjects: Identity, Culture, and Health in Twentieth-Century Britain*, Oxford: Oxford University Press.
Todorov, T. (1977) *The Poetics of Prose*, Oxford: Basil Blackwell.
Townsend, S. (2017) *The Secret Diary and Growing Pains of Adrian Mole Aged 13 ¾*, Harmondsworth: Penguin.
Vignola, N. (2024) *Rewire: Break the Cycle, Alter Your Thoughts and Create Lasting Change*, Harmondsworth: Penguin.
Waterloo Road (2011–2015; 2021–) [TV Series], BBC.
White, M. and Epston, D. (1990) *Narrative Means to Therapeutic Ends*, New York: WW Norton.
Williams, R. (1974) 'A lecture on realism', *Screen*, 18(1), pp.61–74.
Wolf, E. and Antonis, B. eds. (2023) *Independent Women in British Psychoanalysis: Creativity and Authenticity at Work*, Abingdon: Routledge.
Yorke, J. (2013) *Into the Woods: How Stories Work and Why We Tell Them*, Harmondsworth: Penguin.

1

STORIES OF DEVELOPMENT AND CHANGE

Theories and practice in schools

Storytelling and therapy are about change. A protagonist or client needs to acquire or overcome something, go on some sort of journey (even while sitting in a chair), encounter obstacles and antagonists and eventually change by obtaining the thing they need or overcoming the challenge in front of them. Some stories, and clients, show us this process through plot, one event after another. Others show us this journey from the inside out, engaging us through empathy with the protagonist's struggles. As a therapist, I provide a reflection of the inside of 'the plot' for my clients if they are stuck on the outside.

As I suggested in the last chapter, writers have had a wealth of character types and story tropes to draw upon from as long as stories have been told. Psychological theories of personality development and change have, from the nineteenth century onwards, added to the repertoire. We all know what we're referring to by 'the terrible twos', 'teenage angst', 'identity crisis' or 'midlife crisis'. These are mainstream ideas, but they originate in developmental theory, in the idea that across our lifespan we not only age but also 'develop' in a series of stages.

The dominant assumption about development in the middle of the twentieth century was 'maturation', that we simply develop through different stages. The now commonplace idea that our environment has an impact upon our growth became more accepted after the Second World War. Freud, of course, most firmly embedded the theory, central to psychotherapy, that the adult personality is determined by childhood experience. In Freud's 1905 *Three Essays on the Theory of Sexuality*, he proffered the view that children are born with 'a libido', an energy that seeks out a different object to satisfy it at different stages of development: the oral, anal, phallic, latent and genital stages (Richards, 1991). To emerge into adulthood without 'neurosis' or 'fixations', the child must resolve each stage unimpeded.

DOI: 10.4324/9781003715122-3

Much subsequent developmental theory reworks, contests or elaborates upon this fundamental premise.

Developmental theory in teacher training

English secondary schools most commonly teach children from ages 11 to 16, the stage when, second to toddlerhood, the most rapid physical, psychological, neurological and emotional changes of our lives take place. I suggested in the introduction that the post-war expansion of education and the 'creation' of more adolescents meant that there were more young subjects from a range of backgrounds available for the scrutiny of those with an interest in their inner worlds and the changes they undergo. The hefty educational reports of the 1960s overseen by John Newsom, Bridget Plowden and Lionel Robbins gave weight to the insights of developmental psychologists to make their cases for a reset of secondary modern schools and the expansion of preschool and university provision. Each of them made their case for change on more than economic grounds, noting the inner worlds of children, adolescents and young adults at each stage of education.

Given the intensity of change in young people from age 11 to 16, it might make sense, then, to make space in teacher training or 'continuing professional development' for teachers to reflect upon who they might encounter in their classrooms and how their own developmental history might help or hinder their relationships. Conversations I have had with current and former secondary teachers about their training and their exposure to developmental theory reveal that this is not universally the case:

> We did one day a week in Uni, and I was in placement schools the other four days. The one day was split into a morning of difficult topic teaching and the afternoon was a mix of a child psychologist, Jim, and a chap who was an ex-head and an Ofsted inspector. With Jim we did a little on child development. I'd say roughly six hours, and the rest of his sessions were more about the acquisition of knowledge. Any other CPD was in our placement schools, and we didn't touch on anything about child development. It was all about lesson sequencing and updates on legislation and policy creation.
>
> (Christian, Head of a secondary academy, on his teacher training in the late 1990s).
>
> I did a one-year PGCE in 1994, the last year of that course before training went into schools. My training was about my subject specialism and behaviour management. There was nothing on child development. When I got my first job I was quickly put in charge of students' pastoral care even though I was newly qualified. Sometime later I delivered a training day for

> Teach First students on aspects of child development. They were too busy eating sweets to pay attention.
>
> (Amanda, former secondary teacher, current child and adult psychotherapist).
>
> I did teacher training at Manchester Metropolitan University. It was a two-year PGCE training course to be a Maths teacher starting in September 1993 and finishing in July 1995. I was taught in Uni and did teaching practice in school. There was no emphasis on child development at all.
>
> (Paddy, retired secondary Head of Maths, Greater Manchester secondary school).

The nature of teacher training has some bearing on the capacity of schools for reflective practice. For its first 150 years, from the turn of the nineteenth century, teacher training oscillated between on-the-job practice and some form of college training (Robinson, 2006). The early twentieth century saw the model of elementary school 'pupil teachers' – who were basically, 'able' elementary school pupils moved to the front of the class – phased out and the launch of training colleges, overseen by newly formed Local Education Authorities (LEAs). Between the wars, there was debate about whether training had become too theoretical, and that debate has resurfaced every time training moved out of schools and into colleges or universities.

The Butler Act of 1944 dispensed with 'uncertified' teachers and envisioned an all-graduate teaching profession. After the Second World War, the growth and improvements in education for the population were shadowed by the expansion of Education as a broader field of study, an academic discipline in its own right, in both universities and training colleges. The Robbins Report into Higher Education of 1963 attempted to bring university and college teacher training into alignment: universities were to offer postgraduate courses while four-year BEds were provided by colleges. After the James Report in 1972, teaching was to be an all-graduate profession. From the late 1980s, with government suspicions of 'left-wing' universities and colleges indoctrinating teachers, the tide began to turn back to 'on the job' training and more prescriptive curricula for aspiring teachers, coinciding with the launch of the National Curriculum after the Education Reform Act of 1988 (Robinson, 2006). Teacher training routes have expanded and diversified ever since, as has the debate about the merits of theory versus practice.

Looking back from 1944 to the present, the 1960s stand out as a moment when teaching was being promoted as a profession, when training had the space for theory *and* practice. That school counsellor training was launched for teachers with at least five years' experience is consistent with this outlook, and that that training disappeared in the 1970s is consistent with the backlash against this short-lived period of trust in the teaching profession as practitioners who could cope with theory, self-reflection and practice.

Good levels of development

During my own secondary school years from 1977 to 1982, my teachers ranged from borderline sadists to attuned and supportive pedagogues. Some of them will have trained in the 1960s; I cannot imagine what sort of training, if any, others had. Eager to avoid being shouted at, shamed or hit, I was very much what transactional analysis calls an 'adapted child': following rules, looking for approval from adults, shapeshifting with peers so not to be rejected (Berne, 1964). Perhaps as an adult I became a school governor and counsellor to put myself back into school in a different way. In my therapeutic work with secondary school-age clients, I am aware at times of my teenage self looking for acceptance, alongside the adult who is attending to their needs. Internally, I can feel myself appealing to an indifferent client like the mother in *Mean Girls:* 'I'm not a regular mom, I'm a cool mom'. When my adapted child meets a 'free child', one who doesn't play by the rules or feel the need to comply with the codes of the counselling room, I can also feel my 'critical parent' arriving. The critical parent is the rule giver, who storms in at these moments to protect my own adapted child who is feeling shamed by the free child in front of me. I am keen not to be seen as a teacher, but at times crave the status and authority that teachers, theoretically, have in school. If I was unaware of these tensions, I could quickly start laying down the law, which is hardly going to facilitate an effective and boundaried therapeutic relationship. Many teachers, I suspect, are caught in this dynamic but only have time to look at the child in front of them, not at themselves, to diagnose the problem. And that child is often viewed, developmentally, as a fully developed adult in a badly designed uniform who is 'making poor choices'.

Current teachers are well-equipped with the 'classifications' of their cohort (gender, ethnicity, pupil premium status, prior level of attainment…). It would be an interesting but unviable task to attempt to classify a class of Year Nine students according to 'developmental' ideas. Some of the physical changes of puberty are, of course, visible, but everything else lies beneath the surface. In some ways, the increasing awareness around neurotype is forcing ideas of 'brain development' into the foreground of discussions about secondary schools, but as yet schools' capacity to respond to the new information is lagging. The many processes that make the teenage years so overwhelming – and potentially joyous – are only really addressed in schools when something goes wrong and then in mainly disciplinary ways.

Even though the processes of adolescent development stay largely below the surface in secondary school policy, the basics of developmental theory underpin school structure and curricula design. Even the most psychology-sceptical pedagogue will be using ideas which at some point originated in developmental theory. The separation of 'Early Years and Foundation Stage' (EYFS) and Key

Stages One to Four ('infants', 'juniors' and 'seniors'), for instance, is based on a very basic developmental assumption: that children of different ages have different learning needs and capacities.

Developmental psychology has an obvious presence in early years' education. The framework for EYFS describes the expected physical, social, emotional and cognitive development of the under-fives and prescribes the means by which staff should support these processes. The prescriptive element of the framework, of course, has been contested by practitioners, and the assessment of the 'baseline' attainment of four- and five-year-olds once they reach Reception as a means to hold schools to account is much questioned. However, it is accepted that during these years, children change rapidly, and that schools and nurseries can and should understand and support these changes. By secondary school, developmental ideas fade from policy and curriculum formation, even though the 'stage' through which 11- to 16-year-olds are passing is nearly as turbulent as toddlerhood and the consequences when things go wrong can be catastrophic.

Recent reports which inform education policy are telling in the different language they use when referring to EYFS and secondary school. The Education Policy Institute's annual report in 2023, for instance, focuses on the 'attainment gap between disadvantaged pupils and their peers' (Education Policy Institute (EPI), 2023). It refers to 'development' at EYFS and 'attainment' at secondary level, without pausing to reflect on the shift:

> To measure children's development at age 5, we use the statutory teacher-led assessments against the early years foundation stage (EYFS) profile. To assess overall attainment at the end of secondary school – known as key stage 4 – we measure pupils' average GCSE grade across English and Maths.
>
> *(EPI, 2023)*

The independent charity, the Education Endowment Foundation (EEF), which is 'dedicated to breaking the link between family income and educational achievement', provides 'evidence based' toolkits and resources for schools. Their literature refers to supporting 'development' for EYFS and 'teaching and learning' for primary and secondary stages. The EEF's resources include a toolkit for 'behaviour management', which draws on some 'developmental' ideas, such as Sarah Jayne Blakemeore's work on the teenage brain (Blakemore, 2018) and the impact of Adverse Childhood Experiences (ACEs) (Felitti and Anda et al., 1998), both of which I explore below. Most emphasis in the toolkit is on classroom management and the least time-consuming solutions to behavioural disruption. The Timpson Review (Timpson, 2019), commissioned by the former Education Minister Damien Hinds to explore exclusions, is wide-ranging in its findings and recommendations, but seems to have been adopted superficially and rapidly cast aside by a government failing to deal with post-pandemic schooling and reverting to acceptance of suspensions, exclusions and 'no excuses' culture.

While 'evidence based', the 'evidence' upon which educational reports of recent years rely is largely quantitative, formulated in a circular fashion from exam results across different categories of students (based on gender, ethnicity, disadvantage, special educational needs and disabilities (SEND), etc.). None of them, as Peter Mandler points out, have the weight of the 1950s' and 1960s' Crowther, Newsom, Robbins and Plowden Reports with their 'vast apparatus of expert testimony, social surveys and in-depth analysis' (Mandler, 2020, p.11). Newsom (CACE, 1963) on secondary moderns and Plowden (CACE, 1967) on primary education addressed child and adolescent development and the broad context in which it occurs. They made recommendations for an array of other services to support children's development in schools, whose expertise would not be reasonably reproduced by classroom teachers. Writing at a time when the welfare state was growing not receding, the Newsom and Plowden researchers could assume that a support system of social workers, educational psychologists, youth workers and 'child guidance' services would be available and 'just' needed to be streamlined to work effectively with and in schools. Conversely, recent reports silently assume skeleton and over-stretched external services and resort to rather limp offerings about 'whole-school' initiatives to improve attainment, like this empty rhetoric from the EEF's behavioural improvement toolkit:

> Whole-school changes usually take longer to embed than individually tailored or single-classroom approaches. However, behaviour programmes are more likely to have an impact on attainment outcomes if implemented at a whole-school level.
>
> *(EEF)*

When schools succeed or fail on their examination outcomes, they cannot be blamed for prioritising measures which lead to best attainment for most students and shoehorn in 'interventions' for students for whom growing up safely might be the best they can attain.

Perhaps the challenges of adolescence seem too unwieldy to be addressed meaningfully in education policy. Adolescents are in many ways 'liminal' beings, unstable and unknowable to themselves and others. When they start secondary school, they leave behind but still occupy the smaller more stable iterations of their primary school selves. They are moving towards, but don't yet inhabit, their adult bodies and identities. Internally, this can be experienced as loss, grief, euphoria or disorientation. It is a kind of haunting from the past and a divination from the future. Put like this, it's no wonder that Year Nine Maths lessons can be so hard on everyone.

Developmental theory in counselling

As a counsellor, my work is of course informed by developmental psychology. Its theories provide the framework for the change that clients seek (be that relief from distress, recovery from trauma or to move towards self-awareness and new ways of being). It is important for me to understand how someone came to adulthood, or in the case of teenage clients, how they're making their way there (in terms of family and social support, other relationships and schooling). I need to understand what is helping or impeding their growth and have a framework to repair past injuries (for instance, a traumatic event or damaging early relationship) and help them to integrate these experiences into their future, instead of avoiding and reenacting them. For this, I value the insights into developmental processes from Freud onwards.

Critics of developmental psychology draw attention to the context, the blind spots and negative implications of its theories. They argue it can offer an overgeneralised picture of 'normative' development, which is inattentive to diverse populations and ignores the conditions in which people 'develop'. Erica Burman questions the 'objectivity' of developmental psychology (Burman, 2007). She exposes what she sees as its 'regulatory' function and challenges the slippages between 'description' and 'prescription'. I recognise that developmental theory or any framework for psychological therapy has a 'shadow side' that can be co-opted for social coercion. In recent years, for instance, NHS counselling has been prescribed in the service of getting people back to work, off pain clinic waiting lists or as an alternative to hormone replacement therapy for menopausal women. Counselling can certainly support the unemployed, those in pain and those undergoing a physiological transition, but it cannot stand alone as a 'technique' and should not be imposed upon people. In these contexts, counselling can be used to reframe the distress caused by social inequality as a personal lack of motivation or physical and emotional pain as 'negative thinking'. In schools, 'counselling', or the 'skills' associated with it, can be recruited to reinforce behavioural management techniques, as an 'intervention' to promote children's capacity for 'self-regulation' and resilience or to improve attendance. These are necessary and helpful skills, but children require a broader context than a short-term counselling relationship or a self-help questionnaire to develop them. For some children and teenagers, the school environment itself is difficult to tolerate, or the circumstances of their broader lives need time and sustained attention.

Carl Rogers and humanistic development

Counsellors are not in fact mythical agents who can change the course of someone's life by pointing the way through the underworld. When counselling has the space to address the nuances of a client's development, it can be a transformative process in which an individual finds out they have 'a self' which is not solely in the service of a role, a relationship, an organisation or a society. Paradoxically, the process of discovering this 'self' allows them to enter more wholly into roles, relationships, organisations and society. This was the ethos of my initial training in humanist, person-centred counselling, based on the work of the American psychologist Carl Rogers. Rogers, who was both a psychologist and a pedagogue, was part of a post-war movement to 'rebuild' citizens from the inside out. Rogers' work did not propose 'stages' of development, rather a series of principles: the 'self-concept', the 'undifferentiated' and the 'differentiated self', the 'fully functioning person', the 'ideal' and the 'real self' (Rogers, 1959). Underpinning all these principles of development is the idea that an individual is an organism with an 'actualising tendency'. In the right conditions, in relationships which are founded on 'unconditional positive regard', the organism will grow into an 'authentic', 'congruent' person, whose internal and external experiences match. These principles of development underpin the 'core conditions' of person-centred therapy. The therapist is imagined as a 'congruent' person, the client (not patient) as in a state of 'incongruence' which diminishes as they experience the therapeutic relationship (unconditional positive regard and accurate empathy). As the client is regarded as intrinsically motivated towards their own wellbeing and the expert in their own life, the therapist's role is non-directive and facilitative.

Rogers was influential in education as well as in therapy and his therapeutic principles apply to his pedagogical approach. In his 1969 collection of essays, *Freedom to Learn*, which was addressed to student teachers and their educators, Rogers made a case for learning which is not 'from the neck up' but which involves 'feelings or personal meanings' and has 'relevance for the whole person' (Rogers, 1969, p.4).

This 'experiential learning' has 'a quality of personal involvement', is 'self-initiated' and is 'evaluated by the learner' in the sense that it meets their needs and leads them towards what they 'want to know' (p.5). Rogers describes the principles of 'discovery learning' which were set against the standardised curricula and testing in the American educational system of the 1960s. Such progressive pedagogy had also made its way into English education, partly due to the recommendations of The Newsom Report of 1963 and the Plowden Report of 1967. The insights provided by these wide-ranging reports into secondary modern education and primary schools contributed to the development of the training courses in school counselling (based partly on Rogerian principles) for teachers. These reports have a firm belief in the connection between state education and children's growth in many domains.

Development through attachment and play

When I trained to work therapeutically with children, the curricula used attachment theory as its developmental base (its model for how children grow) and play therapy as its 'mechanism for change' (to support them when there has been a disruption or the conditions of their lives are not 'optimal' for healthy growth). Drawing on the work of British psychiatrist and psychoanalyst John Bowlby from the late 1940s onwards, attachment theory focuses on the development of the self in relationship (Bowlby, 1969). Bowlby saw development as a process *between* (inter) rather than, as in Freudian theory, a development *within* (intra) the individual. He proposed 'stages' of infant-parent attachment, where in the early months the child has an indiscriminate bond with its caregiver, followed by an emerging preference for the parent, towards an active 'proximity seeking', and eventually to an alliance between caregiver and child. The relationship is formed through the parent's emotional availability, attunement and responsiveness to the child. Ruptures in this process lead to ruptures in the child's attachment system and difficulty in forming secure relationships. Later theory proposes a multiplicity of attachment bonds throughout the lifespan and the potential for the repair of ruptures, including through the relationship with a therapist who shares the characteristics of the attuned parent.

Play therapy was first developed in the middle of the twentieth century by the early proponents of child psychotherapy, Anna Freud, Melanie Klein and Margaret Lowenfield (Landreth, 2012). Like attachment theory, play therapy is also built on developmental principles, matching language and symbolic forms of expression (art, sand play, puppetry, small world play) to the 'stage' of the child. The child's 'stage' may spontaneously arise through the therapeutic play, and it may not correspond with child's chronological age. By attuning to the child as they symbolically express a conscious or unconscious emotional struggle, the therapist can help the child to work through a developmental gap. The principles of attachment theory are embedded in play therapy.

Bowlby's work on attachment has drawn criticism from numerous directions, principally for its insistence on the maternal-infant bond which has been read as a ruse to get mothers back into the home after the war. The work of Bowlby's contemporary paediatrician and psychoanalyst Donald Winnicott has come in for similar criticism. Winnicott's BBC Radio talks from the 1940s to the 1960s, which formed the basis of his book *The Child, the Family and the Outside World* (Winnicott, 1964), popularised many psychoanalytical ideas about child development and parenting. Winnicott coined the notion of the 'ordinary devoted mother' (handed down to us as the 'good enough parent'), the 'holding' relationship (literally the mother's physical and emotional protection of the infant often invoked as a metaphor in therapy for the safekeeping and protection of the client's experiences over time) and the 'transitional object' (the child's symbolic substitute for the mother, like a soft toy or blanket, which allows for increasing independence). Again, Winnicott posits an inter-relational process of child development, summed up in the provocative statement that 'there is no such thing as a baby'. For Winnicott, the mother's attention and capacity for play brings the child safely into contact with the world beyond itself. The absence of such maternal attention leads to the child's distorted relationship with reality.

Bowlby and Winnicott's work *is* conservative in its assumptions about gendered roles within the family. Its culturally specific observations about child development (its disregard of the social context of the child and the family) are, like many other aspects of developmental psychology, offered up as universal truths. However, their work is part of a movement within psychoanalysis to understand development in relational terms, based on observations of children. As I noted above, this was a movement away from Freudian ideas based on his work with adult clients in his nineteenth-century Viennese consulting rooms. Bowlby and Winnicott were part of a group of therapists who wanted to shift attention from the *reported* childhood experience and internal life of the middle- and upper-middle-class adult to the *observed* world between the adult and child, including the working-class adult and child.

Behaviourist change

This view of the 'inter' world, the complex give and take of relationships, differs from other strands of developmental thinking which were emerging alongside them. Behaviourists, for instance, focused neither on the 'intra' nor on the 'inter' worlds, but on the observable field of behaviour, how it is learned and can be modified. Russian psychologist Pavlov's theory of 'classical conditioning', in which subjects *learn* to respond to stimulus with a corresponding behaviour, was elaborated on by American psychologists John Watson and B.F. Skinner in the early to mid-twentieth century (Skinner, 1953; Watson, 1930). Watson applied classical conditioning to the domain of parenting, and popularised behaviourist ideas in magazines in the 1920s to show how promoting an association with a stimulus can teach children to behave in a particular way. He notoriously dismissed demonstrations of parental affection.

Skinner added a new dimension to behaviourism with his observations of so-called 'operant conditioning'. His experiments demonstrated that teaching a consequence of an action (negative or positive reinforcement) can change motivation and modify behaviour. This approach to 'behaviour modification' is still alive and well. The Department for Education's last behaviour advisor, Tom Bennett, proposed that schools adopt behaviourist principles, dubbing so-called 'restorative' approaches which try to address the contexts in which children live, 'fashionable' and 'ineffective' (Wood, 2024).

Cognitive change

If behaviourists saw the infant as a blank slate, then cognitive psychologists, facilitated by new scientific possibilities of observation, saw the infant's brain as 'pre-programmed' with a range of undeveloped skills and information just waiting to be 'optimised'. It is from cognitive developmental theory that we get the idea of the child's 'potential' and the cultural fear that the child will not 'maximise' it.

After the 1944 Education Act, the work of cognitive psychologists Piaget and Vygotsky informed teacher training and the curricula of the post-war state schools, and their ideas still inform the EYFS framework (Piaget, 1929, 1959; Vygotsky, 1962). Rather than an inevitable process of maturation, child development was now presented to the education sector as a series of stages, where physical, cognitive, emotional and social growth could be mapped on to chronological age and supported. For Piaget, these were the sensorimotor (up to two years), preoperational (two to seven), concrete operational (seven to eleven) and formal operational (12 to adulthood) stages. Inevitably, these stage 'descriptors' pass into the prescriptive basis of standardised testing ('milestones', key skills, levels and the endless euphemisms for passing or failing that have been generated to make the way we organise schools seem fair and natural). As Laura Tisdall has demonstrated, there was slippage between terms used to describe 'normal' chronological development and class-based development (Tisdall, 2020). Tisdall argues, for instance, that the emphasis on the 'concrete operational' (a stage that Piaget put at ages seven to eleven, denoting the beginnings of abstract thought but rooted in simple classification of objects) in the curriculum of secondary modern schools in the 1950s illustrates the way that normative ideas about development are bound up with assumptions about social class and the limitations of the working-class children who largely made up the secondary modern cohort.

While Piaget conjured up a child who was independently developing through these stages (in a process of equilibrium, accommodation and assimilation), Vygotsky proposed that cognitive development is also a social process; his 'zone of proximal development' (now referred to as 'scaffolding') involved observing children's present capacities and planning curricula to challenge beyond them. For both Piaget and Vygotsky, learning is derived from children's own experience, though Piaget saw this as an individual process and Vygotsky understood it to have a social dimension. Vygotsky's influence can be seen in 'peer learning' where one child assists another in a task, or where adults are encouraged to listen to their children read.

Change across the lifespan

Although Vygotsky's theories have a more 'social' dimension than Piaget's, they are not really 'about' social development, or children's development as social beings. This aspect of development was explored by the American child psychoanalyst Erik Erikson, in his writing from the 1940s onwards but principally in his 1959 book, *Identity and the Life Cycle* (Erikson, 1980). Here, he mapped out 'psychosocial' development, recalling and reworking Freud's psychosexual model of development. Erikson outlines 'the elements of a really healthy personality' from the point of view of the 'conflicts, inner and outer, which the healthy personality weathers, emerging and re-emerging with an increased sense of inner unity' (p.52). He describes these conflicts and their resolution as the way in which the individual comes to 'master life's outer and inner dangers', a series of monsters to overcome. So, in the early months, the infant must overcome mistrust and master trust, an ability to rely on oneself and others. In later infancy, the child negotiates shame and doubt (instilled from the social world) to achieve autonomy, a sense of being guided from within and without. Later childhood involves traversing 'initiative versus guilt' and 'industry versus inferiority'. Once initiative and industry have been established, 'Youth begins...all sameness and continuities relied on earlier are questioned again' (p.94). The adolescent searches for 'a new sense of continuity and sameness' and must 'refight many of the crises of earlier years' (p.94).

Erikson emphasises the social aspect of this process, describing how 'the growing child must...derive a vitalising sense of reality from the awareness his individual way of mastering experience is a successful variant of the way other people around him master experience' (p.95). The failure to master this task underpins what Erikson, in the language of his time, refers to as 'delinquency': an inability to settle on a socially recognisable way of 'mastering experience' and subsequent over-identification with 'the heroes of cliques and crowds' and a 'clannish' intolerance of difference (p.97). Grounding his argument in contemporary American culture, Erikson blames consumerism, the creation of the 'synthetic personality' in a 'you are what you can buy' culture, and an education system focused on 'making the grade' rather than aspiring to higher values and goals (p.100). Erikson's way of framing adolescent development recalls Evan Hunter's 'sensational' 1955 portrait of American high school, *The Blackboard Jungle* (Hunter, 1955).

Erikson is unusual in focusing on lifelong development and describes three further stages of growth: 'intimacy versus self-absorption' in young adulthood; generativity versus stagnation in midlife (what the Canadian psychoanalyst Elliott Jacques coined 'the midlife crisis' (Jacques, 1965)) and finally 'integrity versus despair and disgust' – acceptance of the lifespan and the people within it. Lack of resolution of each of these conflicts leads to a sense of inadequacy, or what Erikson calls an 'unhealthy' personality, a person who, in narrative terms, succumbs to the monster or the shadows.

Development across the ecosystem

While Erikson launched latitudinal 'lifespan' studies, the Russian-American psychologist Urie Bronfenbrenner placed individual development in a cross-section. His 'ecological systems theory' was driven by a need to take the study of child development out of the laboratory and into a complex, multidirectional series of 'systems' (the micro, meso, exo, macro and chrono systems), visualised as a series of concentric circles with the child at their centre (Bronfenbrenner, 1979). These systems include the child's genetic characteristics and temperament, immediate family context, the contexts of the people in the child's life, the culture in which the child lives and the changes over time in the child's culture and society. In current practice, such understanding shows up in 'Team Around the Child' work, developed in the early 2000s from an idea by Peter Limbrick where a small group of people from school and external services and parents or carers work together, to meet a child's particular needs (Limbrick, 2007). Such an approach comes under strain, however, when state support is poorly resourced.

Regulation and mindset

As a school governor, at primary and secondary levels, I hear of key ideas that are popular at any given time in teaching and that have their roots in developmental psychology. A current favourite is the term 'metacognition', which was coined by the developmental psychologist and follower of Piaget, John Flavell, in the late 1970s (Flavell, 1979). Metacognition describes 'thinking about thinking', an intentional, reflective practice which is promoted in schools to prompt students to plan, monitor and evaluate their learning. Another popular idea is Albert Bandura's theory of 'self-regulation', the monitoring and adjustment of behaviour by reflecting on its social influences and consequences (Bandura, 1991). Metacognition and self-regulation both assume or aspire to create a self who can learn a series of cognitive skills to overcome emotional reactivity and behavioural impulses. Developmental psychologist Carol Dweck's 'growth mindset' has also been taken up in schools to achieve similar ends. In a book of that name, subtitled 'How you can fulfil your potential', Dweck argues that 'beliefs' about ourselves determine the way we approach learning, challenges, obstacles and failures (Dweck, 2006). These beliefs fall into two categories: the 'fixed mindset' that personality, intelligence and skills are innate and unchanging, or the 'growth mindset', which believes that these things can develop, be adjusted and 'optimised'. In this model, everything is teachable, and 'risk and effort' are the mechanism for growth. Developmental process and systemic thinking, the relationship between self, other and systems, are entirely missing from this model.

Mind and body: trauma and ACEs

From psychosexual to psychosocial growth, from attachments to interconnections in a system, from 'blank slate' behaviourism to 'potential'-based cognitivism, the theories of psychological development themselves develop in their context and according to what knowledge of the developing self is discoverable at the time. Technological developments have shifted our sense of how we develop. From the 1980s, increasingly detailed brain-imaging fostered new understanding of brain development, and the interaction of the brain and the environment. The impact of this technology was felt strongly in the understanding of traumatic experiences on the brain. Bessel van der Kolk's *The Body Keeps the Score* traces the advent of new brain-scanning techniques in the early 1990s that enhanced our understanding of the way the brain processes information (van der Kolk, 2014). Functional magnetic resonance imaging (fMRI) allowed scientists 'to watch the brain as it processed memories, sensations, and emotions' (p.39). fMRI screening revealed that trauma affects the 'Broca's area' of the cortex, one of the speech centres of the brain. Effectively, trauma is a preverbal experience and cannot be healed verbally. The understanding of trauma on the brain has had an impact on treatment, with mind-body techniques like Eye Movement Desensitisation and Reprocessing

(EMDR) proving highly successful. Schools and other organisations which claim to be 'trauma-informed' need to become 'trauma responsive'; this means not just responding sympathetically to children who have experienced acute or chronic traumatisation but by creating environments which support children's recovery at a physical and emotional level.

Training which is commonly available to schools is based on an understanding of 'ACEs'. This was a term coined by a team of researchers led by Vincent Felitti and Robert Anda (Felitti and Anda, 1998). Between 1995 and 1997, they conducted interviews with adults about seven categories of adversity in childhood (physical, sexual and emotional abuse; witnessing domestic violence; living with someone who was mentally ill; living with someone who abused alcohol or drugs; the imprisonment of a member of the household). The team found a correlation between the number of ACEs reported and the severity of mental and physical ill health in the adults. The categories have been increased to include loss of a parent due to bereavement or estrangement and experiences of poverty, racism and violence in the child's community. It is recognised that not everyone exposed to ACEs has poor outcomes but for some the impact is traumatising and requires an approach like that used to treat post-traumatic stress disorder. Again, the focus on training in schools is to raise awareness from a safeguarding point of view, to allow staff to alert and seek support from other agencies (social services, Child and Adolescent Mental Health Services (CAMHS)). The capacity to respond therapeutically is beyond the resource and capacity of many schools and, in fact, of those agencies.

The adolescent brain

Scanning has enhanced our understanding of the impact on the brain of traumatic events and has led to the mapping of the brain throughout the lifespan. Recent books on adolescent neurological development emphasise the adaptive qualities of 'the teenage brain', to counteract the prevailing narratives of disfunction and crisis. In her study *Inventing Ourselves,* Sarah Jayne Blakemore uses neuroscience to update straightforward chronological definitions of adolescence (the teenage years) or biological and social markers (beginning at puberty, ending when 'an individual attains a stable, independent role in society' (Blakemore, 2018, p.2)). In these accounts, the turbulence of adolescence is attributed to hormone surges of puberty and new social roles. Blakemore adds brain development – 'changes in brain structure and function' – to the understanding of adolescence, and, somewhat optimistically, hopes that this new understanding will have implications for social and education policy (p.6). Blakemore notes that the key changes in the brain involve the reduction of grey matter, synaptic pruning, increased 'social brain' (heightened self-consciousness), difficulties with seeing the other's point of view, the hypersensitivity of the limbic system to the rewards of risk taking and the ongoing development of the frontal cortex, which means that impulse control is still not fully available. Those 'poor choices' evoked in school behaviour policies look much less like choices than survival in this context.

Daniel Seigel's work provides an account of neurodevelopmental theory, describing the order in which the brain develops: brain stem (breath, movement), emotional centre and frontal cortex. Therapeutic practice, he argues, should mirror this developmental process, first engaging the body through breath and movement, then emotion through empathic reflection, then rational processing and decision making. His 2013 book *Brainstorm* offers the practice of 'mindsight', a form of mindfulness, to calm the storms of adolescent development (Siegel, 2013). He coins the term 'MWe' to describe the interpersonal quality of brain and mind development, recalling the work of the post-war developmental theorists who understood emotional and psychological development as a relational process.

Two recent books have explored the plasticity of the developing brain, both to celebrate its powers of recovery, redirection and 'rewiring' and to illustrate the vulnerability of the developing brain to being rewired against one's will. The latter is the premise of the American social psychologist Jonathan Haidt's *The Anxious Generation* in which he harks back to the 'freedoms' of childhood pre smartphones and paints an alarming picture of the impact on mental health on adolescents whose brains have been 'hacked by technology' (Haidt, 2024). Nicole Vignola puts a more optimistic spin on the same idea in *Rewire*, in which she describes how we can 'change the narrative' and 'hack' our brains into better habits, including regulating dopamine uptake by reducing the use of smartphones (Vignola, 2024). The idea of children merging with smart technology, signalled in the application of these terms 'hacking' and 'rewiring' to humans and technology, has been alarming enough to have sparked the concern of parents' groups who want action on children's access to smart phones and by some school leaders who have banned their use during school hours. As I suggested in my introduction, these apocalyptic narratives about Generation Z and Alpha's use of digital technology need further exploration, as we are at risk of throwing out the baby, the potential of new forms of connection with the bathwater of new forms of technology.

In this selective account of some trends in developmental psychology, mainly from North America and Britain since the Second World War, I have highlighted the underlying assumptions about how people grow and change, particularly during adolescence, and what can impede or enrich that growth. I have also highlighted the way that they inform educational practice. In the way I have presented the theories, there is an echo of a developmental process: from theories focusing in ever increasing circles on relationships between mothers and infants, to learning capacity in childhood and adolescence, to family, social and ecological systems. The arrival of scanning technology has taken developmental theory inwards again, to observe brains and nervous systems, and infers new knowledge about minds. The shift inwards in developmental theory has coincided with, and perhaps contributed to, the understanding of the self as an 'identity', a bespoke model of personhood defined from the inside out.

Some theories have been so absorbed into the mainstream as to seem like common sense. We seem to accept, for instance, that teenagers struggle with 'impulse control' because of the peculiarities of brain development during adolescence, or that being isolated from a friendship group can feel life threatening to a 13-year-old. We seem to struggle, however, to support the teenagers going through these difficulties, in the places where most of them spend a lot of their time: in secondary schools.

What do they do there? Behind the counselling room door

Schools, because they are working with large groups, are built on reductive behaviourist and cognitive models of development: rewarding good behaviour, punishing bad, maximising input and output of knowledge. The forms of reward and punishment have evolved since the 1950s (principally because corporal punishment was outlawed in 1988) as has the understanding of cognition, informed by neuroscience and the growing knowledge of the physiology of the developing brain. However, due to the emphasis on exam results as the measure of their success, and the increasing panic about a 'crisis' in conduct provoked by the COVID-19 lockdown, schools are locked in battle with the double-headed monsters of attainment and behaviour. Elsewhere on the school battlefield are a declining number of school counsellors, social workers and educational psychologists, patching up the wounded one at a time and with little contact with their leaders.

The varying fortunes of in-school counsellors are partly an issue of resource but also of confidence in what is happening behind the counselling room door. Unless a school counsellor is integrated into the culture of the school, their work can seem at best mysterious, at worst a complete waste of money. When headteachers are accountable for attainment, attendance percentages, staff retention and squeezed budgets, it seems reasonable that the 'tasks' of a school counsellor – possibly the only people in school who have no accountability targets – are delegated to staff who have other roles in the school: (safeguarding leads, pastoral heads, teaching assistants, mentors). So, what's different about a school counsellor? What are they doing in there?

Children and young people competencies

The role of school counsellor has crossed between 'careers' guidance and life skills to the provision of emotional and psychological support. Since the first training courses were established for teachers to become school counsellors in 1965 (and disappeared in the 1970s), counsellors have formed therapeutic alliances with the students in their care, framed by the ideas of theorists and practitioners of psychology and psychotherapy and the developmental theories outlined in the last section. Developmental theory tells the story of change; therapeutic models integrate these stories and offer ways to restore unfinished processes, to redirect 'maladaptive' (unhelpful) growth and repair damage.

It may seem obvious to state that therapeutic work with children and young people (CYP) is different from working with adults. Although those over the age of 13 can be deemed competent to consent to therapy, anyone under 18 is usually 'referred' by an adult, with the inevitable power imbalance that such a process implies. I am registered to practice with the British Association of Counselling and Psychotherapy, so must have particular 'competences' for CYP work (core, generic, basic, specific, meta and organisational). The first core competence is 'knowledge of development in children and young people and of family development and transitions'.

As we have seen, there is no unified theory of child or family development. Development is described with different emphasis with variable degrees of 'scientific' method; critics like Burman have demonstrated how developmental theory does not simply 'describe' what happens to the growing child but in some respects *shapes* developmental processes (Burman, 2007). Nevertheless, to work therapeutically with CYP demands working knowledge of developmental processes and alertness to the difference say, between neurotypicality, neurodivergence and developmental trauma (which will affect the appropriateness of a particular therapeutic approach).

The sense of purpose of school counsellors has shifted across time, depending in part on wider shifts in the understanding of mental and emotional health but also on the context of schooling. With each new government and each new set of priorities, the school system shifts as do the expectations of staff and students. Counsellors, of course, do not have the burden of shepherding their charges towards the 'primary' goal of secondary education (five good GCSE passes including English and Maths?). While teaching staff focus on honing cognitive skills and behavioural management, counsellors can roam more freely. For this and many other reasons, counsellors are at the dispensable end of school staffing when budgets are tight. Under financial constraint, emphasis on 'standards' ratchets up and attitudes towards behaviour become more draconian (see the rising numbers of suspensions and exclusions in a system that just a few years ago was full of promise to restore the losses wrought by the pandemic).

The beginnings of school counselling

The first training courses for school counsellors in England were launched in October 1965, the same month that Tony Crosland, Labour's education secretary, recommended the conversion of all existing state secondary schools (grammars and secondary moderns) to comprehensive status (DES, 1965). For many commentators, comprehensive schools were not a progressive development in the English education system. The grammar and secondary modern schools which they mostly, but not completely, replaced were understood to support different kinds of development for different kinds of children: academic or vocational. Comprehensive schools, it was feared, would impede the development of these different kinds of children by providing a one-size-fits-all environment. Those in favour of comprehensive schools emphasised the social and environmental factors that shaped some of those developmental differences. As Crosland saw it, a disproportionate number of middle-class children took up grammar school places because of their social and economic advantage rather than their innate academic ability (Crosland, 1956).

At a conference about school counselling in 1968, a Professor for Education, Robin Pedley, describes the comprehensive system and school counselling as interdependent (Lytton and Craft, 1969). The complexity inherent in comprehensive schools, he argues, demands the presence of adults who are not preoccupied with the business of teaching to help students of a range of abilities and backgrounds to navigate the parts of the large and complex system. They would be there to put humanity into the comprehensive machine.

Mental health services for children and adolescents

The development of comprehensives and school counselling is enmeshed in ideas about the relationship between social equality and the healthy development of children. While school-based counselling was inspired by American models of school guidance, it also had a history in the growth of mental health provision for children and adolescents in the UK. In the nineteenth century, the mental health of children and adults was treated in the same way, in publicly funded asylums, provided for by the County Asylum Act and the Lunacy Act of 1845 (Barrett, 2019). In 1927, in a move towards recognising the differing needs of children and adults and different degrees of mental health difficulty, the first child guidance clinic was set up in East London. The clinics were staffed by psychiatrists, psychiatric nurses, psychologists and social workers and funded by charitable and private donations. After the Second World War, over 300 child guidance clinics were established throughout the country, now funded by the NHS. Child guidance clinics and educational psychologists feature frequently in the post-war stories about the new secondary modern schools, sometimes as satirical nods to progressive trends in state education or as social commentary on the difficulties faced by post-war pupils.

It wasn't until 1987 that a unified mental health service for children and adolescents, combining hospital, clinic and community support was established. Child and Adolescent Mental Health Services (CAMHS) was organised into a four-tier system which was meant to overcome the problems of inconsistency of provision throughout the country and to take care of differential needs. Schools – like other community-based services like general practitioners and health visitors – were considered as a Tier 1 service, providing the 'universal' oversight of children's mental health. School-based counsellors would sit at Tier 2. But funding for school counsellors would come from school budgets and in England (unlike in Wales) there has never been a statutory mandate to provide them at all.

The growth of school counselling

While counselling is offered by the NHS, it has a history separate to mental health provision. It was also originally different from psychotherapy, which began in Europe and originally at least was seen as an esoteric pursuit for the leisured and wealthy, allowing for the endless exploration of the hidden psyche. Counselling in Britain was first found in the practice of the Marriage Guidance Council in the 1950s and the practice overlapped with social work casework. As these contexts suggest, counselling at this period was a form of moral and social guidance, geared to adjusting the client to the outside world rather than understanding their inner world. Under the influence of American humanism, it became predominantly 'client-centred therapy', facilitating the client's self-actualisation. This form of counselling diversified first under the influence of behaviourism (which later developed into cognitive behavioural therapy and other behavioural and cognitive offshoots) with its more directive emphasis. Psychotherapy and counselling are now much more intertwined as integrative models borrow frameworks which were once very different kinds of practice.

The early push towards putting counsellors in secondary schools came from a variety of sectors – education, social care, mental health – which perhaps explains why early discussions about school counselling were preoccupied with the difference between counselling and other ways of 'helping'. That the first cohort of school counsellors were teachers who undertook local education authority-funded training further explains the amount of text devoted to the differences between teachers and counsellors in the ensuing years, as I'll explore in future chapters.

After the first school counselling courses began, a Schools Council Working Paper reviewed the landscape in 1967 (Schools Council, 1967). The paper reflects 'how broad the thinking on curriculum is at this time' (p.iii). At a moment of rapid growth in interest and training in school counselling, it notes that the intention of the paper is 'to encourage teachers to clarify their own attitudes and to examine the nature and effectiveness of counselling or similar procedures in their own schools' (p.iii). The paper draws on information from institutions providing training courses: Universities of Keele and Reading (the first to set them up), Exeter, Leeds and Manchester; Department of Education, Department of Social Administration, Tavistock Institute, schools, colleges of education and the National Foundation for Educational Research. The authors found that, at that time, school counselling involved a wide range of activities and specialism 'based on an intuitive rather than a defined philosophy or career structure' (p.1). The focus was, they thought, too diffuse: 'it is perhaps important that purely educational interests [as opposed to welfare, youth employment, health and medical services] should play a more central role in shaping the future of school counselling than is at present the case' (p.1).

In 1967, 46 school counsellors came out of the various institutions, a number that was expected to rise to 80 counsellors per annum by 1968 (Schools Council, 1967); by 1970 there were several hundred school counsellors in England and

Wales and nine full-time courses (Bor et al., 2002). In that year the Association of School Counselling was established, signalling a move to the professionalisation of counselling. By 1973 there were 18 courses but by the1980s university courses had dwindled and LEAs wanted teachers to absorb the counselling role as part of their teaching practice. The late 1990s and early 2000s saw rising acceptance of school counsellors again, partly in response to new bureaucratic demands on teachers that left less time for pastoral care and expectations arising from the 1989 Children Act. Training routes were no longer restricted to teachers and came from diverse sources. In 2014, Nick Luxmoore noted that he knew of only one specialised training course specially for training school counsellors (Luxmoore, 2014). The numbers of counsellors in English schools from this time on are vague. A 2016 survey of teachers from the Department for Education 'suggests' that 70% of secondary schools in England offer counselling services to their pupils, and current numbers look similar, though what 'counselling services' means is variable.

Progressive bullies and other school counsellors in fiction

In the school stories of the 1950s, before the advent of school counsellor training, we see references to child guidance centres, careers guidance, youth justice, social workers and even HM inspectors who stand for the new welfare provisions of the post-war state. *Carry On Teacher* (1959) brings a child psychiatrist into the school and lampoons the new theorising around children's behaviour. In later stories, school counsellors tend to be well-meaning and dilapidated, just as social workers are heavy handed and cold and school inspectors (at least from the 1990s on) bureaucratic and malicious. They are supporting roles, outshone by pastorally gifted teachers and outwitted by street smart teenagers.

Poppet Bruce, the RE teacher at Bagley Hall in Jilly Cooper's *Wicked!*, is 'determined to impose total political correctness' on the school and frequently intones with undisguised glee when difficulty arises that a pupil will no doubt 'need counselling' (Cooper, 2006). All-seeing Barbara Covett in Zoe Heller's *Notes on a Scandal* rubbishes all the Local Authority initiatives associated with 'wellbeing' as progressive bullying (Heller, 2004). In J.K. Rowling's *Casual Vacancy*, set in the idyllic but riven town of Pagford, Tess Hall, the 'head of guidance' at Winterdown comprehensive, cuts a downcast and collapsing figure, in 'clothes of a homespun, craft variety, and… jewellery of beads and wood' (Rowling, 2012, p.41). After 60 years of hessian wearing, handwringing intrusion, *Sex Education*'s Jean Millburn gives school counsellors a welcome albeit unorthodox rebrand (*Sex Education*, 2019–2023).

In the chapters which follow, I have incorporated the views of school counsellors from guides written from the late 1960s. Alongside the stories from popular culture, they capture something of the 'norms' and outlying ideas about adolescence and the role of schools to shape, contain or nurture their teenage charges. Some story tropes, character types and plot structures remain unchanged from the 1950s to the present ('progressives' and 'traditionalists' stand-off in most fictional staff rooms). Others are updated or adapted for new contexts (egotistical academy sponsors put a new spin on overreaching governors, for instance). The stories themselves shape English secondary schooling. Some, like the secondary modern school stories of the 1950s, are explicit in this ambition, to persuade their readership to demand more for 'the left behind' and, in their own storytelling, to model 'good' forms of reading to counteract the malign influence of American popular culture. Other stories are the means by which ideas about 'development' circulate in popular culture and occasionally hit a note that is heard by the political centre. Episodes of *Grange Hill,* for instance, were discussed in the House of Commons and their 'Just Say No' anti-drugs campaign made it to the White House. The recent storm around the Netflix drama *Adolescence* reached Downing Street but the relational aspects of the drama are lost in the rush to easier solutions (*Adolescence*, 2025). Phone bans in schools would be quicker and cheaper to implement than a wholesale reshaping of state secondary schooling to support or even acknowledge the developmental processes of adolescents.

The following chapters are reminders that current conversations around adolescent mental health and the place of schools in its 'healthy development' has a history, not just in psychological discourse and educational policy but in the stories of popular culture. Those of us who attended a state secondary school in England some time since the Second World War, as teachers, counsellors or pupils, have stories which contribute to the broader 'state school story', so some of those stories, collected from family, friends and clients, are also represented here.

References

Adolescence (2025) [Television Series], Netflix.

Bandura, A. (1991) 'Social cognitive theory of self-regulation', *Organizational Behavior and Human Decision Processes*, 50(2), pp.248–87.

Barrett, S. (2019) 'From adult lunatic asylums to CAMHS community care: the evolution of specialist mental health care for children and adolescents 1948–2018', *French Journal of British Studies*, XXIV-3, https://doi.org/10.4000/rfcb.4138

Berne, E. (1964) *Games People Play: The Psychology of Human Relationships*, New York: Grove Press.

Blakemore, S.J. (2018) *Inventing Ourselves: The Secret Life of the Teenage Brain,* London: Transworld.

Bor, R., Ebner-Landy, J., Gill, S., and Brace, C. (eds.) (2002) *Counselling in Schools*, London: Sage.

Bowlby, J. (1969) *Attachment and Loss: Attachment*, Vol. 1, New York: Basic Books.

Bronfenbrenner, U. (1979) *The Ecology of Human Development: Experiments by Nature and Design*, Cambridge, MA: Harvard University Press.

Burman, E. (2007) *Deconstructing Developmental Psychology,* 2nd ed., Hove: Routledge.

CACE, Central Advisory Council for Education (England) (1963) *The Newsom Report: Half Our Future* London: HMSO, https://www.education-uk.org/documents/newsom

CACE, Central Advisory Council for Education (England) (1967) *Children and Their Primary Schools (The Plowden Report)* London: HMSO, https://education-uk.org/documents/plowden

Carry on Teacher (1959) [Film] Thomas, G. dir., Beaconsfield: Beaconsfield Productions.

Cooper, J. (2006) *Wicked!* London: Corgi.

Crosland, A. (1956) *The Future of Socialism*, London: Jonathan Cape.

Department of Education and Science (DES) (1965) 'The organisation of secondary education', *Circular 10/65.*

Dweck, C. (2006) *Mindset: How You Can Fulfil Your Potential*, New York: Random House.

Education Policy Institute (EPI) (2023) 'Annual report: Social mobility and vulnerable learners', https://epi.org.uk/publications

Education Endowment Foundation (EEF): https://educationendowmentfoundation.org.uk

Erikson, E.H. (1980) *Identity and the Life Cycle,* London: W.W. Norton and Co.

Felitti, V.J., Anda, R.F. et al (1998) 'Relationship of childhood abuse and household dysfunction to many of the leading causes of death in adults. The Adverse Childhood Experiences (ACE) Study', *American Journal of Preventive Medicine*, 14(4), pp.245–58.

Flavell, J. (1979) 'Metacognition and cognitive monitoring. A new area of cognitive-developmental inquiry', *American Psychologist*, 34, pp.906–11.

Haidt, J. (2024) *The Anxious Generation: How the Great Rewiring of Childhood is Causing an Epidemic of Mental Illness,* Harmondsworth: Penguin.

Heller, Z. (2004) *Notes on a Scandal*, London: Penguin.

Hunter, E. (1955) *The Blackboard Jungle*, London: Constable and Co.

Jacques, E. (1965) 'Death and the mid-life crisis', *The International Journal of Psychoanalysis*, 46, pp.502–14.

Landreth, G. (2012) *Play Therapy: The Art of the Relationship*, 3rd edn., Abingdon: Routledge.

Limbrick, P. (2007) *Family-Centred Support for Children with Disabilities and Special Needs: A Collection of Essays,* Interconnections, https://tacinterconnections.com

Luxmoore, N. (2014) *School Counsellors Working with Young People and Staff: A Whole School Approach*, London: Jessica Kingsley.

Lytton, H. and Craft, M. (1969) *Guidance and Counselling in British Schools: A Discussion of Current Issues*, London: Edward Arnold Publishers.

Mandler, P. (2020) *The Crisis of Meritocracy: Britain's Transition to Mass Education Since the Second World War*, Oxford: Oxford University Press.

Piaget, J. (1929) *The Child's Conception of the World*, London: Routledge and Kegan Paul.

Piaget, J. (1959) *The Language and Thought of the Child*, 3rd edn., London: Routledge and Kegan Paul.

Richards, A. (ed.) (1991) *Three Essays on the Theory of Sexuality and Other Works: The Penguin Freud Library*, Vol.7, Harmondsworth: Penguin.

Robinson, W. (2006) 'Teacher training in England and Wales: past, present and future perspectives', *Education Research and Perspectives*, 33(2), pp. 19–36.

Rogers, C.R. (1959) *Client-Centred Therapy*, London: Constable.

Rogers, C.R. (1969) *Freedom to Learn*, Columbus, OH: Charles E Merrill Publishing Company.

Rowling, J.K. (2012) *The Casual Vacancy*, London: Little, Brown.

Sex Education (2019–2023) Television Series, Netflix.

Schools Council (1967) *Counselling in Schools: A Study of the Present Situation in England and Wales*, Working Paper No. 15.

Siegel, D. (2013) *Brainstorm: The Power and Purpose of the Teenage Brain,* London: Scribe.

Skinner, B.F. (1953) *Science and Human Behavior*, New York: Macmillan.

Timpson, E. (2019) *Timpson Review of School Exclusion* https://assets.publishing.service.gov.uk.

Tisdall, L. (2020) *A Progressive Education? How Childhood Changed in Mid-Twentieth - Century English and Welsh Schools,* Manchester: Manchester University Press.

Van der Kolk, B. (2014) *The Body Keeps the Score: Mind, Brain and Body,* Harmondsworth: Penguin.

Vignola, N. (2024) *Rewire: Break the Cycle, Alter Your Thoughts and Create Lasting Change*, London: Michael Joseph Penguin.

Vygotsky, L.S. (1962) *Thought and Language,* Cambridge: MIT Press.

Watson, J.B. (1930) *Behaviourism*, New York: Norton.

Winnicott, D. (1964) *The Child, the Family and the Outside World*, Harmondsworth: Penguin.

Wood, P. (2024) 'Teachers accuse behaviour tsar of "sniping from sidelines" over schools crisis', *The I Paper*, 6 January.

PART 1
Rebuilding

2

THE ORDINARY DEVOTED TEACHER AND THE SECONDARY MODERN IN THE 1950S

In 1948, at the age of 15, my mother Mary Howard left St Theresa's Roman Catholic School for Girls in Stockton-on-Tees, an all-through elementary school established in 1909. She'd wanted to leave earlier, but the 1944 Education Act put a stop to that by raising the leaving age. All I remember her telling me about her school days was her fear of the rooftop playground, her terror of the nuns and her impatience to leave. Hers was not a story of school-time growth but of war-time survival. I don't know how much St Theresa's was improved by the new provisions for secondary modern education. By then Mary was working at Sparks' bakery and enjoying her independence away from the nuns and the school rooftop. There was an anti-authoritarian part of my Mam, which she put to use in the defence and support of her children and her grandchildren. The teacher who dared to thrust a spoon in my brother Martin's mouth to make him speak more clearly met this part of her (Martin went on to be an accomplished linguist). Mary's authoritarian war-time schooling may have shaped this unwillingness to accept condescension towards her children. I'm happy to have inherited the same disposition.

Fighting the monster of ignorance

Although Mary did not feel the joy of being kept in school for an extra year, this is a point in the history of English schooling that is rich with the energy of post-war renewal (albeit scarred by post-war deprivation). Viewed optimistically, the secondary modern that St Theresa's became was symbolic of the ideals of

DOI: 10.4324/9781003715122-5

democracy, universal citizenship and of the welfare provisions that were enshrined in R.A.Butler's 1944 Education Act.

The Butler Act was part of the government response to the Beveridge Report of 1942, which was itself an 'overcoming the monster' plot. It defined the 'five giants on the road to post-war reconstruction': want, disease, ignorance, squalor and idleness (Beveridge, 1942). With its provision of free education for all up to the age of 15, the goal of the Butler Act was to overcome Ignorance, but its ambition was to vanquish all five giants. Local authorities were to be responsible for 'the provision of free medical treatment for pupils in attendance at any school… maintained by them' (Butler, 1944, p.48). They were to provide 'milk, meals and other refreshment' (p.49). If a child could not attend because of inadequate clothing, the authority was required to offer it (p.51). Facilities for 'recreation and social and physical training' were to be secured and maintained (p.53). Local authorities were granted 'power to ensure cleanliness' (p.54) (to inspect for risks of contamination). They were required to provide transport to their maintained schools and pay the travelling expenses of any student who needed them (p.55); to make provision for children who are unable to access education due to 'disability of mind' (p.57); to prevent children's employment impeding their health or educational opportunity (p.59); to limit the hours children can work (p.60) and to prohibit the payment of fees for education provided by local authority schools (p.61).

The Butler Act paid attention to families' material need and extended educational opportunity to a greater number of children. But psychological and emotional health were also core. In 1948, the World Health Organization defined health as 'a state of complete physical, mental and social wellbeing and not merely the absence of disease or infirmity': similarly, education is not merely the absence of ignorance (World Health Organization, 1948). The 1948 Children Act shows a similar understanding of good health, as it required local authorities to provide more than food and shelter to promote the wellbeing of children in their care (Children Act, 1948).

These pieces of legislation are statements of pastoral intent, informed in part by 'welfare psychology' and the idea of emotional capital: that is, an understanding of child development as relational and environmental which was popularised during and after the war by psychotherapists and pedagogues like John Bowlby, Donald Winnicott, Susan Isaacs, Ruth Thomas and others.

The pastoral intent of the Butler Act is often eclipsed in commentary which, understandably, focuses on the selective and hierarchical structure of schooling that it enshrined: the tripartite system. The Act did not provide one kind of good quality school for every child. Unable or unwilling to provide the 'grammars for all' that some asked for (perhaps due a mismatch of supply and demand), the Act came up with an offer to improve on the existing elementary schools but to maintain the distinction between 'grammar school children' and the rest, who would attend secondary moderns or technical schools. Access to state grammar schools would no longer require a fee or a scholarship earned through passing the 11-plus;

attendance would be free but would be determined for all by a selective test. The ground for keeping the selective test and establishing the tripartite school system was prepared in a series of reports. 'Modern psychologists' had provided evidence for the Spens Report of 1938; they found that measurable general intelligence decelerates at age 11 and falls away more or less completely at age 16 (Spens Report, 1938). Here was the rationale to offer different kinds of education to those children who were measurably of greater general intelligence than 'average' or 'below average' children. The Norwood Report of 1943 consolidated these views, categorising children's aptitudes as those who could cope with abstract reasoning, those who were better at more applied tasks and those who related to the world in more concrete ways (Norwood Report, 1943). The curricula of grammars, technical and secondary moderns were thus to mirror the 'fixed' developmental capacity of the children who attended them.

There are echoes here of Piaget's 1938 theory of stages of cognitive development: the concrete operational stage of the 7- to 11-year-old who understands what is in front of them, and the formal operational stage of the adolescent who has a capacity for abstract reasoning (Piaget, 1959). By the logic of the Spens and Norwood Reports, as most children were to be taught in secondary modern schools, where teaching was to be based on concrete experience, most children up to the age of 15 had the cognitive capacity of a pre-adolescent.

The New Secondary Education

Labour's first Minister for Education, Ellen Wilkinson, put a progressive spin on the tripartite system and the contentious secondary modern. In the Foreword to *The New Secondary Education*, a pamphlet distributed by the Ministry of Education in 1947, Wilkinson defends the new system from those who see it as a device 'for keeping intact a class system of education' (The Ministry of Education, 1947, p.6). She makes her case on the grounds of the diversity and child-centredness of the new system: 'these plans put the child first;...their variety is designed to suit different children, not different income groups; ...they aim at educating the child by the awakening of its interest' (p.4). While some children might be interested in an academic education, she argues, others 'get fun out of a carpenter's bench or a bricklayer's trowel, or satisfaction out of the risk and adventure of the mine' (p.4). This surprisingly jaunty case for selecting children at age 11 for a life of 'risk and adventure' down a mine is part of her broader case for parity of esteem for academic and vocational education. Wilkinson's defence of the new system has at its heart the strained idea that the interests and aptitudes of the individual child will be catered for in a system that is segregated by means of a selective test that most will fail at age 11; a test that was actually designed to identify suitable candidates for grammar schools, not to discern the 'interests' of the rest.

Ken Jones has suggested that Wilkinson was doing her best to sound hopeful about a system that was already in place (Jones, 2016). It is significant that her idealism is framed around the interests of the individual child not the social and economic needs of its class and that she foregrounds the 'awakening of its interests', not the provision of skills or knowledge as the broader purpose of education. The language of this Labour minister resonates with contemporary progressive pedagogy and child-centred psychology. The weaponry to overcome the five giants (want, ignorance, disease, squalor and idleness) is internal and subjective as well as material and measurable.

Crank philosophy and progressive nonsense

In the 1950s, a number of novels were written by teachers (Edward Blishen, E.R. Braithwaite, Michael Croft and John Townsend) about their experiences in the 'new' English secondary moderns. At the centre of most of these stories is the progressive secondary modern teacher. He (for these novels were written by and about male teachers) is a pastoral figure who intuitively offers to his students what might now be called 'emotional capital': self-esteem and empathy. The arrival of school counsellors was over a decade away, but the case for schools to be attuned to their students' emotional and psychological needs was being carved out in part in these stories and in psychological studies of the 1940s and 1950s.

We tend to know that ideas from one domain have entered the mainstream of popular culture when they are subject to satire. Educational and developmental psychology is given this treatment in the 1959 film *Carry on Teacher!* (1959). Leslie Phillips plays Alistair Grigg, an educational psychiatrist who has been deployed by the Ministry of Education to conduct a week of observations at Maudlin Secondary Modern School, as research for his forthcoming book *Contemporary Juvenile Behaviour Patterns*. He is accompanied by one of Her Majesty's Inspectors, Felicity Wheeler, whose views on the causes of and remedies for children's disruptive behaviour are quite different to Grigg's. The staff likewise have conflicting views on 'behaviour management'. The Head, Wakie (played by Ted Ray), is opposed to corporal punishment while the Maths teacher Grace Short (played by Hattie Jacques) is a strict disciplinarian.

The real focus of *Carry on Teacher!* of course is not behaviour management but the 'hilarious' impact of the slapstick pranks of the adolescents who are trying to sabotage beloved Wakie's application to another post in a shiny new rural school. There are also 'romantic' subplots involving the two visitors, the PE teacher Sarah Allcock, played by Joan Sim, and science teacher Gregory Adams (Kenneth Connor). However, it is not an irrelevance that the psychiatrist and the inspector drive the plot and that the setting is a secondary modern school.

The psychology of welfare

Grigg's research for *Contemporary Juvenile Behaviour Patterns* is a satirical nod to the growing research into adolescent behaviour and the workings of 'the adolescent mind'. The works of psychoanalysts and paediatricians John Bowlby and Donald Winnicott popularised ideas about juvenile deprivation, which were particularly pertinent after the war and were implicit in the new welfare state. They showed early home life as a potential source of psychological and emotional damage, most notably in Bowlby's findings of the impact of 'maternal deprivation' (Bowlby, 1952). Bowlby's theory of attachment and Winnicott's invention of the 'ordinary devoted mother', broadcast into the homes of Radio Four (then called the Home Service) listeners between 1943 and 1962, were to provide the antidote to this lack (Bowlby,1969; Karpf, 2014; Winnicott, 1949, 1991).

The adolescents in the secondary modern school stories are often cast as 'deprived'. Their homes lack the Winnicottian ordinary devoted mother and in the novels this absence is compensated for by the attention of the 'ordinary devoted teacher', usually a man. The representation of this pastoral relationship comes to define the purpose of the post-war state school, particularly the secondary modern, in progressive discourse. The school is implicitly tasked with making up for what the post-war working-class home does not provide for the working-class adolescent.

Bowlby and Winnicott both worked with families from a range of backgrounds. John Bowlby, paediatrician and psychiatrist, worked at the London Child Guidance clinic from 1936 to 1940. At the start of the war, Bowlby contributed to the Cambridge evacuation survey, and reported on the impact of mass evacuation on children. He became the head of the Children and Parent Department at the Tavistock Institute after the war. He anticipated the increased demand for people to work with children that arose from the 1948 Children Act and built up the Tavistock's resources in training for practitioners of child and adolescent mental health care. While at the Child Guidance clinic, he worked with children (some as young as five years old) who were referred for stealing and he recorded his thoughts in his 1944 publication, 'Forty-Four Juvenile Thieves: Their Character and Home-Life' (Bowlby, 1944). His principal finding was that a significant proportion of the children had experienced either prolonged periods of separation from their mothers before the age of five or a breakdown of the maternal relationship. He concluded that 'maternal deprivation' was a significant factor in their propensity to steal and a commentator in Bowlby's later report *Maternal Care and Mental Health* speculated that 'their stealing was an attempt to secure love and gratification and so reinstate the love relationship which they had lost' (Bowlby, 1952, p.47). This kind of perspective, which looked for an emotional root for criminal behaviour, would raise the eyebrows of less psychologically minded commentators in the ensuing decades.

Bowlby had been asked by the World Health Organization to prepare the report on maternal care as part of their investigation into the welfare of homeless children. His findings that 'the prolonged deprivation of the young child of maternal care may have grave and far-reaching effects on his character and so on the whole of his future life' (p.46) were contentious amongst many working in adult psychiatry, who dismissed the relationship between childhood experience and poor mental health in adults.

Bowlby's work has often been perceived as part of an ideological ruse to stop women working outside the home in the post-war period, a line of argument neatly contested on grounds of its ahistoricism by Denise Riley (Riley, 1979) and Mathew Thomson (Thomson, 2013). Bowlby *was* myopic in his emphasis on the mother-child relationship, barely mentioning absent or negligent fathers, presumably in part because the parents he worked with most often in his clinics were mothers.

Bowlby's observations on childhood experience as the forerunner of adult difficulty should not be dismissed because they seem so obvious now. His insistence that the 'origins of mental disturbances' can be found in 'intimate domestic events' is a rejection of what he called 'the German school of psychiatry', which 'stress[es] *constitutional and inherited* factors, at times to a point reminiscent of Calvinistic predestination' [emphasis mine] (Bowlby, 1952, p.13). Nurture, especially maternal nurture, continued to be the focus of Bowlby's developing ideas on attachment, because he rejected the idea of 'faulty stock' as the foundation of poor mental health. Further, his arguments about 'delinquency', which also indicted negligent mothers, would be used to counter moral panics about adolescent criminality and to encourage more liberal sentencing for those brought before the magistrates (a theme that gets developed in the secondary modern stories). Conservatism and progressivism sit together in his work, as they do in many of the representations I explore in this book.

Donald Winnicott (1896–1971), paediatrician and psychoanalyst, worked at the Paddington Green Children's Hospital in London for 40 years, where he built up a substantial case history that informed his writing on mothers and children. During the Second World War he was a consultant paediatrician to the children's evacuation programme and with his wife, psychiatric social worker Clare Britton, worked with child evacuees. His expertise was sought in the compilation of the 1948 Children Act and his contribution can be seen in the Act's emphasis on family support and understanding parent-child relationships.

Between 1943 and 1962, Winnicott was a regular on BBC Home Service. His nine-part series, 'The Ordinary Devoted Mother and Her Baby' (Winnicott, 1949), encapsulates what were to become the Winnicottian developmental ideals: democratic relationships, intuitive care and psychological growth through play and maternal attunement. In his weekly broadcasts, he conjured up an 'intimate' relationship with the imagined Home Service-listening mothers and embedded his ideals in the home, or more particularly, the mother-infant pair. Winnicott's broadcasts debunk regime-based parenting theory and promote 'the ordinary mother's' confidence in her own intuitive relationship with her baby. The baby is a 'going concern': an organism that has within it the material for its own healthy growth. The mother both provides and *is* the environment in which the baby fulfils its own promise. When the mother takes pleasure in responding to the baby's needs (because it is pleasurable to do so) and attends to the infant as a discerning person not a bundle of reflexes, the ground is prepared for a healthy subject to grow.

The patrician tone of Winnicott's commentary on 'bringing up baby' makes his work sound like a conservative conduct guide for middle-class women. Winnicott's mothers are never tired, or poor, domestically abused or dealing with several young children at once (unlike, presumably, the women he saw in his clinics). But, like Bowlby, Winnicott was emphasising a new way to understand infancy, as interpsychic (existing in relation to another) not an intrapsychic phenomenon (occurring within the mind of the child). His talks imagine the optimal environment for the emerging self of the infant which forms in the relationship between the internal world of the baby and the social world (in these talks the 'social world' is the child's mother). As Sally Alexander has pointed out, this 'social' orientation of Winnicott's psychological work, like Bowlby's, made it controversial in psychoanalytic circles and more progressive than subsequent criticism has allowed (Alexander, 2012).

Winnicott's 'ordinary devoted mothers' are disembodied, context-less; Bowlby's mothers bear sole responsibility for the good mental health and lawfulness of future citizens. However, there is transformative potential in their emphasis on emotional development as relational and environmental. If child development as they argue is not predestined (through 'stock' or genetic inheritance), relationships and environments can be shaped to help children flourish: an ambition that, at least partially, underpinned the post-war welfare state and the new secondary education system.

A *New Era* in home and school

A series of novels set in recently formed secondary modern schools in London dramatise the 'aftermath' of the Butler Act, capturing its ambition and its limitations. They use the language and commonplace ideas about good child development that was being promoted by child-centred psychologists, pedagogical theorists and in progressive educational journals like the *New Era*, the journal of the World Education Fellowship which, for a large part of the twentieth century to the present, has focused on the promotion of child-centred education (*New Era*, 1920–).

The novels are narrated by or from the perspective of new teachers who had been trained in post-war emergency schemes, and tell the story of what secondary moderns stood for. They conjure up the classrooms and home lives of working-class adolescents in post-war London (some the children of Irish immigrants like my own dad and those from other post-colonial nations).

The stories, by writers including Michael Croft, Edward Blishen, John Townsend and E.R. Braithwaite, plot the transition from the elementary schools that accommodated most children, like my mother, before and during the war to their ostensibly 'progressive' and modernised post-war successors. These schools theoretically provided the space to test out new ideas about schools, teachers and children and to prepare the citizens who would rebuild the post-war nation.

The novels echo the northern 'kitchen sink realism' of writers like John Osborne and Shelagh Delaney rather than the tradition of school-based British fiction that was set in public schools, like James Hilton's *Goodbye, Mr Chips* (Hilton, 1934) or Thomas Hughes' 1857 novel *Tom Brown's School Days* (Hughes, 1999). Only Braithwaite's *To Sir, With Love* (2005) survived in print much beyond the 1950s. There were film versions of *Spare The Rod* (1961), which starred Max Bygraves, and *To Sir, With Love* (1967) starring Sidney Poitier. They were marketed as sensational stories like the American high school story, *The Blackboard Jungle* (Hunter, 1955), about the violent and depraved 'inner-city teen'. In fact, most of the novels read as a riposte to sensationalism and appeal to the readers' empathy with the 'deprived' students.

The historian Laura Tisdall provides a powerful reading of these novels as part of 'the well-documented 1950s moral panic about youth', in relation to 'the popularised psychological concepts of "normal" and "deviant" child' and the implementation of 'progressive educational ideas that artificially limited working-class pupils' horizons' (Tisdall, 2015). She contextualises the novels in 1950s news stories in which secondary moderns are battlegrounds between delinquent youths and permissive teachers and puts them in the tradition of progressive education debates (Davis, 1990; Pearson, 1983). Such narratives, Tisdall argues, offer a more sympathetic and optimistic view of the teaching relationship but ultimately characterise working-class adolescents as intellectually limited and immature while casting the teachers as heroic rescuers.

The ordinary devoted teachers

Bearing Tisdall's critique in mind, there is still something to be said for the reconfigured teacher-child relationship imagined in these novels. As the child of two parents who had nothing but fear and contempt for pre- and war-time teachers, I am intrigued by the image of the benign and committed young men who stand for the new kind of teacher in these novels. My mother Mary feared the nuns of St Martin's and my dad, Martin, who was brought up in Irish-speaking rural Connemara in the West of Ireland, described his schooling, which ended at the age of 13, as basic and brutalising. Neither of them recalled a nurturing presence in their school lives. But such figures are alive and well in post-war fiction and, as the following story of the father of my friend Vivien and her sister Valerie illustrates, in post-war Lancashire.

John Cheetham was born in 1920 in Orrell, near Wigan, and from the age of 11 attended the local grammar school. In 1938 he embarked upon a Geography degree at the University of Leeds, only to be called up to serve in the Sixth Royal Tank Regiment during the Second World War. Captured in North Africa, he was held as a prisoner of war in Italy and kept a copy of Shakespeare's Tragedies in his inside pocket throughout his imprisonment and subsequent escape into rural Italy. After his service, he completed what he referred to as his 'war degree' and having qualified as a teacher got a post in 1946 at the secondary modern school in Radcliffe, Greater Manchester. In the 1950s he was appointed to the headship of another secondary modern school, near Bolton. Although his degree was in Geography (which he put to use when his 'Rucksackers' expeditions introduced urban children to walking in the Peak and the Lake District), his real love was literature and later in his career he developed training material, *The Poetry File*, to help teachers provide lessons in creative writing. Vivien remembers talk at the tea table of Richard Hoggart (much-admired) and of Cox and Dyson's hated Black Papers, and Pelican editions of Bowlby on the bookshelf. John became an education adviser for Lancashire County, sitting on headship appointing committees and overseeing the conversion of grammars and secondary moderns to comprehensives across the county. In 1967 he was awarded the office of the Order of the British Empire (OBE) for his services to education.

Michael Croft, author of *Spare the Rod* and eventual founder of the National Youth Theatre, had been a Burnage grammar school boy before serving in the Royal Air Force during the war (an experience mirrored in his protagonist John Sanders). *Spare the Rod* (Croft, 1954) was inspired by Croft's brief experience as a trainee teacher in London secondary moderns in 1950. While its principal focus is on the harsh discipline in schools, the novel also follows its protagonist's struggles in forming relationships with the children and 'engaging the interest' of his jaded and sceptical charges in a secondary modern that, in the words of its headmaster, is still at heart an elementary school.

The author of the 1955 novel *Roaring Boys* (Blishen, 1977), Edward Blishen, was a conscientious objector who taught in secondary moderns in North London and who sat on the editorial board of the left-leaning educational journal *Forum: for the discussion of new trends in education* (*Forum*, 1958–1990). *Roaring Boys* explores the class-based culture gap between the masters and students and the protagonist's attempt to bridge it by, in the words of Ellen Wilkinson, 'waking the children's interests'. Both Blishen's and Croft's protagonists cultivate 'intuition' as a means to enter the world of their students. This paradoxical process – cultivating something that comes 'naturally' – echoes Donald Winnicott's counsel to the 'ordinary devoted mother' who will know what to do with her baby if she lets go of prescribed ideas about parenthood.

The Young Devils (Townsend, 1958) by John Townsend takes a more cynical and conservative view of the secondary modern. Like Croft and Blishen, Townsend had been a teacher after the war and found the ambitions of the 1944 Act left unrealised, due to staff shortages, large class sizes and poor amenities. While Croft and

Blishen still invest in the progressive child-centred ideal – to awaken the interests of the children – Townsend despairs of the secondary modern's poor academic standards. In the authorial preface, he rails against the failure of mass schooling 'to combat the influence of television, films, the sickly exhortations of "pop" singers'; the popular culture associated with the mythical delinquent teenager. Townsend's narrator is sceptical both about 'this psychological age [where] so much importance is attached to environment and happy human relationships' (*TYD*, p.47) and the schools in which those relationships are meant to be forged. While, he says, the emphasis of 'educationalists' is on combatting the 'terrible home conditions' of the pupils, they 'conveniently forget to criticise the conditions existing in many "difficult" schools which directly contribute to breeding "dead-end kids"' (*TYD*, p.131). There is no road to Damascus conversion for Townsend's narrator as he becomes more authoritarian and defeated as the story proceeds, and reflects finally on 'the nerve-wearing daily struggle faced by each teacher to maintain order and discipline' (*TYD*, p.214). He leaves the school gate pretty much as he entered it: sure of the dangers of mass education.

E.R. Braithwaite's *To Sir, With Love* (Braithwaite, 2005) is interestingly poised between Croft's and Blishen's idealism and Townsend's conservatism. Braithwaite, who was born and educated in what was then British Guiana, served in the RAF and became a teacher after looking for work as an engineer in England after the war. In his fictional reworking of this experience, his protagonist Ricky recalls the overt racism of his post-war job search. An interview for a senior engineering post comes to an end when the prospective employer admits he cannot countenance placing Ricky in 'a position of authority' over 'a number of our English employees' (*TSWL*, p.33). Ricky is confronted with the 'black skin' which 'had not mattered' during his six years of service in the RAF.

A chance meeting with an elderly man in St James's Park (in narrative terms, Ricky's 'donor' who redirects his journey) alerts him to the 'desperate need' for teachers, especially in the East End of London and muses that education authorities are unlikely to be bothered about 'the colour of people's skin' (*TSWL*, p.43). When Ricky bristles at the idea that he is being recommended to a 'tough area' because of the colour of his skin, the old man chides him in the terms of a post-war optimist who sees a 'new breed of professional and scientific men' emerging from the 'slums and alleyways' of the city (*TSWL*, p.43). (The urban alleyway is often imagined as a place of transformation in stories about working-class adolescents as I'll illustrate further in Chapter 9.)

Ricky has some way to go before he can integrate the old man's world view. When we first meet Ricky, on the Aldgate bus, travelling to his first day as a teacher at Greenslade Secondary, he is very much the middle-class product of a colonial education. He is shocked by the bodies and manners of the white working-class passengers, particularly the women, who are 'thick-armed, bovine,... heavy-breasted' and remind him of 'peasants in a book by Steinbeck' (*TSWL*, p.1). Though he concedes condescendingly that they have 'their own kind of dignity'

(*TSWL*, p.1), the impression they give of London's East End is a long way from that he garnered from the writings of 'Chaucer and Erasmus' or his knowledge of the 'Sorores Minores' (*TSWL*, p.5), the nuns of Aldgate's Order of St Clare; women who are no doubt less corporeal than his fellow bus passengers.

Ricky's literary map of London, which has already been stained by racism, is shredded further by the vulgarity of its working people. Ricky, therefore, is not immediately receptive to the 'progressive' views of Mr Florian, the head teacher of Greenslade Secondary, who explains of his pupils that 'the very nature of their environment' inhibits their 'spiritual, moral and physical growth' (*TSWL*, p.25). The task of the school, he says, is to understand and relieve those pressures. Ricky, who is subjected to their racism, sees only the privilege of their whiteness, not the deprivations of their class.

The students' racism and Ricky's class-based contempt are worked through in the novel, but rather uneasily. While the 'tension' between Blishen's and Croft's protagonists and their antagonistic charges is released when the teachers learn to empathise with the students, Ricky 'connects' with his pupils through the more traditional educational means of inculcating shame and bodily discipline.

Storytelling as emotional capital

The more sympathetic secondary modern stories offer a form of emotional capital in their means of representation. In their 'realism' they seek to represent the students back to themselves. The stories are to be what Edward Blishen's teacher-narrator calls 'adventure and comedy extracted from our own daily background' (*RB*, p.254), of which the middle-class child has plenty, rather than the more plentiful stories of the 'fantastic and exotic' found in the school library. Croft, Blishen and Braithwaite create a kind of 'psychological realism', with their representations of students and teachers who develop self-awareness in the context of their relationships with one another. The teacher's sense of self and professional competence develops across the narratives as he is increasingly able to attune to his students' needs just as the initially torpid students come to life under his attention. This trajectory echoes contemporaneous ideas about 'healthy' child development and 'good parenting' from Bowlby, Winnicott and others of the 'independent school' who were moving away from Freudian and Kleinian psychoanalysis with its emphasis on Oedipal battles and the psychic violence of the mother-child pair. The latter, by contrast, was the psychological basis of William Golding's 1954 *The Lord of the Flies* (Golding, 1954), the story of boarding school 'evacuees' surviving on an island after a plane crash. While Golding's was a Freudian, 'intrapsychic' allegory of the students' internal descent from civilisation to savagery, the secondary modern school stories emphasise the inter-relational aspects of self-development. The Independents' relational and observable theories were at the heart of the post-war welfare state in which wellbeing was cast as emotional *and* material, subjective *and* objective.

They were powerfully articulated in debates about post-war education and the stories that teased out their aspirations and shortfalls.

The novelty of secondary modern schools and the fascination and fear that they and their adolescent charges provoked made them a good source of fiction and an emblem for post-war society. As fiction, the novels explore educational and welfare policy from an imagined 'inside' (albeit from the adult not the child perspective). They provide fictional adolescent subjects for developmental psychology and historicise that subjectivity in their portraits of a particular time and place. Part of the comedy and tragedy of the novels relies on the gap between the 'crank psychology' (pedagogical theory) doled out in teacher training colleges and by local authority inspectors and the 'reality' of classroom management which relies on 'intuition'. Their protagonists eventually prove themselves to be above 'theory' but the influence of the 'pragmatic and relational ideals' (so, theory) of contemporary child psychotherapists informs the way they describe their relationships with their students.

'Trying to fetch along the wrong people'

Even the most progressive of the novels' protagonists do not really question the premise of the selective test that failed to select the children in front of them. They liberally use epithets such as 'backward', 'dim' and 'dull' (p.37, p.187) to describe their charges, echoing the pathologising language of contemporary child psychotherapy and educational discourse. An early edition of *Forum*, for instance, opens with an article by a teacher at Peckham Girls' School, London, entitled 'Experiences with a backward class' (Partington, 1959). The article seeks to dispel the myth that so-called 'backward' children (a designation derived from reading age tests at age 11) cannot succeed in education and describes the methods used to increase the girls' literacy. Eventually, writes Partington, they left school with qualifications and as 'happy, confident and responsible individuals', testament to 'the principle on which comprehensive education is based; that within our young people are powers and possibilities as yet unrealised' (Partington, 1959, p.84).

In the novels, questions arise about children who seem out of place in the secondary modern environment: those who passed the 11-plus test but whose parents were 'terrified of expense, or anxious that their sons should receive only a minimum amount of education' (*RB*, p.284); or who started at the grammar school but were bullied out. But all assume it is natural to segregate the children at age 11 and focus instead on the challenges of the increased leaving age, the poverty of resources and the existential purpose of the secondary modern school.

The new purpose as Ellen Wilkinson saw it – to awaken the interests of the child – is far from universally accepted by all of the fictional school staff. For instance, Blishen's protagonist is confronted with 'the private school view' on the extension of the education franchise when he bumps into a former colleague:

'I mean – this Education Act!' said Gibson. 'Rather like there being classical concerts in sports arenas, don't you think? Trying to fetch along the wrong people' (*RB*, p.274).

Like the Act's democratic ambitions, the new 'welfare' responsibilities that it imposes on schools crop up frequently and with irritation. In Townsend's *The Young Devils*, one teacher rails against the hypocrisy of parents' complaints about teachers who administer corporal punishment while they are 'quite willing to let us supervise their kids' dinners, give out milk, make sure they eat their vitamin capsules, hand out toilet paper, collect savings, take them on outings and teach' (*TYD*, p.194). Jenks, the head of Croft's Worrell Street, is so preoccupied with the bureaucracy of the school's welfare duties – keeping a clean register, distributing milk, taking dinner money – that he by-passes relationships with his students entirely.

The schools in these novels are not the panacea to war-time loss that the Act imagined. The new teachers are trained in post-war 'emergency training schemes', to meet the demand created by the Butler Act and find themselves teaching alongside pre-war elementary school teachers whose careers have survived the war but who feel the strain of their new responsibilities. Croft's John Sanders has some sympathy with his 'disappointed, embittered' colleagues when they say that 'their work was more difficult now than before the War, that the conditions were worse, the children wilder, more backward, unstable...War's depredations did not end with an Armistice' (*STR*, p.97).

In the secondary modern stories, the survivors of the elementary school system and most of the new recruits are ineffectual and are unable to 'relate' to their students. The protagonists of *Spare the Rod* and *Roaring Boys* and Braithwaite's Ricky heroically persevere in inhospitable conditions to become 'relevant' to their adolescent students. They cast off the methods and defensive personae of the pre-war staff (none of whom is a Mr Chips) and embrace new kinds of relationships with their students: kinds of attunement, intimacy and familiarity reminiscent of Winnicott's 'ordinary devoted mother'. These teachers are tasked with making up for the deprivations, maternal and otherwise, that their charges suffer outside of school and at the hands of their colleagues. They are new kinds of men who broaden the idea of the nurturing adult; not mothers, not fathers, but new kinds of professional teacher-carers. They are legitimised in what is encoded as a feminine role (recalling Richard Hoggart's description of the 'brainy' grammar school boy who exists in his mother's world) by their conventionally masculine experience of war (Hoggart, 1957).

Blishen's protagonist comes to understand that his progress as a teacher will depend on his understanding of 'the world' of his pupils, just as Winnicott's mothers will enter 'the world' of their infant. When he struggles to engage with one of his students, he reflects that 'my trouble with him was in fact trouble with myself. I didn't understand the school, or the boys, or the district; I wasn't a teacher at all' (*RB*, p.20). He lurches from class to class, failing to make much impression, and eventually identifies his problem as one shared by all the teachers in Stonehill Street where 'two worlds clashed':

> The masters and the boys had very different backgrounds...even though a teacher managed in the end to master the manners of his charges, it was always an act of mastery and never an act of intimacy.
>
> *(RB, pp.63–4)*

It is not just that class divides them, but that the teachers exacerbate the difference by 'trying to master' the students' 'manners'. Mastery makes strangers of the teachers and monsters and thieves of the pupils. In this narrative, intimacy and familiarity will overcome the material and emotional deprivations of the children's lives and so bring the 'two worlds' of teacher and student into contact.

In an episode that recalls Bowlby's account of the young thief as one who steals back that which was taken from him in the maternal relationship, Blishen describes a student called Rigby, 'the school's most conspicuous criminal':

> Like so many of the boys at that time, he was one of the disasters of the war. There had been no continuity in his life at all, nothing from which he could draw the most elementary conception of moral behaviour. The world, taking his father away to its battles, taking his mother away for a long series of war-time liaisons, had given him huge examples of theft.
>
> *(RB, p.82)*

Like Rigby, other children in the novels appear in the 'Juvenile Courts'. Traditionalists like Jenks put their criminality down to their 'bad stock', but these stories emphasise the prior, emotional thefts the children have suffered. In *To Sir, With Love*, Ricky accompanies young Fenman to Court where he is charged with a stabbing offence. Much to Ricky's embarrassment, the Chairman of the Court blames the 'cranks and dreamers ... pursuing an educational course which over the years of trial had achieved nothing to recommend it' for the 'delinquents' he sees before him (*TSWL*, p.118). Rather than be shamed into rejecting the Greenslade ethos, however, Ricky leaves the court 'conscious of a feeling of increased responsibility for the young people who were in my care for nearly six hours each day' (*TSWL*, p.119).

To understand their students' behaviour, the teachers need to understand their lives and bring social context to the abstract developmental theory of the training college. So, when the student Harkness confides in John Sanders about the death of his brother in the war and his father's descent into alcoholism, the 'afternoon was suddenly alive and rich with meaning. In a flicker of time the formal relationship of master and boy collapsed' (*STR*, p.125).

The 'collapse' of the 'formal relationship' is precisely what the advocates of corporal punishment in these novels fear. When *Spare the Rod*'s Sanders arrives at Worrell Street, long-serving teacher Mr Gubb assures him 'It's common sense you need here. Common sense and discipline' (*STR*, p.79). Gubb, a former master-joiner who came into teaching when his work dried up before the war, exhorts Sanders to 'get down to practicalities' (*STR*, p.79). Gubb's 'practicalities' involve frequent and sadistic acts of violence committed on pupils, characterised by Sanders in Freudian terms as a fetishistic psychological flaw: 'were the weals he raised reflected also in his own consciousness; or did he relish his task and seek satisfaction from it as the drug addict craves for his lovely treacherous weed?' (*STR*, p.74).

In *To Sir, With Love*, the head teacher Florian is at the other end of the authoritarian-permissive scale and does not authorise the use of corporal punishment at all (hence the indictment by the Chairman of the Juvenile Court). His school embraces a 'disciplined freedom, that state in which the child feels free to work, play and express himself without fear of those whose job it is to direct and stimulate his efforts into constructive channels' (*TSWL*, p.26).

Underlying these poles of belief about discipline are attitudes towards democracy and the purpose of the secondary modern school in shaping future citizens. Jenks, the defeated Headmaster of Worrell Street, invokes a class-based psychology when he claims the pupils are predestined to failure. Rejecting the progressive *New Era* or *Forum* world view, he sees the school as:

> a combination of a reformatory, a pathological ward, and a menagerie. They can talk as much as they like on the Town Council and at the Association conferences about developing the mind of the modern child, but in this part of the world it does not apply … We deal with instincts – bad ones mostly, animal in some case.
>
> *(STR, p.151)*

While Jenks and Gubb cane their way into authority, imposing restraints on what they see as the instincts of the mob, the idealistic young teachers Bickerstaff and Alcock fail to make contact at all with their working-class students. Despite Bickerstaff's 'course in Child Psychology' he 'could not talk their language' (*STR*, p.98) and Alcock 'understood the theory of teaching [but] could not reach the children because she was unacquainted with their world' (*STR*, p.99).

Sanders works hard to acquaint himself with 'the world' of the children, but the causal connection between progressive, child-centred teaching methods and broader social democracy is frequently satirised and called into question by his colleagues. The world weary Murry succinctly deflates the link between progressivism and citizenship, when he advises his friend to dole out clippings from beauty magazines for the girls and football pools for the boys; this, he quips, is 'training them in citizenship and increasing their sense of responsibility at the same time' (*STR*, p.199). Sanders too is ambivalent about the potential of his students to become citizens worthy of democracy. In an exchange with the 'irrelevant' head

Jenks, Sanders begins by taking a stand against his view of the students as unteachable but his noble defence of his pupils quickly gives way to a less confident view of their autonomy and potential as citizens:

> They would be the subject of Gallup polls, would pick their judgement from the inane leader-column or the smiling personality on the television screen; they would assess the importance of their lives through the sporting pages of the newspaper with the largest circulation. Ineluctably, unalterably, they would be The People.
>
> *(STR, p.160)*

Even this indictment of the heirs of democracy is not based on their 'stock' nor their 'animal instincts': it is rooted in Sanders' fear of the lack of critical distance between the future citizens and the media ('they would be The People' implies a slippage between citizens, the working 'People' invoked by the hard Left, and the newsprint they passively consume).

Cultural capital

Each of the novels is querulous on the impact of television, cinema and comic books on psychological 'development'. Blishen's teacher is vigilant in his search for contraband comic books and tears up these enemies to education when he finds them, which, as Ken Jones notes, echoes Blishen's support for a campaign by the NUT in the early 1950s against imported American horror comics (Jones, 2016, p.66). In the diaries kept by his pupils, the teacher notes their frequent references to watching television and bemoans its addictive and pacifying effect when 'swallowed wholesale':

> Opera, drama, quizzes, ballet, parlour games, the whole gamut. Much of it was received with disgust ... The mere fact of television concealed the pain until the mesmeric occasion was past.
>
> *(RB, pp.265–6)*

This is not the 'moral panic' about popular culture that is often associated with representations of adolescence and delinquency in the 1950s. The new 'attuned' teachers fear more their students' passivity and inability to discriminate: they fear their incapacity to be full citizens.

In *Roaring Boys*, the school's new libraries, visits to museums, trips abroad and dramatic performances, what Bourdieu would later call cultural capital (Bourdieu, 1977) and which are recurrent tropes in the school story, are offered as the antidote to the objectifying mesmerism of television, 'pictures' and comics. While cultural capital has connotations of social improvement, in these stories new experiences are also characterised as emotional capital, an integration of the adolescents' subjective and objective worlds. A trip to Paris, for instance, is described as a 'step out of the slumminess' of the boys' lives (a socially improving experience) and a way to discover already pleasurable things in a new environment (an emotional and psychological experience): the boys' aim 'was to search Paris for approximations to pleasures already known at home, to take photographs and collect souvenirs' (*RB*, p.233). By experiencing the newness of Paris through the familiar activities, the boys' worlds are 'enlarged' but not overwhelmed. These are the kinds of 'small doses' Winnicott recommends for the successful integration of the 'two kinds of reality': the infant's internal world and the external social world (Winnicott, 1991).

For Winnicott, emotional and psychological health is the capacity to 'feel both kinds of reality at once'; it is the interplay between the infant and the mother that allows the internal and external worlds to be integrated. For the 'unfortunate man' whose mother 'made a mess of it all' either 'the world is there, and everyone sees the same thing, or else everything is imaginary and personal' (Winnicott, 1991, p.74): reality for such a person is entirely objective or entirely subjective. In Blishen's novel, one such 'unfortunate' who cannot integrate the social and subjective world is a boy called Bunce. To his teacher, Bunce 'represented something peculiarly distressing in the air of Stonehill Street...the reluctance to participate actively in life that was to be found, in some degree, in so many of the boys' (*RB*, p.89). Bunce and his parents are 'as dreadful an indication of something wrong in society as the impotent comic grotesques of Gogol and Chekhov were of a malaise in nineteenth-century Russia' (*RB*, p.90). The boy would suffer 'from nameless fits of fear' (*RB*, p.89), his 'large and collapsed mother' would intone of 'an enormous vagueness of agonies and disasters' that kept him from school, while his father existed in 'some ultimate limbo of incapacity' (*RB*, p.90). The Bunces are the comic grotesques of post-war London, whose malaise is a traumatised subjectivity, detached from and overwhelmed by the reality of the objective world.

'Something warmer than a pedagogue'

In Blishen's description of the school, the creation of a library, readings, performances and expressive art are presented primarily as an antidote to trauma, and as psychological and emotional enrichment rather than as mechanisms of social mobility: they offer a coming to life as a subject rather than a step up a social ladder. Blishen's protagonist notes that the 'Bohemian naturalness' that is unnecessary in a grammar school where 'most boys are fully supplied with consultable adult acquaintances' (ordinary devoted mothers?) (*RB*, p.346) is core to the task in Stonehill Street: 'there was a great deal of basic healing of the spirit to do before one could begin to appeal to the academic disciplines' (*RB*, p.346). The new secondary modern teacher must be 'something warmer than a pedagogue' to meet 'a fundamental Stonehill Street need' (*RB*, p.346).

Through his students' art and writing, Blishen's teacher comes to find out what their material and experiential deprivations are. Asked to paint a picture called

'Where I live' (*RB*, p.371) and to draft a design for a proposed new secondary modern, the boys come up with sketches of 'what they were missing' (*RB*, p.378): they reel off wish lists of gardens, playing fields, decent toilets, chairs to sit on in assembly and 'the decent homes their fathers and grandfathers hadn't had' (*RB*, p.380). They yearn for 'the world as a beautiful place'; 'the experience of coming to school and finding no bewildering gap between that and the world outside' (*RB*, p.384): they desire the integration of their subjective and objective realities.

Real women, real men and teachers

In the contemporary discourse on deprivation and children's mental health, the mother is the arbiter of plenty and scarcity. Bowlby and Winnicott wrote from their clinical experience, and that experience was of observing mothers and children. In the secondary modern novels, mothers of students feature here and there, usually as sources of their child's poor development. This lack is made up for by the young men who falteringly offer democratic relationships in place of the authoritarianism of their predecessors and sometimes of their students' fathers.

Women in the schools are often notable and suspect for not being mothers. While the 'marriage bar' had been formally lifted for women teachers in 1944, these novels represent the uneasy marriage of traditional femininity and professionalism as seen through the eyes of these ambivalently masculine male teachers (Oram, 1996).

John Sanders, for instance, sees salvation for the floundering young theorist Miss Alcock 'in having children of her own. Otherwise, her future was arranged. She would become inescapably, unalterably, and always recognisably, a schoolmarm' (*STR*, p.99). Miss Dabbott, whose age 'belied the outline of small, firm breasts', arouses Sanders' curiosity: 'What story there, John wondered? What waste of love, or Lesbos? self-hate? Sterility?' (*STR*, pp.51–2). A female Head appears in *The Young Devils* though she is predictably aberrant: Miss Fibbs' 'face was without make-up, and though she smiled continuously she gave…the feeling that it would not be necessary to scratch very deep to find another person' (*TYD*, p.101). Absence of cosmetics does not make this woman 'natural' and, like Croft's Jenks, she is more preoccupied with school administration than cultivating relationships.

Braithwaite's Greenslade Secondary finds it difficult to keep male teachers or, according to their most respected teacher Grace Dale-Evans, to appoint men worth keeping: 'those twerps tootle off to a training college and somehow acquire a certificate, a licence to teach, and then they appear in a classroom looking like last week's left-overs' (*TSWL*, p.107). Rick, 'big and broad and handsome', is welcomed as a new kind of man (*TSWL*, p.107). Unlike the other schools, Greenslade has plenty of female staff. Ricky introduces each of them like a Miss World commentator: 'attractive figure'; 'mannish appearance'; 'slight figure'; 'white-haired matron'; 'full-figured, elegant' (reader, he marries her) (*TSWL*, pp.12–6). These women are experienced, brisk and competent, and some of them are explicitly described as maternal, in particular, Dale-Evans ('attractive figure') who, 'with her ready, listening ear and proven, sound advice, was both teacher and mother to these girls' (*TSWL*, p.20). As this 'ordinary devoted mother' is in place in Greenslade, Ricky can embrace a more traditionally masculine identity and set out to 'disprove the distaff view that the men teachers were inadequate for the job' (*TSWL*, p.64). He struggles to understand what kind of man his students see him as, however. When he upbraids his student Jane Purcell for swearing ('Do you use such words when speaking to your father?' (*TWSL*, p.64)), her Eastenders-like riposte makes it clear that he does not have paternal authority: 'You're not my bleeding father' (*TSWL*, p.64). Pamela Dare's attraction to him is explained by Dale-Evans in terms of his difference from 'their fathers and brothers and neighbours' (*TSWL*, p.107). This distinction is both his kindness and the more ambivalently read difference of his black-skinned, masculine body.

Ricky's colonised body

As a middle-class man, Ricky experiences his own body as more 'decent' than the bodies of the working-class men, women and children of East London, which often provoke in him a visceral disgust. But seeing himself through the gaze of the white working-class and post-war British community, his own body becomes suspect and paradoxical. Ricky has seen how his black, masculine body is associated with 'inexhaustible brute strength' while what is expected of him is 'a courteous subservience and contentment with a lowly state of menial employment and slum accommodation' (*TSWL*, p.37). While, as a colonial subject, he was welcomed to serve in the RAF and found his race no bar to relationships with women during the war, in the post-war years he is not trusted as a citizen or a man:

> It seems as though there were some unwritten law in Britain which required any healthy, able-bodied Negro resident there to be either celibate by inclination, or else a master of the art of sublimation.... We were to be men, but without manhood.
>
> *(TSWL, p.92)*

His experience of racism makes Ricky less sympathetic than the protagonists of the other novels to the deprivations of his working-class students. 'Hungry or filled, naked or clothed, they were white' and therefore privileged. Teaching them would be 'a job, not a labour of love' (*TSWL*, p.25).

Of course, Ricky's trajectory will be to develop empathy with the students, to enter their world and indeed for his work to become a 'labour of love'. A 'turning point' comes in a physical confrontation, when, in a bout of boxing with one of his young antagonists, Denham, Ricky lands a punch in the boy's solar plexus. Ironically, it is Ricky's physical dominance over the class ringleader rather than his democratic pedagogy, or Blishen's 'healing of the spirit', that changes his relationship with the class. Post-punch, the students show 'more attention, obedience and respect' and he finds himself liking them (*TSWL*, p.81).

While Sanders' and Blishen's protagonists develop an atmosphere of familiarity in their classrooms, Ricky puts in firm boundaries and rules of conduct and 'decency' based on his own experience of school in British Guiana. His colleague Weston, who is never reluctant to make racist and class-based quips in Ricky's presence, makes fun of his request that the students address each other as Miss and Mister, dubbing it as 'some sort of experiment in culture for the millions' (*TSWL*, p.83). Despite this put-down, Ricky persists and eventually he secures the students' respect: 'they now accepted the things I said completely' (*TSWL*, p.89).

The novel ends with Ricky reconciled to the unruly adolescents of Greenslade, some of whom, he reflects, 'would make the grade', some 'would always have difficulties', while the rest 'would be decent folk, living decently without too much ambition or aggressiveness or anything' (*TSWL*, p.184).

This imagined future populated by these 'decent folk' sits uneasily with the bleak prophecy of his girlfriend's father for any children Ricky and she might have: 'They'll belong nowhere, and nobody will want them' (*TSWL*, p.174). Mr Blanchard's view chimes with the racist epithets about black teachers, children and members of the local communities that are littered, uncriticised, throughout the rest of the secondary modern novels. In the film version of *Spare the Rod*, the closing scene sees the parents of Olive Thomson (described in the novel as 'a curly-haired half-caste girl'), thanking Sanders for treating their daughter with kindness. 'I just treated her like everyone else' he says, but the fact that he is thanked for doing so speaks volumes about the endemic racism of schools that were adjusting poorly to post-war immigration and the dual-heritage children of servicemen.

What they're missing

Views about fixed intelligence and the limited intellectual capacity of the working-class adolescents and children of immigrants in these secondary modern stories are explicit. The novels contribute to the mythmaking about the post-war 'inner city', the 'problem school' and the 'delinquent' working-class adolescent, and largely reproduce the hegemonic sexism and racism of post-war Britain (though Braithwaite forcefully challenges the latter). At the same time, they unsettle the sensational headlines on which they were sold. They share an emerging language about the relationship between home life and school life, between family and child, school and local authority, post-war democracy, welfare and citizenship. The inexperienced but 'exceptional' male protagonists are tasked with making up for the 'deprivations' of the pupils' home (and school) environments. The children do not live in homes where the 'ordinary devoted mother' has listened to Donald Winnicott, but their new teachers have imbibed enough understanding of attunement to become 'ordinary devoted teachers': part parent, part pastoral guide.

These novels are not documentary realism, but they are an alternative to, and rejection of, the fictional and imaginative world that the children consume in cinema, television and comics. Their narrators are part 'middle-class' rescuers and part a throw-back to the idealised teacher of pre-war fiction, but they are also off-course post-war trainees, washed up in a place where, like their charges, they feel they do not belong. The pupils are often too large for their desks and are too many for the teachers to get to know. They flounder and struggle even to remember the pedagogical and psychological theory that their experienced peers ridicule. The novels sketch the mismatch, then, between the ambitions for modernised secondary education of the 1944 Act and the infrastructure that was to nurture them. These novels capture, in Blishen's words, 'what they're missing' but idealistically start to imagine what might replace that absence: an idea of a teacher-pupil relationship that makes up for the deprivations of war-time and home life. While Townsend throws up his hands defeated at the scale of the task, Croft, Blishen and Braithwaite explore a traumatised working-class subjectivity. They characterise new pastoral teachers who try to elide the difference between the worlds of teacher and student through intimacy, and integration of subjective and objective, the real and the imaginary, the literal and the symbolic.

The work of pedagogues and psychotherapists like Bowlby and Winnicott promoted an 'environmental' understanding of child development and emphasised the necessity of emotional capital. They did not challenge an implicitly class-based view of intelligence or selective education, but as we will see their ideas provide part of the argument for comprehensive education in the following decades.

Abbreviations

RB, Blishen, E. (1977) *Roaring Boys: A Schoolmaster's Agony*, London: Cedric Chivers.
STR, Croft, M. (1954) *Spare the Rod*, London: Longmans.
TSWL, Braithwaite, E.R. (2005) *To Sir, With Love*, London: Vintage.
TYD, Townsend, J. (1958) *The Young Devils,* London: Chatto & Windus.

References

Alexander, S. (2012) 'Primary maternal preoccupation: D.W. Winnicott and social democracy in mid-twentieth-century Britain', in Alexander, S. and Taylor, B. (eds.) *History and Psyche: Culture, Psychoanalysis, and the Past*, Basingstoke: Palgrave Macmillan, pp.149–72.

Beveridge, W. (1942) *Social Insurance and Allied Services* (Beveridge Report), London: HMSO https://www.parliament.uk/about/living-heritage/transformingsoceity/living learning/coll-9-health1/coll-9-health/

Blishen, E. (1977) *Roaring Boys: A Schoolmaster's Agony*, London: Cedric Chivers.
Bourdieu, P. (1977) *Outline of a Theory of Practice*, Cambridge: Cambridge University Press.
Bowlby, J. (1944) 'Forty-four Juvenile Thieves: their character and home-life', *International Journal of Psychoanalysis*, 25, pp.19–52.
Bowlby, J. (1952) *'Maternal Care and Mental Health*: A report prepared on behalf of the World Health Organisation as a contribution to the United Nations programme for the welfare of homeless children', Geneva: WHO.
Bowlby, J. (1969) *Attachment and Loss: Attachment*, 1, New York: Basic Books.
Braithwaite, E.R. (2005) *To Sir, With Love*, London: Vintage.
Butler, R.A. (1944) 'An act to reform the law relating to education in England and Wales', *Ministry of Education* https://www.legislation.gov.uk/ukpga/Geo6/7-8/31
Carry on Teacher! (1959) [Film], Thomas, G., dir., Beaconsfield: Beaconsfield Productions.
Children Act (1948) https://www.education-uk.org/documents/acts/1948-children-act.html
Croft, M. (1954) *Spare the Rod*, London: Longmans.
Davis, J. (1990) *Youth and the Condition of Britain: Images of Adolescent Conflict*, London: Continuum.
Forum: For the Discussion of New Trends in Education (1958–1990), London: Lawrence & Wishart.
Golding, W. (1954) *Lord of the Flies*, Harmondsworth: Penguin.
Hilton, J. (1934) *Goodbye, Mr. Chips*, London: Hodder and Stoughton.
Hoggart, R. (1957) *The Uses of Literacy*, Harmondsworth: Penguin.
Hughes, T. (1999) *Tom Brown's School Days*, Oxford: Oxford University Press.
Hunter, E. (1955) *The Blackboard Jungle*, London: Constable.
Jones, K. (2016) *Education in Britain: 1944 to the Present*, 2nd edn., Cambridge, MA: Polity Press.
Karpf, A. (2014) 'Constructing and addressing the "ordinary devoted mother": Donald Winnicott's BBC broadcasts', *History Workshop Journal*, 78, Autumn.
Ministry of Education (1947) *The New Secondary Education*, Pamphlet 9, London: HMSO.
New Era (1920-) *Journal of the World Education Fellowship*, https://www. newera.ijkie.org/
Norwood Report (1943) https://www.education-uk.org/documents/norwood/norwood1943.html
Oram, A. (1996) *Women Teachers and Feminist Politics 1900–39*, Manchester: Manchester University Press.
Partington, J. (1959) 'Experiences with a backward class', *Forum: For the Discussion of New Trends in Education*, 1(3), pp.82–4.
Pearson, G. (1983) *Hooligan: A History of Respectable Fears*, London: Palgrave.
Piaget, J. (1959) *The Language and Thought of the Child*, 3rd edn., London: Routledge and Kegan Paul.
Riley, D. (1979) 'War in the nursery', *Feminist Review*, 2, pp.82–108.
Spare the Rod (1961) [Film], Norman, L., dir., London: British Lion Films.
Spens Report (1938) *Secondary Education with Special Reference to Grammar Schools and Technical High Schools*, London: HMSO. https://www.education-uk.org/documents/acts/spens/spens1938.html
Tisdall, L. (2015) 'Inside the "Blackboard Jungle"', *Cultural and Social History*, 12(4), pp.489–507.
Thomson, M. (2013) *Lost Freedom: The Landscape of the Child and the Post-War Settlement*, Oxford: Oxford University Press.

To Sir, With Love (1967) [Film], Clavell, J, dir., London: Columbia Pictures.
Townsend, J. (1958) *The Young Devils*, London: Chatto & Windus.
WHO (World Health Organization) (1948) *Constitution of the World Health Organisation.* https://www.who.int/about/governance/constitution
Winnicott, D.W. (1949) [Radion Broadcast], *The Ordinary Devoted Mother*, BBC Home Service.
Winnicott, D.W. (1991) *The Child, the Family and the Outside World*, London: Penguin.

3

THE NATURAL CHILD

The Newsom Report and progressive ideals in the 1960s

In 1967, my eldest brother Patrick was the first in our extended family to sit the 11-plus. He didn't pass and went on to St Aidan's Roman Catholic secondary modern in Stockton-on-Tees. My eldest sister Eileen did the same, going on to St Margaret's RC Secondary Modern in 1969. Both enjoyed their respective schools. Most of Patrick's friends were going to St Aidan's. From the third year onwards, he could wear jeans and sported shoulder-length hair. The school was streamed (stream X, Y and Z) and Patrick was in X, the 'top stream'. He was part of the first secondary modern cohort to sit 0-levels and emerged with five. St Aidan's was featured in the local *Evening Gazette* as the boys in Patrick's year achieved proportionally more O-levels than those in the local grammar. Although he recalls the 'Brothers', the Catholic monks who oversaw the school were 'over-vigilant in their use of corporal punishment', he has fond memories of most of his subject teachers: 'Noddy' Thompson, 'Mogger' Edwards, the English teacher Billy McClean who told the boys stories of his war-time service and Mr Melba the young Geography teacher who took them on trips. School trips included a third-year adventure to Bavaria and a fourth-year journey to Spain, which included a visit to a vineyard, and where the 14- and 15-year-old boys were largely unsupervised. Career support started in fourth year, led by 'canny' Geography teacher Mr Brown. A fifth-year job fair saw representatives from all the local heavy industries on Teesside (British Steel and ICI) come to the school to discuss apprenticeships. A visit to ICI Wilton ('it stank, was big and noisy') confirmed Patrick's decision to pursue academic study and to go on to sixth form college in Middlesbrough. After a period of illness and a stay

DOI: 10.4324/9781003715122-6

in hospital in the lower sixth, however, Patrick decided to leave sixth form and worked for a while in a men's clothing shop. After a fortuitous meeting between our mother and Patrick's former careers teacher Mr Brown, who was concerned that Patrick was not achieving his potential by selling loon pants, a meeting was arranged back at St Aidan's. Patrick mentioned to Mr Brown that his hospital stay had made him curious about nursing. The careers teacher arranged a meeting with his good friend, the Director of Nurse Education at the new local hospital, North Tees General. Patrick was offered a place on the next intake the following May, and so began his 50 years' service with the NHS, first in general then psychiatric nursing and eventually at the top level of senior management.

Eileen's time at primary school had been shared between St John's Roman Catholic School, where all six children in our family were pupils, and the school next door, the Open-Air School. Open-Air schools were originally set up for children recovering from tuberculosis and focused on getting children outside in the 'open air'. Eileen was diagnosed with epilepsy as a toddler; medication left her sleepy and sedated and she was offered a place in the Open-Air school aged five. She has memories of feeling cared for and nurtured there, but by age eight, Eileen was missing being with her siblings at St John's. Our mother intervened and approached whoever were the powers that be to arrange a move back to mainstream education for Eileen's last two years in primary school. Courtesy of the glorious Mr Kelly (who was also my 'Junior Four' teacher) Eileen caught up with the academic skills she'd missed out on. While she didn't pass the 11-plus, she felt ready for secondary school. Her story of her time at St Margaret's RC Secondary Modern (the 'sister school' to St Aidan's) is one of friendship, hockey, short skirts and supportive nuns, including the Head, Sister Mary, Accounts and Commerce teacher Sister Joan and beloved Sister Hilda, who taught French. Eileen left with O-levels, including a much-prized O-level in French, and CSE (Certificate in Secondary Education) equivalents. Her ambition was to become a nurse (inspired by volunteering for the Red Cross while at school) but as that wouldn't start until age 18 she took an administrative job with Stockton Council. Her ambitions for nursing were thwarted when she was turned down on the grounds of her epilepsy. Instead, she carried on working for the council (a job that she loved) until she had the first of her two daughters. Eileen's favourite school story: *Educating Yorkshire.*

Circular 10/65

By the time Patrick and Eileen went through the gates of St Aidan's and St Margaret's, the education system was already moving in another direction. Comprehensive schools had appeared in England as early as 1946, but the wide-scale shift from selective secondary education became government policy in 1965, when Anthony Crosland became Labour minister for education. Crosland's

1956 book, *The Future of Socialism* (Leonard, 2006), had reflected a shift in the Labour Party's position on education. Traditionally, nationalisation was at the centre of Labour's vision and education was part of a welfare system that propped up the lives of the workers. As I have noted, this was the logic of the post-war Labour Education Secretary Ellen Wilkinson's claim in the 1940s that a 15-year-old could be as 'interested' in a mine as anywhere, so long as it was a nationalised mine (Ministry of Education, 1947). In *The Future of Socialism,* education is cast as an engine for social and economic reform, and a selective system was a monstrous obstacle to equality of opportunity. Crosland pointed out that grammar school places went disproportionately to middle-class children, due to social and environmental influences rather than genetic intelligence. For the 'average child', school means poor buildings and overcrowded classes, like those depicted in the secondary modern stories. Crosland had long made clear his broad admiration for the American high school system (as well as other aspects of American life), which he found to be more egalitarian and less class-bound than the system in England and Wales, though he held the Swedish system in even higher esteem. When, as education minister, he had the opportunity to authorise change in the system, his 1965 Circular 10/65, *The Organisation of Secondary Education*, recommended that local authorities convert existing grammars and secondary moderns into comprehensive schools (Circular 10/65). This turned out to be a slow, uneven and, as yet, incomplete process.

Setting the scene for change: the Newsom Report

Some of the preparatory work for the 1965 circular was carried out in the Newsom Report of 1963 (CACE, 1963). The report was produced by the Central Advisory Council for Education (England) and looked at the education of 'average and below average children' being taught in secondary modern schools and who amounted to half of the school-age population. The Report makes a case that the future prosperity of the country depended on improving the education of those children, hence its title 'Half our Future'. It was aimed both at those with authority to act and at a public whose informed opinion would provide the necessary 'incitement' for change (TNR, p.xiv). The Report's recommendations were not about the structure of schools, that is, whether selection should be abolished, but what to do with the large proportion of children and adolescents who make up the school population. The Newsom Report's many recommendations included raising the leaving age for all children to 16 for entrants from September 1965; to increase the appeal to the 'natural interests' of older boys and girls and treat them like young adults (again recalling Wilkinson); to deal with schools in 'slum areas'; to improve pay for teachers and fund better buildings and facilities and to improve teacher training, especially with respect to teaching older pupils and those from areas of deprivation.

At the heart of the report is the belief, despite 'some splendid achievements' in the progress of secondary education, that 'there is much unrealised talent' amongst a large cohort that is 'masked by inadequate powers of speech and the limitations of home background' (TNR, p.3). As in the more 'progressive' views on secondary education in the 1950s, the Newsom Report dispels theories about the fixed and limited innate intelligence of working class and immigrant children only to portray the limiting influence of working-class and immigrant families and communities on their own children.

The Report is explicitly an act of persuasion, 'calling on the support of the public' (TNR, p.xiv) to improve conditions and opportunity for secondary modern students. Its quantitative and qualitative evidence, drawn from headteachers' surveys, is heightened by melodramatic description:

> There is no need to read the melodramatic novelists when there are areas, often near the decaying centres of big cities, where schools have more to contend with than the schoolboy's traditional reluctance.
>
> (TNR, p.17)

In these 'slum areas', the report finds 'mental illness, high crime… delinquency… above average figures for infant mortality, tuberculosis, child neglect and cruelty' (TNR, p.17). These are 'squalid streets…decayed terraces…garish pubs' where young people gather to follow 'the easy goals of group hedonism' (TNR, p.17). The monsters of the Beveridge Report remain undefeated by 1963.

The Newsom Report condenses the findings of the headteachers' surveys into sketches of 'physical surroundings', 'population', 'family life and general social behaviour' in various regions. Here we find broad brush pathologising of immigrant communities. One London neighbourhood has 'narrow mean little streets, badly maintained housing' and 'comparatively large immigration into the area especially from the West Indies, Southern Ireland and Cyprus' (TNR, p.18). Children are found to be 'friendly' but 'confused and bewildered' by the inconsistencies of discipline at home where 'the Victorian concept of father still persists' (TNR, p.18). In the Midlands, a school is plagued by the 'odours of vinegar and beer' from nearby pickle factory and brewery; houses are 'tightly packed'; the presence of 'TV' is noted (TNR, p.17). The description of the population of the Midlands hints again at unease about immigration: the 'tight knit community' consisting of generations of 'old scholars' are being 'rehoused on the outskirts of the city' while the repaired inner city housing is used to 'accommodate coloured [sic] immigrants from India, Pakistan and the West Indies' (TNR, p.18). While the 'coloured population [of Lancashire] frequently change their address', they come from 'better cared for homes than others'. The Irish Catholic community is 'very stable'; 'the people are decent and good-living; there are strikingly few broken homes' (TNR, p.20). The sparse commentary on immigrants from the West Indies, Africa and South Asia compared to the romantic sketches of the chaotic but light-hearted warmth of Irish Catholic life speaks of a trepidation about how to describe the culture of these communities.

The 'welfare of new immigrants' is briefly discussed with reference to school size. The report proposes 'three possible educational solutions' to the problem of integrating 'the new immigrants who are often of different ethnic and cultural groups from their neighbours': attendance at a 'local country school' where they will form a 'distinctive and compact group'; attendance at a 'voluntary school that is virtually their own' like the practice of the Irish Roman Catholics; or 'lose their group identity' by being divided between many small schools, or placed in a big school with a catchment area 'so large and carefully drawn that they cease to be a conspicuous group'. The right decision cannot be settled 'on purely educational grounds' (TNR, p.25). The grounds on which the decision should be taken are not suggested. The silence suggests that 'integration' of immigrant communities is the ideal, as was dominant in debates about 'race' in the 1950s and 1960s. The idea was to distribute children of immigrant communities across schools, and thus to 'dilute' the impact of their own cultural difference on themselves and on the other children in schools. The Black Supplementary School Movement that grew up in cities like Manchester, Birmingham and London in the 1960s, to counteract the systemic racism of state secondaries, demonstrates that the Newsom Report was very much 'of its time' in this way of thinking (Gerrard, 2013).

The authors consolidate 'pen-portraits of 6,202 14-year-old boys and girls' from the surveys into 'profiles of imaginary boys and girls who may be taken to represent the upper, middle and lower reaches of the modern school population' (*TNR*, p.195). These pupils are imagined as, respectively, the Browns, the Joneses and the Robinsons (which suggests that the authors abandoned an attempt to characterise or even imagine children of recent immigrant families altogether). It is in these portraits that we meet Bert, one of the Robinsons, the 'low ability' children:

> Bert was only 5 ft. 1 ½ inches [1.56cm] tall and weighed just 7 st. 7lbs [47.25 kg]. His attainments were very poor when he came to the secondary school...His IQ at the time of the eleven plus was 73. He has one elder brother who went to the same school where he had been a thorough nuisance... Bert himself was a pleasant, cheerful lad on the surface...he lived in a poor housing area, and he and his brother were left to their own devices in the evening while his parents were out. Neighbours reported that quarrels were a regular and noisy domestic feature ... He spent about an hour and a half a day on a paper round, but took no part in any voluntary activities nor did he belong to a youth club.
>
> (TNR, p.216)

Bert's case history is sketched from an account 'supplied by the school' and, like the descriptions of eight other children, adds individual details to the 'generalised profiles' of imaginary boys and girls. The portraits are intended to humanise the data that peppers the report (reading ages and test scores) and garner sympathy for the proposed reforms (increased leaving ages, improved buildings, new media, more children leaving with some sort of certification and attention to the transition between school and work). Proposed curricula for boys and girls are strongly codified (boys are to have access to hands-on experience in workshops while girls are to attend to 'mothercraft') and families' social status is defined by father's occupation. Immigrant families are rated on a scale of relative linguistic and cultural integration. Children from working-class families and migrant families are seen to be trapped by limited communication skills, from which a reformed education system will liberate them. Given the right opportunities in this new system, children like Bert from the overlooked half 'will rise to the challenge which a rapidly developing economy offers no less to them than their abler brothers and sisters' (TNR, p.xiv). The potential of 'the half' will be unlocked by appealing to 'the natural interests of older boys and girls in the work they will eventually undertake' (TNR, p.xiv). The 'natural' interests of a boy like Bert, in work or in anything else, are difficult to discern from his description; implicitly these interests are thwarted by his environment and an improved curriculum is tasked with unleashing his hidden 'potential'.

Meeting higher needs: the arrival of school counsellors

While the Newsom Report is as socially conservative as the Education Act of 1944, its views on how schooling shapes and responds to the inner lives of school children and adolescents represent a considerable shift in the expectation on schools from those set out by Butler. The 1944 Act asks schools to meet what the American psychologist Abraham Maslow in 1943 specified as children's basic physiological and safety needs (Maslow, 1943). The Newsom Report recognises the 'higher' psychological needs (belonging, esteem, fulfilling potential) of all children, not just those who pass the 11-plus. In its proposals for staffing and training, the Report expands the role of the 'ordinary devoted' teachers who were imagined in secondary modern novels and opens a space for a specialised pastoral figure: the school counsellor.

The Newsom Report was the first government paper to recommend school counsellors: 'in large schools, it may not be fanciful to look forward to a stage where there is a full-time counsellor available to advise the pupils throughout their school course and to prepare them for going out into the world' (TNR, p.77). As it would turn out, this was a fanciful ambition. By counselling, the report refers to 'vocational guidance' and 'keeping personal contact with older adolescents and unobtrusively supervising their general welfare' (TNR, p.77). The Report also recommends school social workers and making space in teacher training for the support of children's social and emotional needs.

Looking to America

In 1963, Bob Cant, the Chairman of the Labour-controlled Education Committee for Stoke-on-Trent, made a visit to the US. He and the authority's Chief Education Officer reported the findings of their trip in *American Journey*, including a recommendation that specialised school counsellors should be introduced into secondary schools (Cant, 1963). As Brian Robinson summarises it, Cant pointed out that 'the teacher's job is to teach' and the counsellor's job, 'for which he is fitted by special training, is to study the child's abilities and problems during his school life as a continuous process' (Robinson, 1996, p.13).

Two years later, in 1965, a one-year full-time training course for school counsellors was launched at Keele University; applications were invited from teachers with at least five years' teaching experience for places funded by Stoke Education Authority. In the same year, the Diploma in Educational Guidance was launched at Reading University. The early emphasis of these courses was on vocational guidance rather than what was regarded as the Americanised 'counselling movement', with its emphasis on emotional and mental health. American influence soon arrived, however, in the guise of two Fulbright-funded American professors, Gilbert Wrenn and Gilbert Moore, who would oversee the launch of both new training courses. Further courses would be established in the Education Departments of the Universities of Manchester, Leeds and Exeter and in a range of teacher training colleges, including Westhill in Birmingham, Kenton in Newcastle-upon-Tyne and Edge Hill in Lancashire (Schools Council, 1967).

A 1967 Schools Council Working Paper details the content of the new courses for school counsellors, the numbers who participated and their immediate destinations. The courses are very much rooted in the educational context and were to be connected to other services that would support the students. The numbers are small, but the paper captures a sense that this is just the beginning. However, the tensions that it describes (issues of recruitment, cost, buy-in from local education authorities and teaching staff) and the sense that the breadth of work required to make school counselling viable could have been written yesterday:

> The appointment of a counsellor may afford the school a means of considering and of operating an educational programme which is not simply subject orientated, and which recognises that the curriculum is everything which happens to the child at school. It is easy to exaggerate these possibilities and it is still early days of counselling in this country, but provided the point is kept in mind that the counsellor is swimming with a tide, and not in isolation against it, the reality of the possibilities cannot be ignored.
>
> (Schools Council, 1967, p.30)

A collection of essays presented at a conference on *Guidance and Counselling in British Schools* held in 1968 captures the optimism and trepidation about the new phenomenon of British school counsellors (Lytton and Craft, 1969). Maurice Craft, a sociologist and Senior Lecturer in Education at the University of Exeter, sees the development of school counselling as consistent with the post-war growth of an 'egalitarian political ideology', better living standards and 'an increased demand for extended education and a greater participation by working class children in selective secondary education' (Lytton and Craft, 1969, pp.10–11). Guidance and counselling in schools, he suggests, *are* part of this push towards the democratisation of British society. Amongst other things, a school counsellor is a 'source of skilled help where stresses with social mobility arise' (p.11). However, Craft is at pains to point to the difficult path trodden by the school counsellor and its potential to be used more in the service of the state than the child: offering a 'specialised technique' has:

> enormous liberative potentialities for the individual boy or girl, as well as for the state [and] equally great potentialities for rigidifying the new openness of secondary education …, for closing doors, for pressuring the individual child, and for the invasion of privacy – all in the cause of talent production.
>
> (Lytton and Craft, 1969, p.23)

Counselling here is imagined as a means of harvesting the minds of adolescents for the benefit of the state.

The American origins of school counselling were also a cause of interest and concern for some commentators. According to Hugh Lytton, teacher and educational psychologist, the American system was so varied and flexible, students needed the guidance of staff to negotiate their route through it. Post-war fears of America falling behind in the global education stakes required a system which could nurture American 'talent' to aid the economy. The drive to equalise opportunities opened a space for psychological and emotional support. This was not framed as therapeutic but as help where relationships with family and society are difficult or as assistance to 'adjust'. The transplantation of this American model to British schools raised questions about the difference in the systems (though with the growth of large comprehensives, the 'guidance counsellor' to hold together parts of the system would be useful). Maurice Craft's concern about utilitarian 'talent production', using counsellors to nurture economic and social potential as in the American model rather than alleviate adolescent difficulties was a point of tension.

In the 1968 conference proceedings, the concept of personal counselling (rather than educational or vocational guidance) presents the most confusion: how to distinguish the role of the personal counsellor from social workers, educational psychologists or indeed teachers? Broadly, the 1968 conference contributors agree that there *is* a need for something called personal counselling in schools (though defining the personal proves fraught). In his reflection, Hugh Lytton notes that while Carl Roger's non-directive modality dominated discussion, there was also space for 'existentialist, developmental or behavioural' theories of counselling (Lytton and Craft, 1969, p.103). The pressing issues of the conference were less to do with modality, however, than making counselling relevant to headteachers, making sure enough and appropriate training was available and encouraging local education authorities to employ and support career progression for school counsellors.

An account from the 'coalface' of school counselling, *Teachers as Counsellors* by Alick Holden, was published in 1969. Holden was a deputy head and head of science in a Liverpool secondary school. He also worked for the Marriage Guidance Council (where the British counselling tradition originated) and as a Justice of the Peace, encountering 'young offenders' of the kind popularly associated with state schools. His list of recommended reading for school counsellors reflects this pragmatic, social and moral framework. He emphasises that his book is concerned with 'counselling in the school situation, and its view is common sense rather than clinical' (Holden, 1969, p.5). He aims to help young people become good citizens, uphold family values and promote the orderly running of the school, referring to Donald Winnicott's 1964 book, *The Child, the Family and the Outside World* (Winnicott, 1991), as a framework.

Case histories show Holden as a paternalistic problem solver, keeping his charges on the straight and narrow. The transcripts include long paragraphs of Holden speaking and gnomic interjections from his students. Holden touches on the debate in education circles about whether counsellors should be 'non-teaching specialists' or 'teacher-counsellors': the 'pure' counsellor, he reflects, might think 'formal study is relatively unimportant because he is not involved in it and does not have any responsibility for it' while the teacher counsellor might be too bound up in authority (Holden, 1969, p.94). Holden's patrician tone suggests that, in his case, the latter might be true.

Robert Shields, a contributor to a 1968 edition of *The New Era*, makes a forthright case against the appointment of teachers as 'pupil counsellors' (Shields, 1968). It is 'against the spirit of the age' he writes, to think that anyone has the right to 'advise, guide, induce, inspire' (p.2). As a group, teachers are inclined 'to direct, command, decree' (p.2). Didactic by training or temperament, teachers are not suited to the task of 'listening to the very edge of one's patience, understand to the limit of one's ability and support [the pupil] even while he is making his [sic] own mistakes' (p.2). Shields's broader argument is that as school counselling is regarded as an 'American importation', it is treated with suspicion by local education authorities and school leaders, and if it is adopted at all it will be set up to fail. He compares the careful study that has informed the American model since the 1920s with the British tendency to aim 'at the minimum' (p.2). Counselling, he asserts, should not be absorbed into 'pastoral care' or 'guidance' and counsellors should be, or at least be trained by, psychotherapists, by which he means they must have a capacity for self-reflection. Perhaps drawing on painful experience, Shields warns against assuming that 'anyone who "looks like" a counsellor may be "as good as" anyone else in the job' (p.3). So, 'a neurotic teacher' with an unhealthy interest in other people's problems, 'a clergyman' whose road to moral training is 'sado-mascochism' or 'an inept teacher', who cannot succeed in a classroom but who has a 'bland visage', may all pass as counsellors but are doomed to fail and bring the edifice of school counselling down with them (p.3).

Carl Rogers' *Freedom to Learn*

This commentary on school counselling acknowledges, with some ambivalence, the American influence, but the curricula of the early school counselling courses and the suggested reading in the books written about school counselling are varied. There is a mixture of sociological approaches to British education, educational reports and moral and ethical frameworks for adolescents rather than American counselling theory, though there are references to Carl Rogers' theory of client-centred therapy in numerous editions of *The New Era* from the 1960s. The proceedings of the 1968 conference mentioned that his model dominated discussion. Rogers' work was influential in child-centred pedagogy. The 'self-directed learning' that was much discussed in 1960s' teaching circles, along with non-streamed classrooms and 'comprehensivisation', bears the hallmark of American high school pedagogy, including Rogers' *Freedom to Learn* (Rogers, 1969). There, he explores the principles and practices of non-directive education, with an emphasis on *learning* over *teaching* that would become the mantra of the progressive education movement and that was much derided in the 1970s.

The book captures the urgency of forging new kinds of relationships in schools, driven by Rogers' sense of the pace of social change in the US, racial tensions, 'irrational nationalism', 'the revolt at the secondary and higher education level', an education system mired in its own traditionalism and the prospect of education being taken over by 'profit-making corporations' (Rogers, 1969, pp.vi–vii). He writes with conditional optimism that he relies on 'the potentiality and wisdom of the human being – if this potential can be realised – to bring about the desperately needed changes in education, before it is too late' (p.vii).

With revolutionary zeal, Rogers declares what he means by learning. It is '*not* the lifeless, sterile, futile, quickly forgotten stuff which is crammed into the mind of the poor helpless individual tied into his seat by ironclad bonds of conformity!' but 'the insatiable curiosity which drives the adolescent boy [sic] to absorb everything he can see or hear or read about gasoline engines in order to improve the efficiency of his "hot-rod"' (Rogers, 1969, p.3). Significantly, the pupil that Rogers imagines being inspired by this form of learning is the kind of boy who would feature in the American high school story *The Blackboard Jungle* (Hunter, 1954), a story which in turn would influence the creation of the 'secondary modern schoolboy' in the English stories of the 1950s.

Rogers goes on to describe a process of adolescent development which involves an integration of outside influence and internal subjectivity, in which a student draws 'in from the outside' and makes 'that which is drawn in a real part of *me*' (Rogers, 1969, p.3). If this is to be a valuable experience, the material being drawn in needs to be 'relevant' and sparks a personal investment from the student. In this 'experiential' learning 'the value of what is learned is internal, personal and long lasting'. Rogers hopes that once this type of learning is embraced by the education system, the whole edifice of 'conventional education' will topple: students will set their own assignments; standardised tests will be abolished; grades will become irrelevant.

Rogers sketches examples of the outcome of this kind of learning experience, including a class where non-directive and self-directed challenges proved to be 'stepping stones towards our goal of self-actualisation' and led to a change in the students' 'self-concept…when they discovered they *can*, they did!' (p.2).

Rogers' ideas on the interpersonal and political potential of experiential learning arrived in English schools in quite a muted way. As I'll outline in the next chapter, several 'free schools' appeared in cities like Liverpool and London in the early 1970s and disappeared just as quickly. The fallout from the 'William Tyndale Affair' in 1974, where the attempts of the head and several teachers to embrace self-directed learning and to introduce 'democracy' to the classroom were met with strong resistance, suggests that there was not an appetite for the Rogerian way in the English education system.

The Plowden Report

Rogerian therapeutic principles ('internal locus of evaluation' privileged over outside influence, authenticity, spontaneity and interests deriving from within (Rogers, 1959)) are evident in the way that childhood and schooling was represented in the progressive strand of education debate and more widely in popular culture in the 1960s.

The Plowden Report of 1967, into primary education, was originally commissioned by the Conservative Government in 1963 (CACE, 1967). Emboldened by the Labour administration, particularly the education minister Crosland, to make an egalitarian case for 'child-centred' education for the 'whole child', the Report was perhaps the culmination of the official turn towards progressivism in education debate. It recognised that society was at a stage where help for some children to succeed in education needed to be upgraded from the ambitions of the early part of the twentieth century. Then, free school meals were first introduced. 'Today', Plowden writes, 'their need is for enriched intellectual nourishment' (TPR, p.57). Intellectual nourishment, the report emphasises, can only be digested if a child is free from 'severe emotional disturbance' (TPR, p.18) and schools should play a part in relieving such distress. The Report does not mention school counselling – presumably because the new training courses were aimed at secondary school teachers – but it does call for the expansion of 'child guidance' services (psychiatry and educational psychology), especially to address the geographical imbalance with more services in the south than the north.

Although its remit was to explore the factors which helped or hindered children's primary education, the Plowden Report's commentary extended to the best time for children to transition to secondary school, and the current evidence on the merits and problems of selective testing (generally making a case against). The report drew on the work of psychoanalysts (including Bowlby on maternal deprivation), developmental theorists, especially Piaget on stages of cognitive development, and a wide array of other sources from education, medicine, social sciences, psychology and politics. Most aspects of child development are found by Plowden to be an interaction of a child's 'inheritance…history and …immediate situation' (TPR, p.16) rather than an innate biological unfolding. There are echoes of Newsom's views on the inhibiting effect of some families on the linguistic capacity of their children, especially families in deprived situations and the children of some immigrant families whose first language is not English. Those same families, 'because of poverty, missing parents, or the low intelligence of parents cannot provide security' and children may miss a significant stage in early development (TPR, p.24). Plowden casually, or perhaps optimistically, dismisses racial 'prejudice' as a significant problem between children in primary schools and celebrates the teachers who have worked hard to accommodate the different cultures of their charges. Beryl Gilroy's 1976 memoir *Black Teacher*, which documents her time as a primary teacher and head in the 1960s, tells a different and sobering story of the racism to which she was subject and which she observed in the sector, as I'll explore in the next chapter (Gilroy, 2021).

To counteract inequality amongst cohorts, schools and local education authorities, Plowden recommends 'education priority areas', a new funding formula which distinguishes between areas within local authorities and allocates additional funds to those areas 'in which children and schools are most severely handicapped' (TPR, p.56). Getting to the heart of the child-centred manifesto, she urges that those children must not be endlessly taught 'the three Rs' but must be given time 'for play and imagination and expressive work' (p.50).

A Kestrel for a Knave, a mine for a boy

A child who certainly did not benefit from the Plowden vision is Billy Caspar, the hero of the most celebrated story of adolescence and the degradations of schooling from this decade. Barry Hines's 1968 novella *A Kestrel for a Knave* (Hines, 2000) captures the tension between a romantic view of the natural child with all its emergent potential and the brutality of contemporary schooling that stymies it. Robert Davis has contextualised the story, along with stories written for children in the 1960s, as a reminder 'that many working-class schools in Britain operated in ways far removed from Plowden's principles, serving children and young people whose lives, learning and identities were far from "whole" and integrated' (Davis, 2018). Billy's home and school life are the kind which Plowden and Newsom set out to improve. The representation of Billy mirrors the core belief of these reports in the potential of the 'natural' child whose development is impeded by his urban culture.

Billy Casper is a 15-year-old school leaver from a mining village in Yorkshire. He is reminiscent of the Newsom Report's Bert; as a teacher, the novella's author Hines is likely to have been familiar with the Report. Like Bert, Billy is slight, has an older brother and parents who argued (and in Billy's case separated). Like Bert, Billy does a daily paper round, takes part in no voluntary activities and does not belong to a youth club (much to the chagrin of the Youth Employment Officer who tries to discern Billy's 'natural interests in work' (AKFAK, p.171)). Of course, Billy doesn't reveal to the Officer that he has a passionate interest in the kestrel he keeps in his shed at home and has trained to fly.

From the opening of the novella, Billy is identified with the birds of his neighbourhood gardens. Billy ducks and dives from bedroom to newsagent to paper round, avoiding the blows of his brother Jud and the newsagent's surveillance as he pilfers chocolate. Running from the newsagent with his paper load and stolen chocolate bar he merges, like the thrushes and skylarks, with the gardens and bushes of the housing estate where he makes a newspaper delivery. A thrush runs out from under a rhododendron bush and tries to tug a worm from the soil. Billy uses the moss and grass 'like stepping stones', unwraps the chocolate and sprints back through the gate (AKFAK, pp.16–7).

The natural child

Billy is a 'natural child', an inheritor of the romantic tradition whose writers celebrated the natural world and the qualities of spontaneity and authenticity that were to be found in the rural environment and the child. Carl Rogers was also of this romantic tradition. His 1959 book, *Client-Centred Therapy*, offers a theory of personality and behaviour that is a foundation for the still dominant client-centred therapy movement. He proposes that the child comes into the world in tune with its own needs, with an 'organismic valuing system'. He drew on a line of psychology and philosophy that understood the individual to be physiologically directed towards growth and 'self-actualisation', rather than in the Freudian tradition, which saw the child as riven by atavistic drives and instincts which need to be civilised. In Rogers' accounts, the infant's positive and negative experiences, their pleasures and pains, reinforce the motivation towards growth. The infant 'appears to value those experiences which he perceives as enhancing himself, and to place a negative value on those experiences which seem to threaten himself or do not enhance himself' (Rogers, 1959, p.499). This primary 'organismic' valuing system is supplemented by a secondary set of experiences: 'social experiences, social evaluations by others' (p.499). Out of 'these dual sources – the direct experiencing by the individual, and the distorted symbolisation of sensory reactions resulting in the introjection of values and concepts as if experienced – there grows the structure of the self' (p.501). It is not social experiences and judgements per se that lead to maladjustment. Behaviour that conforms with social norms can be satisfying to the individual so long as they are understood to originate outside the self. The tendency to take on the negative evaluations of others *as if* they were their own (introjection) leads the individual to deny or distort their own experience. For example, an adolescent whose self-concept of gratitude to his parents may experience anger with those parents at a bodily level but denies its existence at a conscious 'symbolic' level or distorts it into a sensation that is consistent with the self-concept: for instance, in a headache (p.505). Person-centred therapy allows the client to attribute the symbolisation of sensory reactions appropriately, to distinguish between values and concepts which have been 'introjected' and distorted to fit with the self-concept and those which have been derived from their own positive and negative experiencing.

For Billy Casper, the self-concept acquired from his experience of his family, his secondary modern school and the mining village where he grew up is wastrel, failure and misfit. 'There's aluus somebody after me', he confides in his hawk, Kes (AKFAK, p.27). To Jud and his mother, he is a nuisance; this is another story of maternal deprivation (in the afterword to the 2000 edition, Hines reflects that he could have made Billy's mother more sympathetic and 'caring' (p.206)). To his headmaster Gryce, and PE teacher Sugden, Billy is an object to be humiliated; to the Youth Employment Officer, he is unemployable. Only the 'ordinary devoted teacher', Mr Farthing, connects with Billy as more than an object. When he coaxes Billy to participate in an English class about 'fact and fiction', Farthing employs Rogerian principles. At first reluctantly, but then enthusiastically, Billy describes to his peers the training regime with Kes, which 'takes weeks' due to the bird's stubbornness and unpredictability. Billy recounts the frustration of thinking he'd taught her something, only to be back where they started the next day (AKFAK, p.83).

Here, the trials of the teacher are represented back to Mr Farthing by his own pupil. When Farthing asks his class to show that they understand the difference between fact and fiction by concocting a 'tall tale', Billy responds with a fantasy of home life with carpets, central heating, mum and dad together, mum not working, food and trips to the cinema (AKFAK, pp.89–90).

Farthing's role as 'ordinary devoted teacher' continues when he comes to Billy's rescue in the fight with the bully MacDowall and Billy trusts him with his 'bottom set' lament. While Farthing tries 'to learn us summat', most of the others call us 'idiots, an' numbskulls, an' cretins', Billy weeps (AKFAK, p.101). When Farthing tries to cheer Billy up by reminding him he'll be leaving school in a few weeks, the boy's 'self-limiting concept' is painfully apparent. In advance of that afternoon's interview with the 'youth employment bloke', Farthing asks Billy what kind of job he would like. 'Out'll do me' Billy replies. When Farthing hopes Billy will try to get something that 'interests' him, Billy resigns himself to having 'to take what they've got' (AKFAK, p.103). Billy doubts he'll be able to follow his 'natural interests' into the world of work.

Billy's story comes to its crisis and downward trajectory when he buys chips and scraps with the money his brother Jud gave him to put on a bet: the horse wins and Jud pursues Billy into school, looking for revenge. Again, the episode echoes the observation of a headteacher from Lancashire in the Newsom Report:

> Gambling is common in phases among the boys… Betting on horses and pools is not infrequent, but then fathers send their sons to the local bookmakers to lay bets and collect winnings, even pursuing them into school to retrieve the money.
> (TNR, p.20)

Loony-coloured phantasies

While the characterisation of Bert/Billy and Jud's pursuit of Billy for the misspent bet suggests that the Newsom Report found its way into Hines' novella, the Report itself is informed by fictional representations of working-class life. It refers to the classic text of the British New Wave, Alan Sillitoe's 1958 novel *Saturday Night and Sunday Morning*, to illustrate the boredom of unskilled labour. Citing Arthur Seaton's description of factory work:

> if your machine was working well...you went off into pipedreams for the rest of the day ...You lived in a compatible world of pictures which passed through your mind like a magic lantern, often in vivid and glorious loony-colour.
>
> *(TNR, p.27)*

The Report paraphrases the novel's description of Seaton's cinematic daydreaming and pathologises it: such 'loony-coloured phantasies' are poor 'nourishment for the rest of their personal lives' and inadequate compensation for the jobs that will 'make as limited demands on them as Arthur Seaton's' (TNR, p.27). The Report's authors believe that the 'potential of these children' could be 'very much greater than is generally assumed'. This potential is not to 'self-actualise' but to 'rise to the challenge which a rapidly developing economy offers no less to them than to their abler brothers and sisters' (TNR, p.xiv). This is a familiarly utilitarian rationale for promoting children's wellbeing but with a promise of equal access for all to 'stimulating' work.

For Billy, who is locked in an unreformed secondary modern whose teachers (except for Mr Farthing) had not encountered person-centred psychology nor child-centred pedagogy, the 'rapidly developing economy' does not reveal itself and he has no desire to take up any of the work that would be offered to him.

Outside of school and home, however, Billy experiences something like the sense of self described by Carl Rogers. In his flights with Kes, Billy experiences a preverbal 'organismic valuing'. The arc of Billy's story moves up towards self-actualisation in his symbiotic relationship with the kestrel. In their training sessions, Billy presents the lure 'an inch before her so that the next wing beat must catch it', synchronising his movements to the bird's (AKFAK, p.139). Mr Farthing gives Billy's experience positive social value when he encourages Billy to put it into words in front of the class. This potential for Billy to grow from this experience is of course short-lived. Kes's death at Jud's hands sends Billy into a traumatised flight. He breaks into the now disused cinema where he had spent his last outing with his dad and his mind moves between the memory of his dad's departure from their home and a fantasy of his own appearance on the big screen, with the hawk in pursuit of his terrified brother. The fantasy ends when Billy goes home, buries his hawk and retreats to the bedroom where his story begins.

In the film version, directed by Ken Loach, the cinema scene is excised. Billy is allowed a moment of popular consumerism, however, in a scene where he reads a copy of *The Dandy* (*Kes*, 1969). He sits on a grass verge overlooking the mine and loses himself in the story of Desperate Dan, whose size and superhuman strength throw into relief Billy's diminutive frame. We are invited to lose ourselves in the comic strip too, as the animation momentarily takes up the whole frame before we return to Billy's 'real world', with the mine looming large.

Loach's adaptation has been celebrated as a social realist masterpiece, with its portrait of a northern, working-class mining community and its fidelity to Hines' social realist ending, where, after overcoming antagonists (in Billy's case, his family, his headmaster and PE teacher) in his relationship with Kes, ultimately things stay as they are, externally at least. The realism that Loach and Hines invest in is a particular kind of emotional realism (Leigh, 2002). Billy is changed by his relationship with Kes and is temporarily supported in this change by Mr Farthing.

Loach's choice of untrained local actors and club entertainers for the cast of *Kes* is true to the production values of social realist artists and resonates with ideas about the 'natural' and 'authentic' self, emerging in developmental and educational theory. *Kes* represents what Leigh refers to as the 'melodrama of protest', using the intensity of emotion to make a case for political reform (Leigh, 2002, p.64).

One of the most memorable figures from the film adaptation, *Kes*, is the sadistic buffoon of a PE teacher, Mr Sugden, played by Brian Glover. The following is the story of John Smith, dad of my friend Bridget and a PE teacher of the same generation as Sugden but from a different mould, another of the 'ordinary devoted' variety.

John Smith was born in 1932 in Canada. As a young child, John and his family moved to England where his father worked in the steelworks. He went to grammar school until the age of 18 and from 1953 to 1955 took a course in teacher training in Sheffield, specialising in PE and Geography. For five years he taught at a secondary modern school in Sheffield. Education was big in the Smith family: John's mum became one of the many unqualified women teachers in the 1940s, his youngest sister Doris became a teacher and elder brother Bob was a headteacher, inspector and contributor to the 1967 Plowden Report.

In October 1959, John applied for a job at a new purpose-built secondary modern school, on the outskirts of Hull, drawn to the sparkling new school gym. To the surprise of his wife Pat, he got the job, and in the bleak January of 1960, John, Pat and their three children under the age of five set up a new life (easier for John than for Pat). Bridget came along in 1964. John was head of PE and added evening duties of football coaching, youth clubs and teaching adult education classes (including to a group of local butchers) to his load. In the late 1960s the school became comprehensive. In the year that the school leaving age increased to 16, John was given responsibility for the group of fifth-year students who were not taking exams and ordinarily would have left at age 15 (the kind of students the Newsom Report had in mind). There was no curriculum in place, so John improvised, taking the group on trips to London (where two of them got lost), on walks and climbs, including to the Lake District where he would supply them with maps and send them out to explore.

Bridget remembers some of the students would arrive at the family home, hoping for a chat with Mr Smith. A frequent visitor was girl called Audrey, who had a particularly difficult home life. In a sign of her affection for her teacher, she named the first of her own children after John.

Eventually John took on more senior management roles in the school, and particularly enjoyed being Head of House, a pastoral and teaching role. By the time Bridget arrived at the school as a student, her dad was regarded fondly as an avuncular figure, which eased her passage through school time adolescence. John retired earlier than he had planned, aged 59, after contracting mumps followed by post-viral illness. After an eventful detour of 35 years, Pat (and John) finally got to return to Sheffield.

This Right Soft Lot

While the Newsom Report is part the implied context of Hines's fictional world, it is an explicit reference point, in Edward Blishen's return to Stonehill Street Secondary Modern in his 1969 novel, *This Right Soft Lot* (Blishen, 1969). The novel revisits the territory of Blishen's *Roaring Boys* and imagines putting into place the recommendations of the Report: making school relevant to older children, connecting them to the workplace and providing extracurricular activity. There are two epigrams to the 1969 edition: one from the Newsom Report emphasising that we cannot 'generalise about the capacity of the average and below average' or their 'potential' until they have been taught 'for a longer period and in smaller classes' (TRSL, p.8). The second, from Brian Jackson's *Streaming: an education in miniature*, provides the novel's title. Quoting an apocryphal parent, it reads: 'In my day when we saw a teacher, we'd shiver in our boots. Them were teachers. Not like this right soft lot they have nowadays' (*TRSL*, p.8).

In the author's note, Blishen describes *TRSL* as a sequel to *Roaring Boys*, giving 'an account of episodes from the four or five years that followed, when he was able, for all the desperate instability that marks such a school, to experiment a little in his teaching' (*TRSL*, p.9). Acknowledging that 'reports enough' have said that 'gross social and educational inequities' mould children like those in Stonehill Street, Blishen hopes that fiction ('the statement of the Case in terms of children, teachers and incidents') might be more persuasive of the need for change (*TRSL*, pp.9–10).

Like its prequel *Roaring Boys, This Right Soft Lot* is narrated from the perspective of an 'ordinary devoted' teacher and emphasises the value – and difficulty – of 'security of relationships' (*TRSL*, p.24). It is similarly structured around comic or poignant descriptions of school life in an overcrowded secondary modern in a 'deprived' part of the city. The incongruity of 'men-sized' boys in classrooms is revisited, but this time to illustrate the need to adapt the school environment and the curriculum to older students and tackle the belief that keeping the boys on at school is an unnecessary delay to their working lives (a key finding of The Newsom Report). The story of Barry Riddle, who leaves school only to suffer at the hands of a harsh employer, illustrates the case for students who might not stay on to do exams but who might be allowed to grow up a little before going to work. Riddle was 'a boy who would never stand on his own feet at any time during his life. But who might have had a faintly better chance of doing so had he stayed under the school roof a year longer' (*TRSL*, p.236). There are stories of boys who would stay on to do exams but also those who by the fifth year would find 'the natural pleasure of being at school' (*TRSL*, p.259).

The protagonist's benign, romantic view of the potential of his charges – blighted by circumstance and environment – clashes with the Hobbesian view of some of his colleagues (that life is nasty, brutish and short and that people are naturally inclined to evil). Mr Bedrock, for instance, believes children are iniquitous, 'infinitely corrupt…[their] natural inclination to be lazy, dishonest…positively evil', kept in check only by 'the most strenuous discipline' (*TRSL*, p.189).

When a teacher's wallet is stolen and the head wants to phone the police, the narrator compares the head's reaction to that of the prep school where he had worked and where 'boyish crimes were described as "traumas", were regarded as delicate faults in health. There were all manner of advisers and specialists who were discreetly called upon, before any thought was given to the law' (*TRSL*, p.212). In the view of this teacher, criminal behaviour and trauma response are in the eye of the fee-holding beholder.

There are extended passages on the merits of being sensitive to the boys' 'interests and preoccupations' (*TRSL*, p.153). The attitude to the boys' reading habits illustrates the pedagogical fault line in Stonehill Street. Mr Newlock, for instance, is a determined enemy of the school library, who views reading as nothing more than an impediment to good posture and a threat to eyesight. The protagonist, conversely, wants to become familiar with the boys' 'spontaneous reading' tastes (*TRSL*, p.147), to encourage them to read popular fiction alongside 'HG Wells and Dickens and *War and Peace*' (*TRSL*, p.53). He wants to exercise the boys' capacity for 'private judgement' (*TRSL*, p.165), to allow them to cultivate a self from their own sensing:

> How shall our boys learn the nature of private judgement … how shall they ever discover the nature of learning, at its heart so private and absorbed and so dependent on provocation, if they do not do this through reading?
>
> (*TRSL*, p.165)

Like the earlier secondary modern novels, *This Right Soft Lot* includes students of 'immigrant families' in its story and is as tentative as The Newsom Report about racism and its antidote. Towards the end of the novel, Blishen introduces Sylvester Chadwick, 'a fiery boy from Jamaica' (*TRSL*, p.242), who is subjected to overtly racist slurs and colonialist condescension. The protagonist hears his colleague Boulder 'roaring away at one of our West Indians' (*TRSL*, p.242). This turns out to be Sylvester, who has come into school wearing a trilby hat. The protagonist holds a debate with his form about whether it constitutes 'prejudice' not to let him wear the hat. When Sylvester replaces his trilby with a baseball cap, the latter is stolen, provoking Sylvester's 'bitter tears', tears 'for more than his cap [for] the whole terror and desolation of losing Jamaica and gaining Stonehill Street' (*TRSL*, p.244). The arrival of more 'West Indian' students lessens Sylvester's 'unfamiliarity' to other students, and the racist name-calling subsides. The 'rubbish of local prejudice', however, persists. Blishen's protagonist echoes The Newsom Report's helpless shrug at the spectre of racism and imagines the only safety is in numbers and the eventual familiarisation of indigenous populations with newer arrivals.

The novel ends as Stonehill Street is to be merged with the nearby girls' school to become comprehensive and the protagonist moves on. His ambivalence about the school's future status is clear. 'Stonehill Street couldn't be allowed to swell into this new thing, into its new comprehensive condition', he reflects, evoking a disease process rather than a restructure 'without some ceremony of farewell, a summing up' (*TRSL*, p.275). His nostalgia sets in before he leaves the grounds. Stonehill Street is a 'roaring, groaning, inept muddle…yet there had been, so often, a kind of honesty' (*TRSL*, p.281). Its failure was in 'to misunderstand …the effort required to lift us all, teachers and boys, above the depression that was the common local response to schooling' (*TRSL*, p.281). But its success was in 'the rough comic refusal of illusion … that made for a sort of disenchanted directness and sometimes for actual gaiety. The school was a failure and essentially it knew it' (*TRSL*, pp.281–2). Although this reads like an admission of defeat, it is rather a refusal to accept some 'lesser education destiny' for the school; the loss of 'acceptance of local reality' in favour of 'dull, conventional, unsympathetically moralising forms of schooling'. Attempts to 'pretend that Stonehill was a middle-class school' (*TRSL*, p.283) would be defeat. To move forward 'you ought to begin with their awkward, growling honesty' (*TRSL*, p.283), to cultivate 'authentic' working-class culture by allowing it to grow rather than concreting over it.

The Blinder

This is the sort of reflection that might more commonly arise when thinking about those sites of working-class social mobility, grammar schools, rather than comprehensives. The tension between 'opportunity' and 'community' that Blishen implies here underpins some of the representations of grammar schools, including Barry

Hines's 1966 novel *The Blinder* (Hines, 1966). Before Barry Hines wrote *A Kestrel for a Knave*, his lament for the children who were first the rejects of the grammar school and then left on the bottom rung of the secondary modern, he created Billy Caspar's antithesis, Lennie Hawk. Lennie, the son of a miner, is in the sixth form of his local grammar school. He is academically gifted, an exceptional footballer and is as charismatic and powerful as Billy is slight and victimised. The novel opens in the school assembly, with the head simultaneously calling Lennie for detention and announcing that he had scored four goals for the England youth eleven the previous evening. Lennie hears neither announcement as he is outside in the rhododendron bush with fellow sixth former, Jenny. The scene sums up Lennie's insouciance; not for him the dramatic tension between attachment to his working-class community and upward mobility to university. His dad wants him to become a professional footballer, and his mam wants him to go on to higher education. Lennie wants to keep his options open: 'I'd like a bit of both' 'Tha wants jam on it' retorts his mam (*TB*, p.25). After football training, Lennie shifts the tea things off the kitchen table to finish his homework before going out to meet a girl. His father Frank sums up Lennie's 'problem' to his colliery mate Bill: 'He's too much bloody talent, that's his trouble. He don't know whether to make a living out of his head or out of his feet' (*TB*, p.25).

Like Billy, Lennie is most alive out of school. For Billy, friendships, family and school come nowhere close to the pleasure of training and flying Kes. As his former friend Tibby says, 'He never knocks about wi' anybody now, he just looks after this hawk all t'time. He's crackers wi' it!' (*AKFAK*, p.78). Similarly, Lennie comes to life on a football pitch. When Lennie's girlfriend Jane accuses him of misanthropy, his response is more tart and a truncated version of Billy's rhapsodic description of training his hawk:

> 'Nobody's right for you are they?' says Jane 'Why don't you run away and find yourself an island somewhere?'
> 'I've found one. It measures a hundred by sixty and they've goals at each end.'
> 'And what about the other twenty-one players?'
> 'They don't count. It's just me and the ball, and the goal'.
>
> (*TB*, p.57)

Unlike Billy, Lennie has the academic ability to succeed in the grammar school system and is personally popular and powerful. If, like the boys in Blishen's novel, Lennie has outgrown school he is not constrained by the school's authority figures. On the contrary, he holds court in the classroom: when he makes an appearance in an art appreciation class, the girls 'looked at each other and blushed. The boys tried to shout him down' while Lennie conducts the hecklers 'like an orchestra' (*TB*, p.8). Lennie's popular authority over his peers extends to his parents and teachers. His father is an ailing collier who wants Lennie to capitalise on his talent for football. His mother wants him to study hard and go to university. Lennie is dismissive of them both. The 'ordinary devoted teachers' are marginal or disempowered in Lennie's story: Mr Rowley the History teacher is constantly outwitted by Lennie, who embarks on an at times violent sexual relationship with his teacher's wife. Mr Brook, whose sexuality is never spoken of but is implied, is infatuated with the sixth former but his feelings are unrequited. The Head, Doctor Bennett, brings Lennie in for a disciplinary chat after he is sent off in a school football match, only to be disarmed by the school star's indifference to school discipline or praise.

His girlfriend Jane is the daughter of D.S. Leary, owner of the town's paper mill and Chairman of the Board at the football club. Lennie is undaunted by Leary's status and lands a punch on his chin after the Chairman warns him off his daughter and slaps him across the cheek.

Lennie's story is a fantasy of the shifting, potentially disruptive, power relations between the newly authoritative working-class grammar student and the confused adults around him. While his sexual prowess mirrors his academic and sporting success, Jane's pregnancy and its termination mark their unravelling. His story ends with a sending off for punching a player who slights Jane's reputation; Lennie is last seen in the director's box, throwing handfuls of cash at Leary as the opposing team secure the win. Lennie will not be bought.

The Blinder is known for its record of a now alien world of professional football, when a player could still be part of his community and his wages wouldn't wildly outstrip that of his mining friends and family (Williams, 2016). And Hines' own life story – working-class grammar schoolboy with a talent for football – is evident in the tale of Lennie, albeit in a superhero fashion. The evolution of Lennie as comic book hero is foreshadowed in Mr Hawk's playful mishearing of the poet Andrew Marvel (whose work Lennie is studying for A-level) as Captain Marvel. But the talented, uncowed working-class grammar schoolboy at the centre of the footballing story has a broader resonance. At a time when progressive pedagogy favoured learning over teaching and person-centred psychology championed self-actualisation, Lennie is a working-class disruptor who overpowers his teachers and those around him with ultimately self-defeating energy. He is too much for those around him and ultimately for himself.

These stories variously focus on boys on the verge of adulthood: the secondary modern boys staying on longer at school and, the grammar sixth former, a man paraded in a school uniform. They are 'naturals', uncontained and unsupported by the state school system. The 'natural' child also haunts the Newsom Report, although there it looks uncannily like the middle-class child, whose speech and literacy is unhampered by the 'limitations' of working-class or immigrant culture. These tensions turn more vexatious in the debate about comprehensive schools in the 1970s, as the next chapter will reveal.

Abbreviations

AKFAK: Hines, B. (2000) *A Kestrel for A Knave*, London: Penguin.
TB: Hines, B. (1966) *The Blinder*, Harmondsworth: Penguin.

TNR: CACE. (1963) The Newsom Report, *Half Our Future: A Report of the Central Advisory Council for Education*, London: HMSO.
TPR: CACE. (1967) *Children and their Primary Schools: A Report of the Central Advisory Council for Education* (The Plowden Report), London: HMSO.
TRSL: Blishen, E. (1969) *This Right Soft Lot*, London: Thames and Hudson.

References

Blishen, E. (1969) *This Right Soft Lot*, London: Thames and Hudson.
CACE. (1963) The Newsom Report, *Half Our Future: A Report of the Central Advisory Council for Education*, London: HMSO.
CACE. (1967) *Children and their Primary Schools: A Report of the Central Advisory Council for Education* (The Plowden Report), London: HMSO.
Cant, B. (1963) *American Journey*, Report for Stoke-on-Trent Education Committee.
Circular 10/65, *The Organisation of Secondary Education*, Department of Science and Education, London: HMSO.
Davis, R. (2018) 'Education, literature and the paradox of "the whole child"', *Research ED*, https://researched.org.uk/2018/09/26/education-literature-and-the-paradox-of-the-whole-child/
Gerrard, J. (2013) 'Self-help and Protest: the emergence of black supplementary schooling in England', *Race, Ethnicity and Education*, January, 16 (1), pp. 32–58.
Gilroy, B. (2021) *Black Teacher*, London: Faber & Faber Ltd.
Hines, B. (1966) *The Blinder*, Harmondsworth: Penguin.
Hines, B. (2000) *A Kestrel for a Knave*, London: Penguin.
Holden, A. (1969) *Teachers as Counsellors*, London: Constable.
Hunter, E. (1954) *The Blackboard Jungle*, London: Constable.
Kes (1969) [Film] Loach, K., dir., London: Kestrel Films.
Leigh, J. (2002) *The Cinema of Ken Loach: Art in the Service of the People*, London: Wallflower Press.
Leonard, D. (ed.) (2006) *The Future of Socialism: The Book That Changed British Politics*, London: Jonathan Cape Ltd.
Lytton, H. and Craft, M. (1969) *Guidance and Counselling in British Schools: A Discussion of Current Issues*, London: Edward Arnold Publishers.
Maslow, A.H. (1943) 'A theory of human motivation', *Psychological Review*, 50(4), pp.370–96.
Ministry of Education. (1947) *The New Secondary Education*, Pamphlet, No.9, London: HMSO. https://www.education-uk.org/documents/mineofed/pamphlet09.html
Robinson, B.D. (1996) 'School counsellors in England and Wales, 1965–1995: a flawed innovation?' *Pastoral Care in Education*, 14(3), pp.12–9.
Rogers, C.R. (1959) *Client-Centred Therapy*, London: Constable.
Rogers, C.R. (1969) *Freedom to Learn*, Columbus, OH: Charles E. Merrill Publishing.
Schools Council (1967) *Counselling in Schools: A study of the present situation in England and Wales*, Working Paper No 15.
Shields, R. (1968) 'Guidance and counselling', *The New Era in Home and School: The New Education Fellowship Journal*, 49(1), pp.1–3.
Williams, R. (2016) 'A glimpse of a forgotten game: how Barry Hines painted a portrait of football's past', *The Guardian*, 25 March.
Winnicott, D.W. (1991) *The Child, the Family and the Outside World*, London: Penguin.

PART 2
Backlash

4

COMPS AND DELINQUENTS

Declining school standards in the 1970s

In 1970, my sister Susan passed the 11-plus and joined St James' Roman Catholic Convent school in Hartlepool. She was kitted out in the brown uniform – pinafore, blazer and hat – that would mark her out on the way to the bus stop through our council estate. Although the local authority had plans to phase out the 11-plus, new girls were assured they would see out their education in the school they had started.

Susan had an uneven start at the convent. She was unhappy and at the bottom of her form in the first year, and our parents started the process of moving her out to the girls' secondary modern. Suddenly, towards the end of the summer term she announced that she was, in fact, enjoying herself and subsequently moved up the academic pecking order. From that point on, Susan recalls 'it was like *Call the Midwife* in a school': singing in the chapel; the inspiring smells of incense and the waxed assembly hall floor; Latin declensions and 'sodality'; French lessons with beloved Sister Seraphina. Sister Seraphina couldn't sing so the class were not taught French songs like their peers in other forms, but she did delight Susan by anointing her with a Gallic pseudonym: Claire Pomme de Terre. My sisters, it seems, have an affinity with nuns that was not inherited from our mother.

This idyllic period came to a dramatic end when the local authority announced that the convent, the boy's grammar St Paul's (attended by my late, middle brother Martin) and three other secondary schools would merge into one comprehensive, All Saints, in September of 1974. Susan remembers that the summer term had ended early, and she and Martin returned to school in

DOI: 10.4324/9781003715122-8

September to massive disruption, including fights between the newly 'merged' students, which meant that the school shut down again until October. From that time, Susan would board the school bus home and hear the refrain 'your Martin's had a fight'. The merger wasn't, it seems, a smooth one. Susan stayed on to sixth form and was offered a place at university (a first in our family) but had other plans and took a job in the local benefits office. A long career followed, first in hospitality, then as a Senior Executive for Health and Safety and multiple Trust Board appointments, including in Colleges of Further Education in Scotland. Susan's favourite school story: *The Prime of Miss Jean Brodie.*

Please Sir!

In February 1972, the last episode of the London Weekend Television sitcom *Please Sir!* aired after four series (*Please Sir!*, 1968–72). The fictional students of class 5C of Fenn St secondary modern had certainly exceeded the compulsory leaving age, which had risen to 16 just as the series ended. Over four series, *Please Sir!* followed the predictable 'antics' of newly qualified teacher Bernard Hedges, played by John Alderton, and his implausible fifth formers. Hedges leaves in series four, before the school merges with nearby Weaver Street secondary and is redesignated as comprehensive, amidst much consternation from staff.

Fenn Street's 'merger' was more than a comic ploy. Since 1965, when Labour Education Secretary Tony Crosland's Circular 10/65 advised local education authorities to replace selective schools with comprehensives, mergers and redesignations were the order of the day. The policy became law under the Labour government in 1976 only to be repealed again in 1979 under Margaret Thatcher's administration. Whatever the legal position, the conversation about comprehensive education was always animated and divisive.

The move towards comprehensives was motivated politically, for Tony Crosland at least, by the sense that selective tests were skewed towards middle-class children. Further, children in secondary modern schools were increasingly demonstrating the academic ability that had been assumed to be the preserve of grammar school children (see my brother and sister Patrick and Eileen in the last chapter). O-level exams sat in secondary moderns, it was argued, rendered the 11-plus meaningless.

Child-centred pedagogy and psychology also fuelled the trend away from selection. As I outlined in the last chapter, the first university training course for school counsellors was launched in Keele University in October 1965, inspired by the American high school system of guidance and personal counselling for students and partly by the need to support students to navigate the new comprehensives. In the 1969 publication of the proceedings of a conference on *Guidance and Counselling in British schools* (Lytton and Craft, 1969), a contributor looks forward to a less stratified society, a more 'flexible' education system and a role for counselling in the new schools. He argues, optimistically, that while comprehensives are bigger and more complex systems than their predecessors, school counsellors who could provide 'an all-round view of the whole child in his [sic] total social setting can ensure that human problems do not jam the works' (p.25).

The Black Papers

In the 1960s, the post-war population boom was still affecting the education sector and the numbers of children in need of school places drove school building programmes and recruitment of teachers. The 1972 White Paper, *Education: A framework for Expansion*, notes that now that the number of children being born has passed its 1960s' peak, the focus can move from the provision of more school places to the offer of longer periods in education for more children and young people. Places were to be offered from nursery (as recommended in the 1967 Plowden Report) to higher education (as promoted by the Robbins Report of 1963).

The direction of travel in the 1950s and 1960s had been towards child-centred, non-selective schools and a widening of educational opportunities. Towards the end of the 1960s, a wave of critique of the perceived consequences of this movement was washing up from the contrary direction. Between 1969 and 1977, Brian Cox and Anthony Dyson, two lecturers in English Literature at Manchester University, and editors of the academic journal *Critical Survey*, launched attacks on comprehensive education, university expansion and progressive educational ideas in special editions of the journal called the Black Papers, so-called as an alternative to official government White Papers (Cox and Dyson, 1969–77). Cox and Dyson believed in the potential of grammar schools as engines of social mobility and saw comprehensives as a backwards step. They took contributions from across the political spectrum and included some florid predictions about the impact of educational change. Cox also appeared on *This Week*, a magazine programme from Thames Television which produced several short films focusing on education matters in the 1970s. In an episode dedicated to the pros and cons of the comprehensive system, entitled 'Could do Better?', Cox raised the alarm on behalf of the 'able' working-class child who would not thrive in the comprehensive system (*This Week*, 1977).

The opening salvo of the first issue, 'Fight for Education: A Black Paper' in 1969, directed at Members of Parliament, conflates 'the introduction of free play methods in primary schools, comprehensive schemes, the expansion of higher education, the experimental courses at new universities' with 'Anarchy', exemplified in student protests in Europe and North America (Cox and Dyson, 1969a, p.1). The catalyst for this catastrophe was a perceived shift in the 'student/teacher relationship'. The article opines that the teacher is now follower not leader, 'decoder' not exponent. In the name of social justice and egalitarianism, it claims, schools and universities are undermining accumulated knowledge, academic excellence and reward based on merit. While not named, person-centred psychology and child-centred pedagogy are implicated in this collapse of authority and civilisation.

As Rhodes Boyson's article in the second Black Paper (Cox and Dyson, 1969b) demonstrates, the contributors were not wholeheartedly against comprehensive schools. Boyson, who at the time of writing was head of a comprehensive in London, saw the potential of the new schools to increase academic opportunities for more children, but he railed against the conflation of educational opportunity and social engineering, arguing that schools cannot remedy social ills or elide class difference:

> Social egalitarians stepped in and clamoured for comprehensive secondary schools for social not academic reasons…Neighbourhood comprehensive schools would in the view of the egalitarians end the class system by educating the Duke's son and the docker's son in the same school, and, in an unstreamed school, in the very same class. It is a pity that the advocates for such schools did not look on the map and note that the Duke and the docker lived in different places.
>
> (Cox and Dyson, 1969b, p.58)

The creator of this egalitarian dystopia evidently hadn't heard of buses.

The separation of the 'social' and the 'academic' runs through the Black Papers: 'brightness' is free of class, race or sex and would be constrained by a system that pins it to such forms of 'identity'. A 1972 book by a group of professors in the Philosophy of Education from the Universities of Cambridge and London takes a similar view. The authors are sceptical about the Plowden Report urging schools to allow children to 'be themselves' and its privileging of 'sincerity, self-expression, freshness, being spontaneous, being "natural" and authenticity' (Deardon, Hirst and Peters, 1972, p.77). Somewhat archly, they ask how a teacher should know what is 'natural' to the child and what is already culturally acquired by the time the child starts school:

> [H]ow is the teacher to discover not just when the required inner agreement obtains but also what the individual nature is with which activities must be in agreement? The educational process appears to have become impossibly private.
>
> (Deardon, Hirst and Peters, 1972, p.78)

Hirst sums up the case of the book in a chapter entitled 'Liberal education and the nature of knowledge': 'a liberal education…[is] based fairly and squarely on the nature of knowledge itself' (p.391). Such knowledge must have an 'objective' foundation and the education which imparts it must be based on 'the nature and significance of knowledge itself, and not on the predilections of pupils, the demands of society or the whims of politicians' (p.393).

The rejection of 'child-centredness' is presented here as a defence of objective forms of knowledge and an education system whose responsibility is to develop children's reasoning capacity not to cater to their 'private interests'. While Deardon et al hold on to their philosophical purity throughout, not commenting on the extension of the educational franchise, the Black Papers often elide the defence of a knowledge-based education system with an explicit defence of a socially elite as well as philosophically pure education sector. Public schools, after all, were founded upon the creation of a class of scholars to whom permanent forms of knowledge, not transient disciplines nor 'relevant' skills, were imparted. Public schools were not designed for social inclusiveness: they were to be unbound by relevance and ostensibly free of social context, while upholding the stratification of society beyond their gates.

Progressivism in retreat

In these defences of knowledge-based education, person-centred progressivism is characterised as a retreat to a private, subjectively based education (which coincidentally encourages more kinds of children to access it). Elsewhere in the state sector, progressivism is seen to be a thing of luxury, an import from esoteric psychoanalysis and the fringes of the private sector, associated with schools which had the resources to pay attention to the interests of the individual children of the middle and upper classes.

This kind of critique, amongst other issues, killed off the local education authority-funded school counsellor training before it was fully established. As noted by Bor et al, at the beginning on the 1970s there were several hundred school counsellors in England and Wales and nine full-time university courses (Bor et al., 2002). Eighteen courses were in place by 1973, and school counselling services were developed by some local education authorities. Despite the increasing numbers of trained school counsellors and the arrival of a professional body to support them (the Association of School Counselling), scepticism about the place of counselling in the state school and lack of government funding saw enthusiasm for the university courses trail off. School counselling would no longer be organised or supported in a centralised way in England.

School counselling in the 1970s

Those writing about school counsellors from the early 1970s were making a case for their own existence as much as developing the practice. Anne Jones was a former teacher, marriage guidance counsellor and counsellor in a girls' comprehensive. In her 1970 book *School Counselling in Practice*, Jones describes the role of counsellors in schools as somewhere between advice givers and psychotherapists (defining the aim of psychotherapy as 'personality change'):

> The school counsellor is more concerned with the development of what is, than with fundamental change; with the here and now more than with the deep and distant past; with making the best of a situation as it actually is, rather than altering the way of the world.
>
> (Jones, 1970, p.25)

This kind of distinction between counselling and psychotherapy still crops up today, but the split does not really hold as firmly as Jones asserts here. Perhaps the strength of the distinction is based on the need to put distance between the pragmatic, school-focused counsellor and the esoteric, inward-focused psychotherapist.

In terms of modality, Jones references American literature on counselling and highlights Rogerian non-directive counselling alongside directive, problem-solving approaches and the 'eclectic' mix of the two. 'Ultimately the counsellor functions not according to a book', she writes, 'but according to himself [sic], yet in a disciplined, informed and professional manner' (Jones, 1970, p.27). In her account of setting up a counselling service in a secondary school, Jones points out that the counsellors had no teaching responsibilities and provided no educational or vocational guidance. Counsellors offered: 'help...through temporary crises... with normal developmental problems ... note[d] signs of abnormal disturbance' and where possible referred on for 'specialist treatment'. The counsellor helps to communicate between 'the school, the home, the community' and is there to 'support, reassure and guide teachers' (p.40). According to Jones, the school counsellor is not child-centred in the sense of providing an intersubjective relationship, unaltered by specificities of place, time or other markers of identity. Jones's school counsellor is an agent in a system, attending to the situation of the relationship with the child and its impact on other relationships and systems.

In his 1974 book, *The Teacher and Counselling*, Douglas Hamblin made a case for counselling as an integrated specialism within schools (Hamblin, 1974). While local education authorities were losing their enthusiasm for school counselling courses and leaning towards counselling as part of a teacher's pastoral duties, those who had been involved in school counsellor training could see its ongoing value. Hamblin had taught on the Diploma in School Counselling at the University College of Swansea. In his book he spells out the relationship between counselling and teaching, shares a model of counselling in secondary schools (with an emphasis on comprehensive schools) and illustrates techniques and problems.

Hamblin is an 'integrator' on several levels. He argues for counsellors to be fully integrated members of school staff (not working in isolation); he sees students' difficulties as internal and systemic (school, home and social environment make up those systems). He is alert to the value-laden aspects of Rogerian counselling. 'It has been held', he writes 'that one of the virtues of the non-directive model is that it is value free. In fact, it seems to encapsulate middle-class values which stress that self-exploration is a desirable activity' (Hamblin, 1974, p.36). He is sceptical that a working-class adolescent would find much meaning in the 'structured permissiveness' of the counselling relationship advocated by Rogers, and, echoing Newsom and Plowden, imagines it would be particularly difficult for 'disadvantaged pupils' with 'restrictive language' (p.36).

Hamblin compares 'the structured permissive relationship' with a 1970 description of the counselling relationship by E.C. Lewis. For Lewis, counselling is:

> a process by which a troubled person (the client) is helped to feel and behave in a more personally satisfying manner through interaction with an uninvolved person (the counsellor) who provides information and reactions which stimulate him to deal more effectively with himself and his environment.
>
> (p.5)

Hamblin emphasises the more active role of the counsellor proposed by Lewis, but there is also more explicit reference to behavioural shifts in the client, the 'operant conditioning' that was popularised by Skinner and was used to promote positive behaviour in classrooms. For Hamblin, counselling in schools should promote 'more adaptive behaviour' as well as self-understanding, protection of the individual student as well as the promotion of the smooth running of the school. The counsellor should support the 'mastery' of developmental tasks that will help the adolescent to move into adulthood (using Erikson's description of psychosocial development). The 'task' of the adolescent is to develop autonomy (p.5). The counselling relationship 'is the basis upon which the counsellor supports the pupil in his ...problem-solving efforts' (p.16). It is a relationship 'based on acceptance of the pupil as he is rather than as we would like him to be' and that helps 'a boy or girl become the best that he or she can be in every aspect of life where the need for counselling exists' (p.20).

Erikson and the psychosocial task of adolescence

As Hamblin's work suggests, it is perhaps Erikson's work and tone rather than that of Carl Rogers that informs the work of school counsellors in the 1970s and the representation of 'the adolescent' in the comprehensive school in that decade. Adolescence in this view is a period of 'crisis' rather than organic emergence. Erikson (who coined his own surname) was born in Germany to a Jewish Danish mother. He lived in Germany until he moved to Vienna where he studied psychoanalysis with Anna Freud. He left for the US in the mid-1930s and practiced as a child psychoanalyst and later developed an interest in the relationship between psychotherapy and anthropology, the intersection between the psychological and the social. This intersection also informed his involvement in a longitudinal study into child development when he was based at the University of California. His book *Identity and the Life Cycle* is a collection of papers from the late 1940s to 1950s which were first republished in 1959 and then again in 1979, illustrating a persistent interest in its themes (Erikson, 1980). In the 1959 Preface, Erikson describes its overarching theme as 'the unity of the human life cycle', in stages, 'prescribed by the laws of individual development and of social organisation' (p.7). In the 1979 reissue, Erikson emphasises his interest in the 'interplay of life history and history' (p.13), the details of individual development and the general movement of social change.

This work is best known for Erikson's delineation of stages of the 'lifespan' and the tasks that must be completed at each stage to ensure the development of a 'healthy personality', like the tasks of Campbell's hero's journey but with less dragons. The stage between childhood and adulthood, 'adolescence', brings challenges, especially, Erikson argues, for those living in complex societies, like post-war America and, implicitly, the UK. He sums up the task of this stage as 'identity versus identity diffusion'. This is a time of consolidation between the continuities of childhood and connection 'with the ideal prototypes of the day' (that is, the social measures of success in a particular time and place) (p.94). Erikson argues that it is not adequate for an adolescent to be given indiscriminate praise nor be restrained from self-expression. The adolescent needs 'wholehearted and consistent recognition of real accomplishment, that is, achievement that has meaning in their culture' (p.95). Without this 'real accomplishment', adolescents are prey to 'identity diffusion' and lapse into 'delinquency' (p.97). For Erikson, identity diffusion is a state of doubt (in his view especially about ethnic or sexual identity), which is exacerbated by being forced to assume 'a role' which approximated the 'inexorable standardisation of American adolescence' (p.97). The resistance to this prototype leads to 'delinquency', to running away 'in one form or another; leaving schools and jobs, staying out all night, or withdrawing into bizarre and inaccessible moods' (p.97). Diagnoses and 'social judgements' only make the problem worse, and adolescents defend against these attempts to bring them back in line with social roles by the temporary overidentification, 'to the point of apparent complete loss of identity, with the heroes of cliques and crowds' (p.97). While Erikson's language isn't ours, he could be describing the process of school avoidance, gang involvement and grooming that our schools wrestle with. Erikson argues that it is a problem particular to democratic societies like America and the UK which insist on 'self-made identities ready to grasp many chances' (p.99). Such identities are difficult to fulfil in complex societies which promote being 'self-made' but simultaneously override the freedoms and 'choices' required by the self-made to function (p.99). This tension produces delinquents, adolescents with no sense of place or purpose; it gives with one hand and takes away with the other. Erikson's proposed antidote is 'a system of education that transmits values and goals which determinedly aspire beyond mere "functioning" and "making the grade"' (p.100).

More popularly, 'delinquency' was associated with lack of discipline, as debated in the secondary modern novels, when magistrates of juvenile courts blamed progressive teaching methods for the wayward teenagers appearing before them. Erikson's account points to something deeper, a contradiction in post-war democracy that leaves many adolescents adrift. Erikson advocates more genuine freedom, not less, to overcome 'identity diffusion'. However, the critical commentary on 'progressive education', and comprehensive schools, in the 1970s argues that it is the absence of hierarchy and authority which produces identity diffusion and adolescents with no sense of purpose: delinquents. Comprehensives, they argue, both relinquish the transmission of 'knowledge' and the social structure that is preserved by the public school and the grammar system.

Early to Bed

In 1975, the screenwriter Alan Bleasdale, who was educated in a grammar school, was teaching in a comprehensive school in Halewood, Merseyside, when he submitted a short screenplay to a BBC competition for new writers. The play, *Early to Bed*, was featured in the BBC's 'Second City Firsts' series. Set in a small town near Wigan, it focuses on the relationship between a young, unhappily married woman, Helen (played by Alison Steadman), and her 18-year-old neighbour, Vinny. Vinny is a grammar schoolboy emerging from adolescence. He cares for his blind mother who wants him to pursue academic success. Vinny is also a runner, and with the support of his 'ordinary devoted' PE teacher secures a place at Loughborough University. The plot has echoes of Hines's *The Blinder*, whose protagonist Lennie is also an academically gifted and athletic grammar schoolboy from a mining town (Hines, 1966). The stories invest the bodies of these young working-class men with skill, power and libidinous energy. While it is Lennie's body, and his swagger, that closes off the route out of his mining town at the end of *The Blinder* (he gets his girlfriend pregnant, ignores his A-levels and throws away his chance of professional football), Vinny has kept up his studies, his care for his mum and his training while having an affair with Helen. The final scene sees him boarding the bus to Loughborough while Helen is left holding his (yet unborn) baby. Vinny, it seems, has swerved the social realist pay off even though, as always, the woman bears the brunt. There is a shift here from the earlier version of this story told by Hines. *Early to Bed suggests* that the grammar school can be redemptive for the working-class adolescent, a passport out of his limiting environment and restraint on his libido. Implicitly, the comprehensive might not offer such opportunity.

The Best Days?

While the grammar school, where the young bodies of the working class are subjected to reason, is often associated with social mobility, the comprehensive school has struggled to shake off its reputation for levelling down. In the mid-1970s, Labour education policy, which was overseen by Education Minister Shirley Williams, continued to champion comprehensive reorganisation. However, the association between comprehensive schools and academic and social decline was made from the top of the party in October 1976, when the Prime Minister James Callaghan gave a speech at Ruskin College (Callaghan, 1976). He decried the erosion of educational standards in secondary schools and launched what Waters and Brighouse call 'the age of accountability' in secondary education (Waters and Brighouse, 2021). Although Callaghan distanced himself from the views of The Black Papers, the media made the connection for him.

Further editions of the Black Papers in 1975 and 1977 fuelled 'moral panics' that were circulated by the tabloids, broadsheets and the BBC. As Peter Mandler has observed, 'One or other of the Black Papers themes – student unrest, indiscipline, the abolition of grammar schools – was hardly out of the media at any time during these years' (Mandler, 2020, p.101). The most striking example is the BBC's *Panorama*, 'fly-on-the-wall' documentary *The Best Days?*, about Faraday Comprehensive school in Acton (Pope, 1977). The documentary, which was directed by Angela Pope and introduced by David Dimbleby, was screened in March 1977 and prompted a 'media frenzy', which has been documented by the Cambridge social history of secondary education project (Jeppesen, 2017). Dimbleby's sombre introduction announces a change in the regular *Panorama* format to indicate the extraordinariness of the content, and the programme proceeds on a grey-tinted route through classrooms dominated by apparently 'disaffected' adolescents (delinquents) and exasperated teachers.

The documentary has no commentary, just headings that indicate the setting of each scene. The episode opens with rain-streaked windows on an unprepossessing 1960s building and adolescent school students hastening across a wet playground at the start of the school day. As with most school stories, we join a morning assembly, populated by barely awake students and a touchingly optimistic teacher introducing the room to Wagnerian opera. The cameras move from class to class, largely following third and fifth formers. Alongside subject lessons is tutorial time, where a young male teacher cajoles his charges into attending the rest of the day's lessons and encourages one young girl to give up smoking. His tone is familiar and genial. In the programme's most notorious scene, the same girl is filmed smoking with a friend (the Cambridge project notes that there were accusations that the crew gave the cigarettes to the girls). Classroom scenes focus on bored and distracted students who occasionally look directly to camera. Teachers are largely seen trying to settle students as they arrive or interact with more reluctant class members. A room called 'The Sanctuary' provides a calming place for students who have been sent out of classes; a conversation between the Deputy Head and a parent reveals that the school does not administer corporal punishment. Two aspiring university students are interviewed by the head teacher while a clipped careers adviser talks to fifth form girls who have all indicated they would like to become secretaries. The adviser spends her time distinguishing between the role of a secretary and that of a typist while the girls zone out.

The final word of the piece goes to two cleaners, who bemoan the state of the gym. 'It gets worse every day!', one exclaims, before she opens the door to the changing rooms and reels in disgust: 'ooh, what a dirty 'ole!'

The absence of commentary means that there is no context. We roll our eyes with the self-conscious adolescents at the attempts of 'progressive' teachers to befriend them or at the frustrated ones who resort to shaming. As in the later generation of school documentaries, it is the most camera-friendly students who make the cut but unlike those later films, *The Best Days?* provides no narrative arc, no heartrending back story and no inspiring redemption. Teachers appear well-meaning but out of their depth. There are no interviews with staff or students: instead, we see parts of a system, like amputated limbs. As the viewer pieces them back together, Faraday seems to stand for the starkest critique of the Black Papers: poor discipline, low expectations, collapsing standards. That most of the students are from white working-class and black communities is left to speak for itself.

Black Teacher

The publication of Beryl Gilroy's *Black Teacher* in 1976 now reads like an intervention in a debate that was polarised around 'academic standards' or social inclusion (Gilroy, 2021). Her intervention was to name the racism in the education system which was evident but colluded with in *The Best Days?* Gilroy had trained as a teacher in British Guiana and studied in London from 1952. Her memoir documents the racism that blocked her way into teaching in England in the 1950s and that faced her throughout her teaching career. She also records the racist abuse doled out to children in her care. This form of explicit prejudice and the more coded version in the designation of a disproportionate number of black children as of 'low intelligence' and 'educationally subnormal' led to the development of the Black Supplementary School movement in the cities, which organised informal tuition and pressure on local authorities to address the abuse at the heart of the system.

Gilroy's description of her own schooling in British Guiana recalls the idea of education as imparting objective knowledge with no attention to the identity of the 'learners':

> No one thought of individual differences, or of regarding the children as handicapped, or disadvantaged or disturbed. No one thought that the various cultures from which we came had any bearing on what we learned.
>
> (Gilroy, 2021, p.20)

She recalls the racism from the Divisional Office that placed teachers in schools and the initial hostility in the classrooms in which she is eventually tolerated. She describes the 'common sense' educational prejudices of some colleagues, like

Mrs Burleigh who, sounding like the 'old lags' in the secondary modern stories, 'was violently against research':

> Research, especially educational research, threatened the future of Britain... All the famous psychologists of the day were raving lunatics who practised academic cannibalism, by devouring all that was sane and good in English education.
>
> (Gilroy, p.68)

Gilroy was an advocate of educational research and psychology and eventually completed a PhD in Counselling Psychology. Her understanding of the 'common sense' traditionalist attitude is inflected with her understanding of empire and slavery. Learning through play, for instance, was something that teachers in the West Indies did not acknowledge. She asserted that behind the authoritarianism of West Indian schooling was 'a concept of worth through work – something that had its roots in the rigours of a slave society' (p.102). Gilroy had embraced 'the new concepts of gaining the willing co-operation of children, and of trying to bring out the best in each and every child' (p.102), which was written off by colleagues as new-fangled nonsense.

Although Gilroy is looking back to the 1950s and 1960s, and her experience was in the primary sector, her commentary foregrounds racism and imperialism as intrinsic to English education throughout the sector. The book's publication coincided with the updating of the Race Relations Act in 1976, which extended the 1968 Act's definition of racism to include direct and indirect discrimination. Gilroy saw both in the state sector and saw it countered in the progressive wings of the independent sector. She chose to send her son Paul to University College School, a private progressive day school in Hampstead. Paul went on to become a prominent scholar in cultural studies who has published widely on race, colonialism and black British and African American culture.

Our Day Out

While the critique of comprehensives seems to be sharpest from those who were nostalgic for grammar schools, those speaking on behalf of students who, in a selective system, would have attended secondary modern schools also found comprehensive schools wanting. In 1977s *Learning to Labour*, the sociologist Paul Willis tells the story of a group of 'lads' at a single-sex comprehensive (a former secondary modern) in the West Midlands (Willis, 1977). The 'Hammertown Boys' (12 leaving age friends) represent what Willis calls an 'informal counter-school culture', inverting the values held up by the authority of the school, which for Willis are reinforced by the coercive powers of the state (the law and the police). The racism and sexism of the group are all explained in terms of counter-school cultural belonging, of class-based opposition to the dominant culture of the school, albeit one colluded with by some of the staff. This radical sociology of the 1970s viewed comprehensives as simple reproductions of the hierarchies of the selective system which intensified the sense of alienation in 'counter-school culture' groups.

The playwright Willy Russell was born and educated on Merseyside. He left school at 15 and after a stint as a hairdresser returned to education to train as a teacher in his early 20s. Russell's *Our Day Out* (televised as part of the BBC's *Play for Today* series in December 1977) dramatises and gives voice to a softer left-wing critique of comprehensives through the character of Helen Kay (Russell, 2002). Helen is the teacher of a Merseyside comprehensive school's 'remedial' class, euphemistically dubbed the 'Progress Class'. A school coach trip to Conwy Castle is overseen by the broadly progressive/traditional pairing of Mrs Kay and Mr Briggs. Briggs tries to organise the children into polite, straight lines while Mrs Kay wants to give them a 'good day out', not an educational experience (Act Two, p.148). She challenges Briggs' determination to get them to pay attention and behave like middle-class tourists and exposes the facade of the 'educational offer' for her low achieving charges. Born to be 'factory fodder', even that future is lost now that the factories have closed (Act Two, p.148). Briggs chides Mrs Kay's 'woolly minded liberalism' (Act One, p.133.). It is all well and good to be 'the great champion of the non-academic' he sneers, but 'you have to risk being disliked' (Act One, p.133). It is a risk he takes and wins.

The play imagines a temporary collapse of the progressive/traditionalist binary and a shift from the official purpose, organisation and hierarchy of school. The children ransack confectionary from a motorway station; smuggle zoo animals onto the coach; students Linda and Reilly make uncomfortable bids for intimacy with teachers Colin and Susan. At the play's climax, Carol Chalmers, a neglected child, contemplates throwing herself off a cliff rather than return home. When she lets Briggs catch her fall, the Deputy Head is temporarily changed. He proposes a trip to the fair and joins in with a singsong on the coach on the way home. His transformation – and by implication the broader release from the order of things – is temporary, however, as he destroys the roll of photographic film that literally and metaphorically exposes his transformation. As the coach pulls up at school, the status quo is restored. The voyage is complete; the return leaves the order unchanged.

Free schools

Helen Kay's ethos echoes that of the founders of the Scotland Road Free School in Liverpool, which was established in 1971 and was run by local teachers John Ord and Bill Murphy (de Castella, 2014). It was one of several such schools set up in cities throughout the country, reminiscent of the Summerhill progressive school but aimed at working-class city children who were 'truanting' from mainstream school. The Scotland Road School cut across the religious sectarianism of the local authority schools in Liverpool and was registered with the authority as

'Education otherwise' and subject to inspections. According to the *Times Educational Supplement* in 1970, cited in de Castella's piece, there was to be no 'headmaster, nor hierarchy' and rules and curriculum were to be arrived at by parents, children and teachers. Parents of children who attended the Scotland Road School were interviewed for an episode of *This Week* and provided a scathing critique of the mainstream system and a ringing endorsement of the free school (*This Week*, 1971a). (This episode also raised questions about raising the school leaving age to 16.) The free school teachers were unpaid, often otherwise unemployed 'helpers'. The building was a disused office above a shop, and the school minibus was a repurposed ambulance. An exhibition in Liverpool's Bluecoat Gallery in 2017 displayed photographs of the school taken in 1971 by John Walmsley, including images of children and adults moving bits of discarded furniture into the building (Walmsley, 2017). As numbers grew, new premises were found. In an interview Ord explains that the ethos was one of freedom not license, freedom in the sense of the children having to work out the rules, 'freedom to help other people', freedom 'in a social sense'. Children were to find their own way to what they learn. Scotland Road children were encouraged to reconnect with the natural world, were taken on trips to rural Wales, to milk cows and carry water from wells. 'History meant visiting Welsh castles', like the children in *Our Day Out*.

In the early 1970s, Liverpool was also an Education Priority Area. These arose from the Plowden Report in 1967 which explored the discrepancies between the educational outcomes of children from different social and economic backgrounds. Liverpool was one of five areas with the designation and was given additional funding for improved school buildings, to attract new teachers and to promote the value of education to families. An episode of *This Week* explored the initiative in Liverpool and focused on community-led preschool playgroups, schemes to increase parental involvement and the integration of schools in their local communities (*This Week*, 1971b).

Grange Hill

In this context, it is unsurprising that Merseyside produced an unusually high volume of writing about schools in the 1970s and beyond, including the work of Willy Russell, Alan Bleasdale, Jimmy McGovern and Phil Redmond. Redmond, the creator of the longest running and most celebrated television school story, *Grange Hill*, was born and educated in Liverpool, though for production reasons *Grange Hill* was set in London. In later years it was filmed in Liverpool and set in an unnamed city.

Redmond, born in 1949, had passed the 11-plus but in what he refers to ironically as the 'Socialist Jerusalem of Huyton', Liverpool, he was 'selected to be part of a group that would form the grammar stream, in the great comprehensive experiment of the 1960s' and was bused across the city to St Kevin's Roman Catholic Comprehensive (Redmond, 2013, p.23). When, some years after his time at St Kevin's, he studied the sociology of education, he began to reflect on comprehensivisation as a 'tragedy' (p.23). Redmond recounts how he was introduced to the ideas of John Holt and Ivan Illich, who respectively critiqued 'a school system that kills children's innate desire to learn' (p.91) and championed 'a system of self-education driven by interest and need, moderated and mentored by peer networks' (p.92), which was very much the ethos of Ord, Murphy and the city's Scotland Road Free School. Through *Grange Hill*, Redmond gave voice to 'how disempowered kids felt in their own education' (p.119). While benign authority figures in the fictional comprehensive would concede to the students' demands, Redmond wanted to show adolescents finding their own way to resolution:

> This was, and always remained, one of the overriding guidelines: that while the kids could challenge the status quo or demonstrate their feelings of injustice, it would always be the figures of authority who facilitated, not provided, the resolution.
>
> (p.119)

In *Grange Hill*, the 'ordinary devoted' teacher emerges when there is difficulty. When Anthony Karamanopolis falls asleep in lessons because he is working into the early hours in his family's restaurant, the art teacher Miss Summers makes a home visit to plea for his schooling to be prioritised. Miss Summers also intervenes when Susie McMahon struggles to live up to her parents' academic expectations. (When Susie's GP rules out a physical cause of her illness, he offers an hour-long appointment to get to the heart of the matter. Heady days.)

Redmond wanted *Grange Hill* to represent the lives of state-educated children, but to transcend the experience of the comprehensive school. He tried to present:

> an approximation of what life at school was like for the majority, never mind whether it was at a comp, grammar, or even a private school. *Grange Hill* worked in this way… it wasn't about education as such, but about all the social interactions formed by the comings and goings between lessons or on the way to and from the school itself.
>
> (p.26)

The school setting gave Redmond the opportunity to bring diverse characters into a shared setting with a common purpose, in what would become known as the 'precinct drama' (p.36). The stories were primarily told from the children's perspective, with cameras at their eye level.

Grange Hill dramatises all the contentions of the Black Papers, voicing their perspective on standards, disruption and permissiveness through the characters of overbearing parents, ambivalent teachers and sometimes overwhelmed students. Teachers draw attention to poor grammar; Susie McMahon's parents compare Grange Hill unfavourably to the grammar school attended by her older brother

David, fret about mixed ability teaching and the poor standard of the school production. However, *Grange Hill* also revels in the strength of the children's relationships and the potential of school as a site of resistance. Redmond's sociologist background emerges in the depiction of *Grange Hill*'s 'oppositional' culture. For instance, in an early episode the arrival of a new head sees the teachers work to rule in protest at new timetabling (foreshadowing the action taken by teachers in the 1980s). Students follow suit, pushing against the prescribed forms of democracy. The authorised school council, with its process of one representative for each year group and one proposal permitted for discussion, frustrates the more radical students. A Student Action Group springs up to protest uniform ('branded like sheep') and segregated seating for children in receipt of free school meals. Eventually, despite the expulsion of the 'ringleaders', pressure wins out. A referendum is called and school uniforms become optional, allowing our hero Tucker to sport his trademark leather biker jacket in form. As Phil Redmond points out, the student demonstrations were viewed by the tabloids as 'a blueprint for how to disrupt schools up and down the country' (p.120) even though the plot lines drew on Redmond's research of what had already happened in schools.

By the time that Tucker Jenkins and Trisha Yates were fastening their Grange Hill ties for the first time in 1977, the humanistic ambition of 1965, for comprehensive schools to attend to the academic and vocational needs of all children, supported by 'in-house' counsellors to keep an eye on the 'whole child', had foundered under the pressure of 'accountability'. In England, the scene was set for an incoherent sector of comprehensives, grammars and secondary moderns. Education was not to be held together by the common and complex cause of 'the whole child' but by a double-headed monster: the national curriculum and Office for Standards in Education (Ofsted).

This period marked the transition from what Brighouse and Waters call the 'age of optimism and trust', from 1945 to 1976, where education was described as a 'national education service locally administered' (by local education authorities) to the 'age of markets, centralisation and managerialism' (Brighouse and Waters, 2021, pp.13 and 19). What was taught and how it was taught became of increasing interest to central government, leading up to the Education Act of 1988.

Fifteen Thousand Hours

Just as the decade seemed to have turned its back on the ideals with which comprehensive education was launched, a piece of research published in 1978 was a beacon of hope about the potential of comprehensive schools to realise their early promise of academic and vocational success and social cohesion. A group of researchers, led by the child psychiatrist Michael Rutter, conducted some investigations in London secondary schools in the late 1970s, asking not whether selective or comprehensive schools best serve children but what common features successful schools share. 'The question here is whether schools were as they were because of the children they admitted, or rather whether children behaved in the way they did because of school influences' (Rutter et al., 1979, p.181). The research was prompted by arguments that schools had little impact on children's life chances, and that home life was the primary determinant of academic success (an implicit finding of the 1967 Plowden Report into primary education). While not discounting the many variables that have an impact on children's outcomes ('we agree … that education cannot compensate for the inequities of society' (p.182)), Rutter's research into 12 London secondary schools concluded that school processes have more impact than had been given credit. School processes are 'those features of the social organisation of school life which create the context for teaching and learning' (p.106). One of the most striking findings was that the 'social mix' of the children had less impact on all children's outcomes than the range of academic ability of the children in the school. Those schools with 'a high proportion of less able children' had a 'high propensity to delinquency': attributable to a range of factors, including low scholastic motivation. Mixing children of different academic abilities, therefore, gave rise to better social outcomes so long as the schools were well managed. In a decade which had foregrounded the losses incurred by the comprehensive system, Rutter's research finds that cognitive, social and implicitly emotional aspects of adolescent development are supported by non-selective, socially mixed secondary schools. This voice struggles to be heard in subsequent decades.

References

Bor, R., Ebner-Lany, J., Gill, S. and Brace, C. (eds.) (2002) *Counselling in Schools*, London: Sage.

Brighouse, T. and Waters, M. (2021) *About Our Schools: Improving on Previous Best*, Carmarthen: Crown House Publishing.

Callaghan, J. (1976) 'The Great Debate, 1976', Ruskin College, https://education-uk.org/documents/speeches/1976ruskin.

Cox, C.D. and Dyson, A.E. (eds.) (1969–77) *The Critical Survey*, London: Critical Quarterly Society.

Cox, C.B. and Dyson, A.E. (eds.) (1969a) 'Fight for education: a Black Paper', *The Critical Survey*, Winter, 4(1).

Cox, C.B. and Dyson, A.E. (eds.) (1969b) 'The crisis in education: Black Paper Two', *The Critical Survey,* Winter, 4(3).

De Castella, T. (2014) 'The anarchic experimental schools of the 1970s', *BBC News Magazine*, 21 October, https://www.bbc.com/news/magazine-29518319

Deardon, R.F., Hirst, P.H. and Peters, R.S. (1972) *Education and the Development of Reason,* London: Routledge and Kegan Paul.

Erikson, E.H. (1980) *Identity and the Life Cycle*, London: W.W. Norton and Company.

Gilroy, B. (2021) *Black Teacher*, London: Faber & Faber Ltd.

Hamblin, D.A. (1974) *The Teacher and Counselling*, Oxford: Basil Blackwell.

Hines, B. (1966) *The Blinder*, Harmondsworth: Penguin.

Jeppesen, C. (2017) 'Best days? Panorama 21st March 1977', *Secondary Education and Social Change in the United Kingdom Since 1945*, https://sesc.hist.cam.ac.uk/

Jones, A. (1970) *School Counselling in Practice*, London: Ward Lock Educational.

Lytton, H. and Craft, M. (1969) *Guidance and Counselling in British Schools: A Discussion of Current Issues*, London: Edward Arnold Publishers.
Mandler, P. (2020) *The Crisis of the Meritocracy*, Oxford: Oxford University Press.
Please Sir! (1968–1972) London Weekend Television.
Redmond, P. (2013) *Mid-term Report*, London: Arrow Books.
Russell, W. (2002) *Our Day Out, Willy Russell Plays*: 1, London: Methuen.
Rutter, M., Maughan, B., Mortimore, P. and Ouston, J. (1979) *Fifteen Thousand Hours: Secondary Schools and Their Effects on Children,* London: Open Books.
This Week (1971a) 'Should education be compulsory?', Thames Television.
This Week (1971b) 'Education priority areas', Thames Television.
This Week (1977) 'Could do better?', Thames Television.
Walmsley, J. (2017) 'Liverpool free school and 2017 reunion', https://www.johnwalmsleyphotos.co.uk/galleries/schools-colleges-universities/liverpool-free-school-1971-and-2017-reunion.
Willis, P. (1977) *Learning to Labor: How Working-Class Kids Get Working Class Jobs,* New York: Columbia University Press.

5

'THERE'S NO SUCH THING AS SOCIETY'

Dysfunctional families and the 1980s' comprehensive

I left St Martin's Roman Catholic Comprehensive in 1982 and carried on to St Bernadette's Catholic Sixth Form in Middlesbrough where I acquired three unremarkable A-levels. The academic confidence I had at secondary school (which was the only confidence I had) dissolved at the sixth form. I attended sporadically, didn't seem to make the impression I had on some of my previous teachers, and felt somehow unformed. Support at college was minimal but, following in the footsteps of older siblings and with the urging of a family who helpfully believed in my academic ability, I somehow applied to university. I missed the grade for my first choice but found the courage to pause and reapply. We didn't call them 'gap years' in 1984, but I took one and arrived at The University of Leeds in October 1985. After a year of living independently in the big city of Newcastle, my edges were slightly less blurry than when I had left the care of St Bernadette's.

In 1981, 15-year-old Paul had been out of school for a while, his absence largely unremarked upon by the Roman Catholic Comprehensive he attended in South Manchester. Things had been tricky at home. Like me he had five siblings, but his mum had been primary carer for most of his childhood and her partner during Paul's adolescence was not a supportive presence. Paul was drawn to a group of older boys and men from his estate and quickly 'progressed' from smoking weed to using heroin, a drug that had only recently been imported at scale into the cities of the UK (Morgan, 2014). Paul was unfortunate to be an early adopter, and addiction would lead him into a cycle of crime and imprisonment until his mid-20s. He broke that cycle, inspired partly

DOI: 10.4324/9781003715122-9

by becoming a father, and made a successful life until poor health brought him to burn out in his early fifties. A creative and self-aware man, he drew on his own resources to recover and improve his physical and mental health. His recovery was helped in part when he wrote his own life story, which helped to understand the relationship between his past and his present. He now wonders how his life could have been if someone had noticed him drifting in his early secondary school years. In the absence of family with enough emotional and material resources to anchor him through his adolescence, where were Paul's social family, starting with those charged with his education?

The family, school and Section 28

Margaret Thatcher's administration brought some significant shifts in education policy. The 1980 Education Act set up the assisted places scheme, providing private school places from public funds, increased the power of parents on governing bodies and ushered in the idea if not the practice of parental choice over school places for their children. Choice was the ideological key word in the 1986 and 1988 Acts. To make schools more transparent and accountable to parents, the 1986 Act required local authorities to make public their curriculum policies and governing bodies were to publish annual reports and hold parents' meetings. In the transfer of disciplinary authority to the family, corporal punishment was abolished in state schools. The year 1987 saw the abolition of the power to negotiate pay which teachers had held since 1965. The 1988 Act ramped up the shift from local authority control of schools with the establishment of the National Curriculum, GCSEs, 'key stages' and further changes to admission arrangements and funding formulae.

The rhetorical transfer of authority from schools to families makes sense in a period of high unemployment and when 'personal responsibility' is prioritised over social support. While families were to believe they had more choice and control over schools, schools were told to uphold a particular model of 'the family'. The Local Government Act of 1988 (which amongst other things aimed to loosen further the link between state schools and local authorities) included in Section 28 the instruction that a local authority 'shall not…promote the teaching in any maintained school of the acceptability of homosexuality as a pretended family relationship' (Local Government Act, 1988). The edict was in force in England until November 2003 when it was repealed by the New Labour government.

This aspect of the relationship between schools and the family would find its way into school stories from the 1990s onwards. In the early 1990s, Grange Hill Comprehensive employed its first gay teacher, Tom Brisley. Tom faces homophobia from staff and students, is thanked by the Head for his 'discretion' about his relationship with his partner Dan while enduring the incessant planning for the forthcoming marriage of a straight colleague (*Grange Hill*, 1992–99). Section 28 is not mentioned directly but it is challenged by Tom's presence in the school. The media coverage of Section 28 is the backdrop for the 2022 film directed by Georgia Oakley, *Blue Jean,* which I discuss in a later chapter. The film charts the impact of the legislation on Jean, a gay PE teacher in a northeastern secondary school in 1988.

School counselling and the system beyond

Thatcher of course redrew the relationship between society and family more broadly. In her infamous interview with *Woman's Own* magazine, Thatcher asserted that 'there is no such thing as society', and that we should imagine community as organic, not organised, relationships between individuals and families (Keay, 1987).

When schools are responsible for upholding a specific image of the family (two parents, one male, one female) whilst being invited to give more authority to families in relation to school matters, there is confusion and tension about where responsibility for children and adolescents lies. This blurring is implicit in the literature on school counselling, where the school system is coming into view as part of 'the problem'.

In the late 1960s and 1970s, there is an implicit understanding in the literature on school counselling that the child and adolescent's family life are pertinent to the counselling session. A 1981 book by former educational psychologist David Galloway signals a subtle shift, by noting that the school itself may be contributing to the difficulties a child presents at school. Galloway offers case histories of 'children whose educational failure or disturbing behaviour challenges their teachers… to question the system they are currently operating' (Galloway, 1981, p.10). Galloway is addressing the status of school counselling and pastoral care in mainstream schools after the Warnock Report of 1978, which proposed greater integration of children with special educational needs into the mainstream system (Warnock, 1978). The report also recommended better partnerships between schools and families of children with additional needs. Galloway points out that this signals a reset of the view that it is the role of the school to identify a child's problems as emanating from 'outside' (usually in the family) and encourages schools to invite in the expertise of the family to help the school adapt its practice. Galloway asserts that 'personal counselling is not always appropriate' and is ineffective 'unless combined with a conscious attempt to deal with the problem where it occurs – in the classroom or the playground' (p.20).

Galloway's case histories illustrate the need for greater integration between services for children and young people and their families. An account of pastoral care at Castle Square Comprehensive School, for instance, starts with the frustration of a first year tutor who is trying to write a court report on a boy in her year but is stymied by inaccessible medical, psychological and social care records. These are held in filing cabinets marked 'confidential' or as knowledge retained by the boy's primary school or members of staff who have left his secondary school. Explicitly, the piece raises questions about access to sensitive records held by schools and the complexity of acting on information about children in large secondary schools, but its underlying message, which runs throughout the book, is about the impact of 'the school system' on the child and staff and vice versa. The school system is like a family system with all the possible dysfunction that implies.

Family systems theory

Family systems theory was forged in the 1940s and 1950s and understood the family not just the backdrop for the individual's difficulties but as the subject of therapeutic intervention. It shifted its focus from the Freudian idea that emotional disturbance originates in the early childhood of the individual. Family systems theory proposes that difficulties, even acute mental illness, are created and perpetuated by the dynamics of the family system, often across generations. In 1978, the American psychiatrist Murray Bowen explored the dynamics of families in his book *Family Therapy in Clinical Practice*, which gathered papers on aspects of family therapy since the 1950s when he had worked with families with a child with severe mental illness (Bowen, 1978). The family system he describes is claustrophobic and enmeshed, almost gothic in its blurring of selves and others.

In a deliberate attempt to align his work with science not philosophy, Bowen used language and ideas drawn from biology: he observed mothers and children in *symbiotic* relationships (characterised as intense cycles of closeness to the point of having merged identities) followed by periods of distance, separation and separation anxiety. This cycle, he observed, had an impact on other members of the family. Fathers would be drawn into the system of triangulation, being pulled closer to the mother when there was distance between the mother and child and cast out when the mother and child merged again. Bowen noted states of *fusion*, the blurring of emotion with intellect, and *differentiation*, the capacity to maintain a sense of self while staying connected to others. Bowen defined the *solid self*, made up of 'clearly defined beliefs, opinions, convictions, and life principles' (p.365), and its opposite *the pseudoself*, 'composed of a vast assortment of principles, beliefs...acquired because it is required or considered right by the group' (p.365).

As a psychiatrist, Bowen set himself outside the systems he 'observed'. He expressed his frustration with psychotherapists for whom the most successful outcome of therapy was free emotional expression and the mechanism for change was working through 'the transference' (the feelings from the past that the client brings to the relationship with the therapist). Bowen makes a trenchant case for the therapist to remain as objective as possible, outside of the relationship with the family. The therapist, he argues, should support the process of differentiation between emotional and intellectual systems and between family members locked into emotionally riven cycles with one another.

The heroism of the school failure

Bowen's families have dynamics which inflict damage upon their members, not through abuse but through misaligned relationships. This is a frightening prospect for those who assume that a family which does not directly abuse or neglect its members is protected against dysfunction. Theories like Bowen's unearth the precarity of the 'family values' that underpinned Thatcherite conservatism and the social order which it upheld. The patriarchal, heterosexual and economically self-sustaining family was the norm against which a range of bogeymen of the popular and right-wing press were measured and found wanting in the 1980s: the working mother; the single parent; the addict; the gay man or woman; the delinquent; the recipient of benefits. These 'types' are all presented as symptoms of a permissive and enabling welfare state, which includes the comprehensive school system.

School stories by Phil Redmond, Sue Townsend and Alan Bleasdale variously challenge this narrative and recast the 'social failures' and their misfit families as heroic: *Grange Hill*'s Danny Kendall and Sammy 'Zammo' McGuire, Sue Townsend's Adrian Mole and Alan Bleasdale's Francis Scully. In these stories, family and school are comic and tragic systems to be survived by the adolescent protagonists. Their schools reproduce the dysfunction of the family system and blame the boys' families for their misdemeanours.

In his memoir *Mid-Term Report*, Phil Redmond wrote of the influence of John Holt's work on schools and childhood when he studied the sociology of education in the 1970s (Redmond, 2013). For Holt, childhood is an 'institution' that is justified by 'idealised pictures of family life which often have little to do with reality' (Holt, 1974, p.27). In a provocation against what he sees as the arbitrary distinction between the rights and responsibilities of adults and those granted to children, he argues for children to be afforded the same rights as adults (to vote, work for money, have financial independence, to direct their own education, to drive, to use the same drugs that adults use).

Resisting authority

Holt's ideas of the family and school as systems which keep children 'subservient and dependent' (p.15) and Bowen's portrait of the capacity of the family system to imprison its members in a dynamic that threatens autonomy and rationality are ripe with gothic imagery, pertinent for the new authoritarianism to the 1980s. Redmond's *Grange Hill* amplifies children's resistance to authority, their struggle to find purpose and the flailing attempts of adults to answer the question 'why should I'? Often at the centre of such battles is bewigged tyrant and languages teacher Maurice Bronson who tries to hold on to an idea of authoritarian paternal control in the face of adolescents with strong ideas about democracy and autonomy. Bronson epitomises Bowen's idea of the 'fusion' of emotional and intellectual functioning, as he flies into rage when rules of his own invention are subverted.

Other staff are more 'pastoral' in their interest in their charges' wellbeing and step into their students' way of seeing. In Bowen's terms, these empathic adults are further up the scale of differentiation than Bronson. Mr Kennedy, for instance, has a healthy gap between his emotional and intellectual functioning. His relationship with Stephen Banks shows a teacher who works out a way to engage a student in decision-making rather than impose a rule upon him (*Grange Hill*, 1986). When Stephen grows a moustache, he is mocked by Mr Baxter and told to shave it off, while Mr Kennedy sets up a competition between them, agreeing to shave off his own bristles and charge the class to guess the weight of their offerings. The same dynamic is repeated in a later episode about sporting rivalry.

Maths teacher Mr King, however, mistakes empathic identification for something far more problematic when he allows fifth year Fay Lucas's adoration to turn into a relationship with him (*Grange Hill*, 1986–87). The bizarre family values of the 1980s come to the fore in this plotline when Mr King's relationship with 16-year-old pupil Fay is treated by Mr Glover, the Chair of the governing body, as the moral equivalent of the failure of unmarried teacher Miss Partridge to disclose the existence of her son on application. In his eyes, both are sacking offences. Mr Glover is a parent governor, a new breed produced by 1980s education policy. He is both an authoritarian parent and a governor who exceeds the boundaries of his authority. As we will see, governors become a more prominent fixture of the school story as the relationship between local authorities and schools continues to be redefined.

The power battles in *Grange Hill* are not just between a single teacher and a pupil. In what Bowen refers to as 'triangulation', a pair of teachers is often embroiled, via a student, in a power battle with each other. Bronson and Baxter, for instance, triangulate with Ant Jones (*Grange Hill*, 1986–87). Ant is sporty and academic and while he is a favourite of Mr Baxter, Mr Bronson belittles and bullies him. When Ant's parents are called into school, they initially repeat the pattern of the teachers: his dad doesn't entirely believe Ant's account of Bronson's bullying, while his mum defends him. After Ant runs away, the extent of Bronson's bullying is revealed, and Ant is taken out of Grange Hill and sent to a private school. The triangle collapses.

The most headlines generated by *Grange Hill* in the 1980s were about Zammo Maguire's heroin addiction. Heroin had arrived in UK cities at the beginning of the 1980s and Zammo's story, eked out across the whole of Season 9 in 1986, was like an extended public information film about the risks of drug use to school-aged adolescents. The cast sang 'Just Say No' for First Lady Nancy Reagan at the White House (Saner, 2016). This snappy jingle was not powerful enough to counter the forces of unemployment, an absence of attuned adults and the fracturing of social welfare that led adolescents, like Paul whose story opens this chapter, into heroin addiction.

Zammo's storyline attempted to provide a context for addiction. Zammo's story is shadowed by another plotline about nicotine addiction and the attempts of a group of students to encourage staff and students to stop, which attempts to 'humanise' the heroin addict and promote broader understanding of addiction. The origins of Zammo's addiction are vague, a symptom of getting in with 'the wrong crowd' and taking an adolescent risk. Zammo's risk taking goes beyond the 'norms' of adolescence, however. In the terms of Bowen's theory, Zammo has constructed a 'pseudo self', adopting the beliefs and behaviours of his peers before he has had time to construct a 'stable self'. His family consists of Zammo and his mum and although her status as a single parent is not offered overtly as a cause of Zammo's vulnerability, the series has other plotlines about single mothers (Miss Partridge, Miss Regan), which give voice to the broader moral panic about single-parent families.

Zammo's story is moving and convincing, but the story of Danny Kendall, which begins in the same series and ends in Series 12, is more unsettling (*Grange Hill*, 1986–89). Danny is small, pale and dark-haired; he seems to come from nowhere, is always alone and appears in the school corridors at odd times. He smokes at every opportunity and has no fear (nor, it seems, much joy, apart from in his talent for graffiti). Like Ant Jones, he is part of a triangle with Bronson but this time the third point is the art teacher Miss Booth. Danny seems to have swallowed John Holt's mantra about children's rights whole and is unbowed by Bonson's insistence that he must accept school rules. While Ant leant on Mr Baxter for support, Danny is reluctant to accept help from Miss Booth. When she attempts to engage him by offering him the chance to repaint a community centre, Danny shrugs off the opportunity. 'I don't do well in partnership' he says, and when pushed for an explanation reveals that he was born a twin, that his brother died at birth and thereafter he felt compelled to go it alone. 'I used up two lives being born', Danny says, immediately before collapsing due to an unnamed illness and being sent to Scotland to recover.

When in a later season an apparently recovered Danny is promised future work with a design company, Bronson makes sure the work doesn't materialise. In fury, Danny steals Bronson's car and is subsequently found dead in its back seat. Pupils respond with ghoulish fascination to his death and probe the boys who found his body about its appearance. There is no 'therapeutic' response to Danny's death, just an announcement in assembly and a proposed memorial service. When the head Mrs McCluskey is informed by Danny's family that a postmortem found he died of a recurrence of an earlier condition, Bronson is exonerated, and Danny's world weariness is somewhat explained.

While for everyone, adolescence is an 'in between' liminal experience, Danny is particularly ephemeral. He wanders the corridors of Grange Hill like a wraith, on the border between life and death. In every scene he pops the balloon of purpose and meaning as ascribed by school and debunks the authority of every adult. Danny Kendall is an archetypal anti-authoritarian, refusing not just submission to rules but any form of engagement. He keeps himself in what Bowen calls the 'emotional cutoff', estranged from the system but still enacting its impact, until it annihilates him. He refuses the 'pseudo-self' offered by peer identification while never achieving the stable self. This was a strong stuff for teatime children's television.

The Secret Diary of Adrian Mole

Danny's refusal of the self that is offered to him by family and school has tragic consequences. A more comic account of this adolescent battle with external authority is found in the diaries of a 1980s comprehensive schoolboy, Adrian Mole. Adrian epitomises the pseudo-self of the adolescent trying to find his place inside and outside of family and school. Sue Townsend's *The Secret Diary of Adrian Mole Aged 13 ¾* was first published in 1982. It records the life of the aspiring poet and intellectual from 1 January 1981 to 3 April 1982, the day that Britain and Argentina went to war over the Falkland Islands. I sat my O-levels that summer.

As she recorded in 'The Mole Story', an addendum to the special 50th Birthday edition of the character of Adrian Mole, Townsend had been crushed by her own experience of primary school and learned to read at home via the services of Richmal Crompton's *Just William* books (Townsend, 2017). When her family was unable to afford the uniform that would be required for her to transfer to grammar school and sit some exams, as encouraged by her Drama and English teachers, she left school aged 15. A single parent to three children in her early 20s, she held down numerous jobs, including a long stint at a youth centre where she tuned into the conversations between the teenagers who attended. She harvested those conversations for her writing.

The Secret Diary and the follow-up, the *Growing Pains of Adrian Mole* (which takes him to age 16), were adapted for television in 1985 and 1987 (*Growing Pain,* 1987; *Secret Diary*, 1985). Less social realism than comic social observation, family and school life are observed through Adrian's eyes and in that 'adolescent, self-pitying voice' that Townsend recalls hearing in her own son's voice when she could not afford to take her children to 'safari parks like other families' ('The Mole story', Townsend, 2017). The diary form, long associated with candid self-revelation and artful self-construction, self-awareness and solipsism, is the archetypal adolescent genre. The comedy of Adrian's diaries lies in the interplay between his aspirations and his vulnerabilities, as he veers between emulating George Orwell and watching *Play School.* At Neil Armstrong Comprehensive in Ashby-de-la-Zooch, Adrian pines for recognition: 'None of the teachers at school have noticed that I am an intellectual' he frets (p.18). He is a conformist but is moved to rebel for love. He is indeed a 'pseudo-self'.

We join Adrian as his parents' marriage is collapsing. His narration ventriloquises the moral outlook of the Thatcherite tabloid press, with its melodramatic demonisation of unemployed 'scroungers' and 'broken families'. Adrian is already shamed by his mother's search for a job: 'I could end up a delinquent roaming the streets and all that …I'll be a latchkey kid!' (pp.22–3). He is bewildered by her emerging feminism: 'My mother has not done any proper housework for days now' as she is too busy reading Germaine Greer's *The Female Eunuch* which 'is full of dirty words' (p.33). He is oblivious to her relationship with newly separated neighbour Mr Lucas. When Mr Lucas and Mrs Mole set off to Sheffield to set up a new life together, Adrian, in the vein of Dickensian waif, tells the school secretary of his mother's 'desertion' and in return receives a form for free school dinners, in the transactional form of state school empathy (p.72). 'We are now a single-parent family', he opines with melodramatic relish. Things only get worse when his dad is made redundant. 'He will be on the dole! How will we live on the pittance from the government?' (p.111).

The political and the personal pull Adrian in different directions (in Bowen's terms, his 'emotional' and 'intellectual systems' fuse). His view of the family is a conservative one: he is desperate for a mum who looks after things and a dad who earns money. Meanwhile, his burgeoning and inconsistent political views are cobbled together from left-wing slogans and personal whim. When visiting his mother in Sheffield he notes that 'I didn't see any knife and fork factories. I expect Margaret Thatcher has closed them all down' (p.90). Mr Scruton, the head of his school, has a portrait of Margaret Thatcher. The left-wing teacher Miss Elf defaces it with a moustache, writes 'three million unemployed' across the cleavage and resigns (p.248). 'I will miss her' laments Adrian, 'she was responsible for my political development. I am a committed radical. I am against nearly everything' (p.248).

Adrian's political radicalism is mainly fuelled by his romantic devotion to his classmate Pandora Braithwaite. Pandora is from left-leaning, intellectual Labour party stock. When Adrian is sent home by Mr Scruton for wearing red socks, Pandora organises a red-sock-wearing protest in solidarity. The protesters receive a lecture from Scruton (who is dealing with a caretakers' strike) 'on the dangers of being a nonconformist' (p.113). As in every aspect of his life Adrian wavers and gives way to Scruton's demands while secretly sticking to his principles 'We wear red socks underneath our black socks. This makes our shoes tight, but we don't mind because principle is involved' (p.121).

Adrian is drawn to 'radical critique' and takes John Holt's *Escape from Childhood* (Holt, 1974) on the train to visit his mum in Sheffield and is delighted on reading *How Children Fail* (Holt, 1969) that if 'I fail my O-levels it will be all my parents' fault' and he will be exonerated (p.258). He is ecstatic, however, when he is made a dinner monitor. 'My duties are to stand at the side of the pig bin and make sure that my fellow pupils scrape their plates properly' (p.98). Adrian's anxious need for approval wage war with his rebelliousness. Eventually, a more 'stable self' emerges through his relationship with Bert Baxter, the 89-year-old 'commie' he befriends through his school's Good Samaritans scheme and with whom Adrian's uncomplicated kindness emerges.

Adrian is comically aware of his vulnerability. In *The Growing Pains of Adrian Mole* which charts his final year at school, Adrian protests when his parents arrange to visit some potential new homes without his knowledge: 'Why didn't they consult me? After all, it is my O-level year and it is most important that I suffer no violent change, trauma or neurosis' (p.480). His wellbeing is rocked when the paternity of both his half siblings, conceived while his parents were separated, is under scrutiny. 'I can't stand this eternal insecurity!' he cries, referring to his particular and general state (p.483).

Adrian's *Growing Pains* concludes at a hopeful moment. The heavy load of O-levels, family breakdown, the prospect of unemployment, nuclear annihilation and the background hum of a 1980s adolescence is lifted by another more cheering adolescent experience. With his parents off at family therapy he and Pandora 'indulged in some extremely heavy petting: so heavy that I felt a weight fall from me' (pp.547–8).

Scully

While Adrian Mole was putting Leicester schooling on the map, Liverpool was to be the setting for another school story about working-class adolescence, Alan Bleasdale's *Scully* (Scully, 1984). The Channel 4 comedy drama ran for seven episodes in 1984 and emerged from a series of radio short stories, a novel and stage and television plays (including a *Play for Today* in 1978). The television series was a follow-up to Bleasdale's *Boys from the Blackstuff* in 1982, which followed a group of unemployed tarmac layers from Liverpool and was a riposte to the right-wing press scourge on so-called 'social security scroungers', those claiming benefits and working short-term contracts on the side (*Boys from the Blackstuff*, 1982). *Scully* revisits Liverpool and the background of high unemployment, a moment when Scully's friend Mad Dog is hoping for another war to give him some prospects.

Bleasdale, who was a Liverpudlian grammar schoolboy turned secondary modern teacher. As I noted in Chapter 4, Bleasdale had written about a schoolboy in his 1975 short play, *Early to Bed*, which had also featured on *Play for Today* (*Early to Bed*, 1975). It covered similar territory to Barry Hines's *The Blinder* (Hines, 1966). *Scully* also looks back to *The Blinder*. Lennie excelled academically and had popular authority in school because of his footballing prowess; Francis Scully has little authority or agency in his own life. He is in the bottom set of a Catholic comprehensive on Merseyside and his ambitions of professional football stay firmly in his dreams. The drama plays with the boundaries between Scully's fantasies and his reality. As he looks at the Liverpool FC posters on his bedroom wall or has a kick-about with his school friends, Kenny Dalglish (then manager of Liverpool) appears, offering words of encouragement. Scully finds these appearances alarming, and notes in a conversation with Mad Dog the difference between the fantasies he is in control of (such as casting the vindictive school caretaker as a cartoonish Count Dracula) and the unbidden appearances of his idol.

Scully talks directly to camera, breaking the fourth wall: this is his only authority in the narrative. We join Scully in the first episode in a meeting with his probation officer who is trying to discern the fifth former's interests and skills (reminiscent of Billy Casper's interview with the youth employment adviser). While Scully's school report notes acting as his notable talent, he eventually shares with the probation officer his dream of professional football. He quickly takes his disclosure back as he expects only derision. This scene includes our first sighting of Dalglish, who briefly takes the place of the probation officer. The Liverpool manager seems to appear when there is tension between what Scully wants and what is.

There are other dreamers in *Scully* or at least characters who cope with their reality by detaching from it, especially Scully's family. Scully's father and maternal grandmother take refuge in alcohol and hangovers; his older brother Tony is referred to as 'the great pretender', notorious as he is for dressing in a suit on match day and signing autographs outside Liverpool FC's ground, Anfield; a 'brain damaged' brother (played by Elvis Costello who also supplied the soundtrack, 'Painting the Town Red') wears a train driver's uniform and only communicates about train timetables; younger brother Arthur dreams of being a girl and wears his mam's clothes. One of the most poignant scenes is between Scully and his mam in the family kitchen. Scully is pleading for some help to stop his dad 'killing himself' with alcohol but his mam has washed her hands of him as Dad stands for her old dream. 'My dreams are dead', she tells her son, and while she doubts the value of the dream Scully has for himself, she tells him not to dismiss 'the dreams other people have for you'.

Scully's best friends, 'Mad Dog', his young brother 'Snotty Dog' and 'Baby Dog' who is carted around in his pram (and occasionally rented out to a local girl who wants her own baby) all live in hope of something else. Mad Dog wants to do 'something big', to be noticed, even if that is to serve in another war like the recent Falklands conflict. Snotty Dog is keen to be accepted by the older boys but is shackled with looking after the family baby. The representation of Mooey Morgan is excruciating. He is referred to as 'simple', 'daft' and subjected to 'slapstick' violence. However, he is the story's emotional savant, undaunted by the bleakness of his prospects, happy just to be with his friends.

Scully's dream of professional football ends because of the barriers he puts up himself. A long-awaited club trial at Liverpool falters when Scully struggles to cope with the presence of the 'real' Kenny Dalglish. Scully squares up to his idol and demands to know why he's been appearing to him: 'It's all been a dream… Why was you there in the first place, you bastard?' Scully pushes Dalglish and the bemused coach gets in his car and drives away. 'I was gonna be just like you!' Scully shouts after him. In tears, he turns to his teacher/mentor Steve, accusing him of betrayal. 'You knew all along I was no good' he says and blames him for prolonging and ending his fantasy.

In a bleak denouement, all of Scully's attempts to escape from his chaotic family life, to find entertainment with his ramshackle group of friends or to find romance end the same way: with nothing. Mad Dog and his little brother take a bus to the Shetlands, via Glasgow, to escape a court appearance. There's no room for Scully or Mooey on the bus, so they go home 'to face the music'. Back home, the great pretender Tony is set to marry his mother's friend Mrs Barrett who's 'worth a few bob', while Arthur decides he's sick of being a girl, and swaps his mother's clothes for a Liverpool strip. 'Sweet dreams' is all the encouragement that Scully can offer to him.

When Scully discovers the caretaker Dracula in a clinch with his mother, he runs despairing to Steve's house. Steve's wife calls out to him, asking who's there. 'Nobody' he replies. 'Nobody?' 'Yeah...nobody'. 'Who shall I say called?' 'Kenny Dalglish...I'm going out to paint the town red'. Scully's final act is to assume the identity of his idol and take revenge on the caretaker, daubing 'Dracula sucks' in red paint all over town.

Scully, Adrian, Zammo and Danny are not the school pin-ups, sporting heroes nor academic high achievers. Their families are variously 'dysfunctional', but they are not vilified by their narratives. They are at best overlooked, and at worst bullied by school authority figures. These stories carry forward the progressive perspective of the state school storyteller of earlier decades, that state schooling matters because it is where the adolescent, including the working-class adolescent meets 'society'. But at a moment when society is being supplanted by what, in 1790, British MP and philosopher Edmund Burke called 'the little platoon', the family and private life, 'state' schooling as a grounding in citizenship or even employment becomes a suspect project (Burke, 1982). If adolescence involves a fragmentation of self (as represented in these stories by Scully's hallucinations, Zammo's drug-induced torpor, Adrian's existential fear and Danny's lost twin) it needs a firm structure against which the young adult can reintegrate. If a family is poorly resourced, emotionally or materially, then social structures matter more. In adolescence, the structure that has the potential to matter most to most adolescents is a state school.

In the lead up to the 1988 Education Reform Act, comprehensive schools were haunted by the ghost of grammar schools (although a good number of those still existed in brick-and-mortar form). While selection was not to be reintroduced, a new centralised curriculum and increased accountability for school standards would come to define the debate about secondary state education for the foreseeable future. The independent sector, while it was marginal in terms of the percentage of children educated there, grew in the 1980s, and cast its shadow over the state system. The stresses on the state sector carried on into the 1990s and the attention of school story tellers turned back to those trying to hold it together, the teachers and the Heads.

References

Bowen, M. (1978) *Family Therapy in Clinical Practice*, New York: Jason Aranson.
Boys from the Blackstuff (1982) [TV Series], BBC.
Burke, E. (1982) *Reflections on the Revolution in France*, Harmondsworth: Penguin.
Early to Bed (1975) [TV drama] 'Second city firsts', BBC.
Galloway, D. (1981) *Teaching and Counselling: Pastoral Care in Primary and Secondary Schools*, Harlow: Longman Group Ltd.

Grange Hill (1986) [TV Series], Series 9, BBC.
Grange Hill (1986–87) [TV Series], Series 9–10, BBC.
Grange Hill (1986–89) [TV Series], Series 9–12, BBC.
Grange Hill (1996–99) [TV Series], Series 15–22, BBC.
Hines, B. (1966) *The Blinder*, Harmondsworth: Penguin.
Holt, J. (1969) *How Children Fail*, Harmondsworth: Penguin.
Holt, J. (1974) *Escape from Childhood: The Needs and Rights of Children*, Harmondsworth: Penguin.
Keay, D. (1987) 'Interview with Margaret Thatcher', *Woman's Own*, 23 September.
Local Government Act (1988) Chapter Nine, Part IV, Section 28,https://www.legislation,gov.uk/ukpga/1988/9/contents
Morgan, N. (2014) 'The heroin epidemic of the 1980s and 1990s and its effects on crime then and now', Home Office Research Report 79.
Redmond, P. (2013) *Mid-term Report*, London: Arrow Books.
Saner, E. (2016) 'Just say no! What really happened when *Grange Hill* met Nancy Reagan at the White House', *The Guardian*, 7 March.
Scully (1984) [TV Series], Channel 4.
The Growing Pains of Adrian Mole (1987) [TV Series], ITV.
The Secret Diary of Adrian Mole Aged 13 ¾ (1985) [TV Series], ITV.
Townsend, S. (2017) *The Secret Diary and Growing Pains of Adrian Mole Aged 13 3/4,* Harmondsworth: Penguin.
Warnock, H.M. (1978) *Report of the committee of enquiry into the education of handicapped children and young people,* https://webarchive.nationalarchives.gov.uk.

6

STRESS IN THE SYSTEM

Opting out and aspiring up in the 1990s

Between 1992 and 1994, three of my nieces began their tenure at St Martin's Roman Catholic School, Billingham. In the decade since I had left, the senior staff had changed, corporal punishment had been outlawed and GCSEs had been introduced. The uniform remained the same. Its reputation in the local area was still good, although as the Catholic secondary from the 'feeder primary' which my nieces attended, no other schools would have been considered. Self-proclaimed 'bookworm' Rebecca went first. Fastidious about her appearance, with just a slick of clear mascara, well-groomed black hair, uniform just so, she was also attentive to her studies. She most enjoyed English and Art, and under the tuition of 'the legend' Mr Curran (who had taught me and my brother Peter over a decade earlier), she excelled in History too. She eventually left school with ten GCSEs, including Maths, which was not a favourite subject, and a spotless behaviour record. What no one had noticed – not least Rebecca herself – was that she was in an unhealthy relationship with her best friend. While the friend could have long hair, Rebecca had to wear hers short. Other friendships were policed and effectively outlawed. Looking back now, Rebecca recognises how unhappy she was but at the time she thought the friendship was normal. Sixth form college provided some loosening of their ties, but it was not until Rebecca, aged 21, had to return suddenly from the friend's wedding in Mexico because Nanna Keane (my mother) had died, that the friendship finally ended abruptly. Rebecca now works as a Corporate Relationships manager for a charity in the northeast, and her work includes outreach to local schools. She now has the language to teach her teenaged daughter what a

DOI: 10.4324/9781003715122-10

good friendship feels like. Favourite school stories: *The Worst Witch* and *Harry Potter.*

Younger sister Jacquelyn started St Martin's two years later. Hair like Ginger Spice and a passion for the girl power quintet, Jacquelyn pushed boundaries and made it her aim never to go to PE. She loved music lessons, but her teacher refused her request to sing a Whitney Houston number for her GCSE performance exam. As friends, fashion and makeup were Jacquelyn's priorities, top set German without her friends was not a comfortable place, so she put herself in middle set. With an ambition to become a midwife, she needed GCSE Maths. She failed and midwifery was now out of reach. Nanna Keane, my mother, stepped in as she had done with her own children, and helped her to find a place as a healthcare assistant after which she found her way into nursing. She is now a health visitor, working with new mothers and the babies she still wishes she'd delivered and has two children of her own. Favourite school stories: *The Worst Witch* and *Clueless.*

In between Rebecca and Jacquelyn came their cousin, my niece Kathryn. She was happy in school, with a flair for English and a talent for the flute. By her third year, she was meeting boys and hanging out with friends while keeping up with her schoolwork. In the battle of Oasis and Blur, she preferred the London boys and went to see them for her 14th birthday in November 1995. Just into the following January, less than halfway through her third year at St Martin's, Kathryn contracted meningitis. She didn't recover. The school dedicated an annual prize in English to her memory.

The loss of Kathryn reshaped our family. Despite their closeness to their cousin, neither Rebecca nor Jacquelyn remember the school providing support for their grief, though this didn't seem unusual at the time. Like them and the rest of our family, I would have loved to ask Kathryn about her own school story and for her to tell me what came next.

From the local to the centre

Just as 1980s education policy redrew the relationship between school and family and attempted to define what family is, so the 1990s remapped the terrain for teaching staff in state schools. The 1985 White Paper 'Better Schools (Relaxing Local Authority Control)' was the soft launch of a new relationship between state schools and local authorities that was to be intensified in the subsequent decades. Higher standards were to be driven by the introduction of a national curriculum, which dispensed with the requirements on local education authorities to devise their own, new standardised tests and increasingly centralised power over state schools by the government. Teachers, under this new regime, were subjected to new forms of training and oversight, arguably, as one critic puts it, shifting from professional to 'technicians', governed rather than autonomous (Leaton Grey, 2007). Workload increased as the volume of assessment grew. A national teachers' strike in 1987 and a prolonged period of 'working to rule' signalled dissatisfaction with pay and the direction of travel of education policy. Hannah Pool, writing in *The Guardian* in 2008 on the day of the first national teachers' strike since 1987, remembers her experience of that first strike as a 13-year-old. Despite being crushed that she wouldn't get to play hockey after school, Pool was thrilled by the inversion of school norms:

> There was something exciting about teachers' strikes, anarchic even. It wasn't just the possibility of the extra day off school, it was the reason why. Here were my teachers, the gatekeepers of authority, refusing to do what they were told.
>
> *(Pool, 2008)*

The perception of teachers as potential rule breakers is a shift in 13-year-old Hannah's 'ecosystem', a term used by psychologist Urie Bronfenbrenner to describe development not as something inherent in and boundaried within the individual but as a series of intersecting structures around the individual, impacting upon them and upon one another (Bronfenbrenner, 1979). If the gatekeepers open the gates, what happens to those on the outside? The Conservative government were in no doubt that authority in the education sector lay with them, not with teachers. To this end, the 1992 Education (Schools) Act initiated a new system of school inspections, under the authority of the Office for Standards in Education (Ofsted). This was to be a break with the older model of local education authority and HMI (Her Majesty's Inspectorate) inspections, which were thought by the government to be inconsistent in their inspection criteria and its application. With a public grading system of schools, the impact on staff has been predictably onerous. In school stories as in life, an Ofsted inspection often provides a moment of narrative crisis. *Ofsted the Musical*, first performed at the Edinburgh Fringe Festival in 2004 by drama students from Hull University, captures the dramatic tension at its height with its setting of a no notice inspection to a musical score.

School counselling and the stressed system

In this context, with diminished trust in local oversight and school leadership, increased workload and arrested remuneration, it is not surprising that one-to-one emotional support for students was not a high priority in schools, although culturally there was increased social acceptance and awareness of counselling and psychotherapy at this point. In her introductory essay to a 1993 collection of essays on counselling in schools, former social worker and counselling trainer Brigid Proctor reflects on the 'explosion' of interest in and change of attitude towards counselling and psychotherapy since the 1970s (Proctor, 1993). She notes the reduced stigmatisation, the increasing professionalisation of counselling and the dissemination of 'counselling skills' into other professions including social work, nursing and teaching. Ironically, it is this spread of 'counselling skills' that may have contributed to the deprioritisation of 'the counselling relationship', with approaches like that described in psychologist Gerard Egan's pragmatic and systematic *The Skilled Helper* finding favour over Rogers' more poetic and philosophical account of change and connection in a deep therapeutic relationship (Egan, 1975). Egan's is very much a 'doing skills' handbook, with clear stages of the counselling process described in detail.

Colleen McLaughlin reiterates that in the 1980s the one-to-one model of counselling in schools came under strain because of spending cuts, an increase in counselling skills for teachers, the emphasis on 'life skills' for students and the debate about the fit of counselling in 'applied settings', where counselling is not the primary purpose (McLaughlin, 1993). 'Counselling', she suggests, was happening at different levels of intensity but through necessity rather than evidence of best outcomes. Overall, there was a shift to 'counselling skills for all' rather than dedicated counsellors for individual students. Capturing this shift, McLaughlin uses Douglas Hamblin's distinction between the immediate, the intermediate and the intensive levels of counselling: teachers using counselling skills in everyday interactions, teachers using counselling skills in a more focused way to work with individuals or groups of students and more 'specialist' counselling provision. McLaughlin emphasises the need for the evaluation of counselling and for a well-communicated school policy. Counselling and guidance she argues should be 'educative', 'reflective' and have a 'welfare element'. It should not be a mysterious process that happens behind closed doors but, as argued by Galloway in the 1980s, integrated into the school's ethos. McLaughlin quotes an HMI review of counselling and guidance in schools, which points out that 'the greatest strength of the guidance lay in its pervasiveness' (p.50) not in its modality. The risk of the idea that counselling should be 'pervasive' is that the 'skills' become so watered down that they are barely perceptible in practice nor reflected upon, which is where many secondary schools still find themselves today.

The school and the ecosystem

Essays in Bovair and McLaughlin's collection focus on the impact of counselling on students, staff and the 'school system'. Graham Upton refers to the school 'ecosystem', drawing on the understanding from family therapy and implicitly Bronfenbrenner's 'ecological systems theory' of 1979 (Upton, 1993). For Bronfenbrenner, development is 'a lasting change in the way a person perceives and deals with his environment' (Bronfenbrenner, 1979, p.3). The 'ecological environment' is, Bronfenbrenner writes, like a 'set of Russian dolls', each structure nesting within and impacted by another. The innermost structure is the 'immediate setting' (home, classroom or in research, the laboratory). The next level is the relationships between the single settings. The third level 'takes us yet farther afield and evokes a hypothesis that the person's development is profoundly affected by events occurring in settings in which the person is not even present' (p.3), such as parents' employment. Finally, Bronfenbrenner argues that particularities within any culture or subculture affect child development, as do changes to those features, such as changes in 'maternity ward practices affecting the relation between a mother and newborn', the effects of which are detectable five years on, or the impact of an economic crisis (p.4). The COVID-19 pandemic is one such recent – and global – environmental shift which will have shown up differently across cultures. The decision in the UK to close schools has had a developmental impact on children and adolescents and on the perception of schools (particularly regarding attendance), which will play out for a generation.

In his 1993 essay, Graham Upton applies Bronfenbrenner's developmental model to the behaviour of children in the 'immediate' setting of the classroom. How a child's behaviour is perceived depends on individual, school and teacher differences; it is situation specific; it derives from the different norms in the school and the family; it is an enactment of underlying emotional difficulty; it is caused by school itself. In this ecosystemic approach, problems are understood as 'interactional' (not solely originating in an individual but in the interactions *between* individuals) and are simply punctuation marks along a sentence, or paragraph, of events. The resolution to such problems requires what Upton refers to as a 'reframe', a change in interpretation, an empathic response to another's point of view and a consequent shift in behaviour. It shifts the locus of the problem from the individual (the child or adolescent) to the system.

Lizzie started high school in 1990. She didn't settle in easily. Lizzie was the youngest child of a large family whose drug use meant that life was unpredictable and unsettled throughout her childhood and adolescence. Her first years in high school coincided with periods when her mum would disappear and Lizzie was left in the care of older siblings who weren't really caring for themselves, let alone Lizzie. At school she remembers the attention of a behavioural support worker called David and the kindness of her art and music teachers who 'knew what was going on'. Unsurprisingly, Lizzie messed about in most lessons and was suspended. By Year Eight, as her home life deteriorated, Lizzie was placed in a residential children's home. She remembers her anger, 'pure shame' and her refusal to go to school. Eventually, her eldest brother and his wife took her in, but she felt less important than their two children and she often ran away. Her memories from the following period are vague but she knows her life was increasingly chaotic and that she was getting caught up in crime and drug use.

At age 13, there were plans to send her to live with her mum who was now in a nearby city. Her mum had poor mental health and when Lizzie had last lived with her, her mum had taken an overdose of medication. Around this time, Lizzie also took an overdose of aspirin and paracetamol. Social services intervened and she was returned to a children's home, from which time on she was involved in crime and drug use. She has no memory of school from this period. From the age of 16 she spent time in prison. 'I was so far gone I didn't know who I was'. She does remember that wherever she was there was someone trying to nurture her, but at the time these attempts had little impact on her behaviour or her sense of self. Lizzie is now over a decade in recovery from addiction, has a long-term partner and works for a drug rehabilitation service. She now feels and values those attempts to reach her during adolescence even if she couldn't at the time.

Workplace stress

As we have seen, 'the system' could have detrimental effects on both students and staff. The 'new right' education policy from the late 1980s, with reduced autonomy and increased demand on teachers, was a recipe for industrial action and for workplace stress. Workplace stress had been recognised as a risk for all employees since the early twentieth century, but late twentieth-century legislation formalised the responsibility of employers to look out for and find ways to mitigate the stresses placed upon their employees. The Health and Safety at Work Act of 1974 placed a 'duty of care' on employers to protect employees from work-related stress. In 1999, the Management of Health and Safety at Work Regulations upped this duty to require employers to make a 'suitable and sufficient assessment' to the risks to their employees at work, including risks of stress.

Brigid Proctor reflects on the 'minting of the word "stress" to cover all sorts of behaviour which would formerly have been called weakness, break down, nerves, and so on' and which has enabled some people to relate less judgementally to their own and other people's emotional and social difficulties (Bovair and McLaughlin p.4). Some of the experiences of working in a school can extend the definition of the word stress to breaking point, as Dave's story illustrates.

Dave came to teaching after completing a Geography degree in the 1970s. He taught Geography and Geology up to A-level and began volunteering as an adult literacy tutor, roles which gave him a sense of purpose. He had attended a 'wonderful' secondary modern in Birmingham, where he completed Duke of Edinburgh awards, competed in annual Eisteddfods and benefited from committed teachers in its small sixth form. This school influenced his view of the role of education throughout his career. His early years of teaching in Manchester were in former grammar schools which converted to comprehensives in the later 1970s. There was little external oversight, and internal planning was minimal. When the school he was teaching in became comprehensive, there was no planning for the new intake. Dave's experience as a literacy tutor caught the attention of the Head and he was asked to set up a 'remedial department'. Dave was given a windowless room, a set of books but no extra pay. Nevertheless, it was a very rewarding experience and provided Dave with an insight into the value of good school management.

In his next school, after a couple of years as a Geography teacher, he was appointed as Head of Year, so would be privy to the life stories of the pupils in his charge, many of which were challenging. Court hearings were numerous. The role had responsibility for corporal punishment, but Dave declared he wouldn't administer it. Others followed suit and the school phased it out a couple of years before it was banned nationally. Although the school was now comprehensive with a diverse intake, its curriculum was still shaped by its grammar school past. Dave was asked to take a lead in setting up more vocational pathways – City and Guilds courses in construction and engineering, for example. The authority was promoting the development of an 'alterative curriculum', and Dave became its coordinator for his school, setting up classes in years 10 and 11 for students with behavioural and learning difficulties. The curriculum was devised by Dave and his team at the school, though they worked closely with other local schools doing the same thing. They set up linked courses with local colleges, work experience opportunities with local employers and organised outdoor activities like abseiling.

During his time at the school a tragic incident occurred, which had major repercussions for the school and its community. There were also serious questions raised about the headteacher, who was eventually asked to leave. Dave was the NUT (National Union of Teachers) representative during this period and while all staff were under stress due to these circumstances, Dave felt significant pressure and eventually sought a complete change of direction. It was only in retrospect, after leaving the school, that Dave recognised the considerable stress he had been under and the absence of support for staff.

Dave was appointed to an advisory team of the local education authority with the brief to develop evaluation and school development strategies in its secondary schools. While he learnt a lot in this role, eventually he wanted to return to the 'chalkface' of school life. He took up the role of Deputy Head in a large secondary school. Along with the school's Special Educational Needs Coordinator (SENCo) he helped to develop an inclusive resource base for SEN. His earlier experience taught him to stay alert to the impact of stress and to separate work and home life. Since his retirement, Dave has remained in education as a governor and is still committed to inclusion and local partnerships between schools. He also volunteers for a charity that supports the homeless.

From *Hearts and Minds* to *Hope and Glory*

The interaction between the school ecosystem and workplace stress is played out in two school dramas aimed at adult audiences in the 1990s: Jimmy McGovern's 1995 four-part series for Channel 4, *Hearts and Minds* (1995), and Lucy Gannon's three season series for the BBC, *Hope and Glory,* which updates the state school story for early part of the New Labour era (1999–2000).

Before McGovern found success as a television writer (with the Liverpool-based soap *Brookside* and the series about a criminal psychologist and addict, *Cracker*), he taught English for three years at a Liverpool secondary school. According to an interview with *The Independen*t in 1995, McGovern had encountered small-mindedness in the staffroom and was given an unforgiving timetable while 'the head of department [got] all the cream' (Sutcliffe, 1995). These experiences informed his representation of 'probationer' Drew Mackenzie at stress-inducing Northfield Comprehensive on Merseyside.

Lucy Gannon had no experience as a teacher, though military policing, social work and nursing gave her insight into public sector and 'frontline' work, which she drew on for series like *Soldier, Soldier* and *Peak Practice. Hope and Glory* transfers to schools her interest in 'making a drama out of the apparently ordinary' and the 'heroism' of people with 'ideals, striving and a feeling of owing something to the world' (Rampton, 1999). In *Hope and Glory*, the narrative is driven by the 'heroism' of headteacher Ian George, a heroism which eventually ends in stress-related personal tragedy.

Hearts, minds and opt outs

McGovern creates the 'ecosystem' of Northfield Comprehensive: a deprived community in Liverpool, a negligent local education authority, a worn-down staff and students infected by the violence, racism and homophobia of their families and their histories. Into this unpromising mix comes 'probationary' English teacher Drew Mackenzie. Drew previously worked in a factory and studied for four years to get to this point, at great cost to his family life with his wife and three young children. With the belief that education was his passport to a better life, Drew arrives at Northfield armed with a determination to transform the fortunes of the students by igniting their imaginations. His arrival, however, coincides with an imminent disruption to the already flawed and fragile ecosystem of Northfield: 'opting out'.

The 1988 Education Reform Act provided a route out of local authority control for state schools, which would subsequently be directly funded by central government, and Northfield is about to embark on consultation with staff and parents. At interview, Drew is advised by the Head that voicing opposition would not be the best support for his application. The Head, meanwhile, is threatened by the local authority's director of education that his relationship with an ex-pupil ('the ink hardly dry on her A level exams' as one teacher quips) might not stay private if he pursues Grant Maintained Status for Northfield. The ecosystem seems to be held together by self-interest.

Drew is not minded to oppose opting out anyway. Having been in union politics while working in the factory, he is unimpressed by the NUT. He is soon alienated from his 'rank and file' colleagues, however, and is the only member of staff outside of senior management to show himself to be in favour of the opt out at a meeting with parents. His colleagues fear the new employment arrangements that come with Grant Maintained Status, which affords more authority to the Head and the governing body, and removes the chain of accountability from the Local Education Authority and local, elected politicians. The point is illustrated sharply when canteen staff give Drew the cold shoulder, knowing that after opting out their work will go to outside contractors.

Drew's alienation continues when he challenges the apathy and cynicism of three of his colleagues who, to him, seem to have 'opted out' of teaching individually: Trevor, a young black teacher who is embittered by the racism in the school and the wider community and engages with teaching only to prepare the black students for encounters with the police; Shotton, an older gay man who drinks alcohol from a tea mug and talks to himself inside the classroom and the staff room, expecting his monologues neither to be heard nor to be challenged; Maggie, a longstanding teacher whose achievements Drew characterises as knitting and handing out worksheets.

What Drew misses is the context of his colleagues' apparent indifference to teaching, the shift in the ecosystem which affected each of them differently. Maggie is an older woman who at some point has become invisible, has lost her ability to connect with students and so delivers information, rather than herself, in the classroom and she knits in the staffroom to keep herself invisible. Shotton has lived in a homophobic culture throughout his life and as a teacher endured the fallout of Clause 28 and the permitted derision it brought. He drinks to numb. Trevor is a black teacher in a city which exploded in riots in the previous decade. The Toxteth riots of 1981 had been a response to discriminatory policing in Merseyside, stop and search policies which disproportionately singled out young black men and the arrest of photography student Leroy Alphonse Cooper. The government's response to Toxteth was the appointment of Michael Heseltine as Minister for Merseyside to boost the infrastructure of the region; this did not erase the memories of Toxteth nor immediately improve the image or behaviour of the police.

Trevor is also working in the aftermath of the Swann Report of 1985, which shared the findings of an inquiry into 'the education of children from ethnic minority groups' (Swann, 1985). The inquiry defined itself as a response to the perceived 'underachievement' of children of 'West Indian' immigrant communities, though it widened its terms of reference to include other 'ethnic minority' students. The report in some ways repeats the problems it sets out to investigate, minimising evidence of overt and implicit racism in schools. It is unable to find data, for instance, to prove or disprove one of the most disturbing claims that led to the inquiry, that a disproportionate number of children of West Indian origin were placed in schools for the 'educationally subnormal'. Similarly, it could find no statistics on the 'ethnicity' of children excluded or suspended from schools and placed in behavioural units. The Swann Report's broad recommendations were improved data and processes to capture the histories of different cohorts of students, and for 'multi-culturalism' in school curricula and teacher training. Multi-culturalism would recognise and celebrate difference rather than seek to erase racism by more systemic means. Trevor's demeanour and his determination to teach a cohort of students what he thinks they most urgently need (protection in the face of racist police practices) speaks of his sense of the failure of such measures to address racism. Antiracism was an overt policy of teacher activists in city schools, especially Inner London Education Authority, and Trevor represents this kind of activism.

A crisis point arrives for Drew when he attempts to illustrate the destructive power of a homophobic slur (issued by a black student to Shotton) by using a racist one. This lands him on a course from which he never fully regains his footing. Drew's ideals come from the 'egalitarian' school of thought on comprehensives: place all the children from the local community, teach them together and social divisions will resolve, as though the particularities of those children's lives would be erased. His colleagues have long since abandoned that ideal.

Viewed out of context, as they are initially by Drew, the classrooms of his colleagues – chaotic, rowdy, lacking focus – seem to represent the worst caricatures of comprehensives by those pressing for selective education. Drew's response is to engage all his students with heartfelt, performative lessons. He tries to persuade Sahira, a girl who will not speak, to read out her work in class, and he reads her silence as modesty. On a misguided quest to discover the origins of the girl's refusal to speak, he discovers not that she is 'culturally' disinclined, but that she is grieving for her dead mother.

Drew is initially out of his depth in reading the children's ecosystems, but when his fluency improves he encounters other kinds of obstacles. When he suggests that Sahira would benefit from the services of an educational psychologist, the Head refuses on the grounds of expense and the stigma of having the school associated with psychological services: 'like a visit from the nit nurse'. As she is recovering from an attempt to take her own life, Drew persuades Sahira and her father that she has the courage to return to school. While, dramatically, this seems to be the moment that Drew's fortunes will start to turn (having learnt the art of the reframe), the Head foils his redemption by not offering him a contract after his probation.

Drew has an opportunity to put his ideals into practice one more time, however, when he steps into the shoes of poor drunken and shrunken Shotton to direct the school production of *Julius Caesar*. Determined to make it 'relevant', Drew engages different factions in the school and seems about to succeed where others have failed when musicians, dancers and performers of different social and cultural groups come together. The Head, however, demands 'Shakespeare as Shakespeare intended'. Drew's parting shot is to pretend to concede, but he plants pupils in the audience who storm the stage to sing a protest song about the school under a hanging effigy of Maguire. Drew's egalitarian dream of the comprehensive ideal is over while the educational ecosystem, which the political left and right have failed equally to reset in a way which will enhance the lives of the children, is set to stagger on. As he leaves school for the last time, he has reclaimed his relationship with his wife, leaving behind the schemes of work, the vertiginous piles of marking and the relentless assaults on his goodwill.

Hope and Glory

Lucy Gannon's *Hope and Glory* swaps McGovern's idealistic probationer for an aspirational 'super head', a product of New Labour's 'education, education, education' mantra which swapped egalitarianism for meritocracy. Difference is no barrier to success and with the right mindset everyone can rise to the top.

The 1998 School Standards and Framework Act was a blueprint for the 'third way' in state education, encouraging secondary schools to become 'specialist schools', which could select some pupils because of their aptitude for, say, modern languages. *Hope and Glory* arrived in this context. It ran for three seasons, from 1999 to 2000, and dramatised one of the new administration's headlines grabbing education policies: the rise of the super head, the overachieving school leader who was to be parachuted in to struggling schools to turn around their fortunes. The super head was a genie without a lamp.

Gannon was apparently inspired by the case of Hammersmith Comprehensive, a London state secondary in special measures which had been 'transformed' by the appointment of Jamaican-born Headteacher William Atkinson in 1995. The school was unironically renamed Phoenix High School.

When Atkinson arrived, only 4% of pupils achieved five top-grade GCSE passes, and the school was reported to be in chaos:

> There were reports of pupils throwing furniture out of windows, setting fire to buildings. And covering every surface with graffiti. There was little evidence that teachers were doing anything more than crisis management.
>
> (Garner, 2010)

Phoenix was a school with high percentages of children on free school meals and with additional needs, and many students left during the academic year because of problems in their home lives. The school community boasted 50 languages. Atkinson's arrival sparked the recruitment of a newly motivated staff body willing to 'go the extra mile' (offering, for instance, extra classes on Saturdays) and according to Ofsted, an 'aspirational outlook' in the school (Garner, 2010).

Atkinson's own story bears some attention. In an interview with *The Guardian* in 2009, he tells the story of how, in 1957, his mother brought he and his two brothers from Jamaica to Battersea, South London, to rejoin their father who had already made the journey. Somehow, seven-year-old William was mistaken for his nine-year-old brother and put in his class. Never having been to school before, William did not speak up and 'was thought to be stupid':

> Two years later, with the mistake still undiscovered, he sat the eleven plus and predictably failed. Shortly afterwards, his real age was at last revealed and, after another two years, he took the eleven plus again and failed again. [Making him] the only teacher in the country to have failed the eleven plus twice.
>
> (Wilby, 2009)

There is, as we psychotherapists are fond of saying, a lot to unpack here. He verifies this improbable origin story by explaining how his parents had to work long and unsociable hours to earn money to buy a property (it was difficult for black families to rent in England in the 1950s) and that the house was filled with lodgers to supplement the family income. With the family of five living in one room, Williams' parents were not well placed to challenge the system.

Gannon's inspirational head is Ian George, played by Lenny Henry. He is Britain's youngest headteacher, feted by the Department for Education for his 'visionary' leadership. George does not have Atkinson's arresting back story. In many ways, he is context-less, though friends and ex-partners appear in some episodes to fill out details of his personal life. Season One opens with George addressing a teachers' and headteachers' conference. He shares the stage with a panel from the Department for Education while speaking on behalf of his beleaguered colleagues. So begins his journey into the New Labour education ecosystem, typified by the (re)invention of the 'Education Action Zones', which were designed to bring together schools, LEAs, local business and parents to improve schools in areas of deprivation. Thus, Ian does the bidding of the DfE, the LEA (personified by the director of education Leo Wheeldon, who we are not sure is George's friend or foe until late in Series Three) and a staff body who are a familiar mixture of cynical old lags (Series One's deputy head Phil Jakes) and forward-looking ingénues (Sally Bell and Kitty Burton). Students are marginal in the first series, growing in significance by Series Three, but throughout, super head Ian George is the centre of the narrative. While he strikes up a relationship with Maths teacher Debs Bryan (who becomes deputy head) in Series One and with parent Clare in Series Three, his commitment to work is a barrier to his private life. An appearance by his ex-girlfriend reveals that the relationship foundered on his preoccupation with work. Somewhat inconsistently, Ian instructs Debs to choose professionalism over friendship with her colleagues. He ends the relationship with Debs when she fails to disclose that her fellow deputy, Phil, has lost a set of exam papers. Ian's relationship with Clare looks to be heading for marriage when tragedy strikes in the final episode of Series Three. The heart problem (metaphorical and literal) which has been flagged throughout the series catches up with Ian when he is in a rooftop standoff with an unravelling science teacher. As Ian tries to talk the teacher down, he collapses and dies in view of the staff and pupils waiting in the playground below. The unsustainable pressures of which the science teacher complained during his classroom hostage-taking breakdown take the super head down just as Hope Park had emerged from 'special measures'.

While Drew was an egalitarian, Ian is a Blairite meritocrat: to the prime minister's call of 'education, education, education' his response is 'aspiration, aspiration, aspiration'. Ian George's predecessor at Hope Park, Mr Bruce, has long since given up on the school and its community. His parting speech is a litany of insults to his charges. Conversely, Ian berates teachers who limit the expectations of the students, who do not, in Atkinson's words, 'go the extra mile'. The score of the series is classical to underpin the fantasy of 'classlessness' while 'diversity' is celebrated. The only time that 'race' is foregrounded is when George accepts a talented former pupil of Kitty Burton's, Liana Andrews, into the school. Her admission raises questions. Leo Wheeldon challenges Ian's acceptance of a black student when he had previously rejected white applicants. Ultimately, the conversation is represented as a test of George's personal integrity rather than a debate about 'positive discrimination'. The weary and cynical deputy Phil is dismayed by Liana's acceptance to a 'mainstream school' on the grounds of her disability. 'I'm sick of all this political correctness', he opines, in the late twentieth-century version of 'anti-wokeness'.

Adam Sweeting in *The Guardian* attacks *Hope and Glory* for its uncertainty of tone and berates Gannon for not being Alan Bleasdale or Jimmy McGovern (Sweeting, 1999). He criticises her for putting 'melodrama' where ideological battle and documentary realism are required: 'maybe education is too pressing and prickly an issue to be liquidised into soap opera, with its inevitable cliches and illogicalities' (Sweeting, 1999). Sweeting evidently did not foresee *Waterloo Road*. *Hope and Glory,* unlike *Hearts and Minds*, is not steeped in the particularities of later twentieth-century state education. It does not, however, purport to be realism. Its references are to other dramas. A conversation between George and his closest colleague, Mike the caretaker, turns into a Top Trumps of school stories they remember: *Please Sir*! *Dead Poets' Society*! *Grange Hill*! *Goodnight Mr Chips*! *The Prime of Miss Jean Brodie*! *Chalkface*! *Hearts and Minds*! (*Hope and Glory*, 2000). Scenes back in characters' homes frequently have *Eastenders* playing in the background and occasionally we hear David Attenborough's tones. Sweeting evokes the film version of *To Sir, With Love*, inevitably likening Lenny Henry's portrait of Ian George to Sidney Poitier's Ricky, and of course finds it wanting. *Hope and Glory* is not, and nor is it intended to be *To Sir, With Love*. *Hope and Glory* begins with the utopian promise that a single, if significant, change in the 'education, education, education' ecosystem, the appointment of an inspirational, aspirational Head, can be socially transformative. *Hope and Glory* holds together the aspirational vision of Blairite legislation (the aspects which genuinely, if temporarily, improved children's access to education, such as Sure Start and the Education Maintenance Allowance) with a melodramatic illustration of its potential consequences for overworked staff. The tragic denouement, when George lays dead on the school rooftop, as staff and pupils wander the playground aimlessly, undercuts that promise and hints at a system so top heavy that it will topple over completely.

Teachers and post-stress

Channel 4's comedy *Teachers* from 2001 to 2004, created by Northern Irish writer Tim Loane, was almost entirely teacher focused. The teachers in question are 'post-stressed' and the school they work in, Summerdown High, could only loosely be called a 'system'.

While not particular enough to be satirical, *Teachers* deflates the Blairite vision. The politics of education carry on outside the comedy while a donkey wanders through the school corridors without remark. The central group of newly qualified staff (English teacher Simon, ICT teacher Kurt and PE teacher Brian) defy the idealistic ingénue trope. *Teachers* takes late 1990s and early 2000s 'lad culture' and lets it play out in a secondary school. The central trio objectify women, drink to excess and pay little attention to schemes of work and learning objectives. They not only eschew the high stress norms of the secondary school but also discard adult responsibility. The first episode sees them break into the school as part of Simon's birthday celebration, inverting the trope of subversive students breaking into the school building out of hours. Simon smokes cannabis with a pupil, is distracted by female students' bodies and eventually leaves teaching to go travelling. There is no 'growth' in his narrative arc, or at least no more than in the adolescent arc of his students. While *Hearts and Minds* and *Hope and Glory* portray the personal costs to teachers of the pressures of the job, the *Teachers* protagonists stress about anything but teaching. These are comic versions of Erikson's depiction of the first stage of adulthood, where the task of the 'healthy personality' is to negotiate the tension between 'love and work' (Erikson, 1980, p.102): Simon, Kurt and Brian haven't emerged enough from their adolescence to succeed in either.

In some ways, *Teachers* is also an absurd, apathetic response to the emerging reality of the New Labour government. Shortly after they came to power, Blair's government established a commission chaired by Ken Robinson, which made its recommendations in a report entitled *All Our Futures: Creativity, Culture and Education*, recalling perhaps the subtitle of the Newsom Report, 'Half our Future' (Robinson, 1999). The commission's recommendations on the 'creative and cultural development of young people through formal and informal education' (p.2) were never really taken forward and, once again, 'standards' dominated the education policy agenda. As Brighouse and Waters note, 'Two years into the Blair government, the quest for "education, education, education" was alleged by some to be "results, results, results" or "targets, targets, targets."' (Brighouse and Waters, 2021, p.47). As Simon, Kurt and Brian know, so long as the donkey in the corridor does not impede the target, they can let it roam.

References

Bovair, K. and McLaughlin, C.(eds.) (1993) *Counselling in Schools: A Reader*, London: David Fulton Publishers.

Brighouse, T. and Waters, M. (2021) *About Our Schools: Improving on Previous Best*, Carmarthen: Crown House Publishing.

Bronfenbrenner, U. (1979) *The Ecology of Human Development: Experiments by Nature and Design*, Cambridge, MA: Harvard University Press.

Egan, G. (1975) *The Skilled Helper: A Problem-Management and Opportunity-Development Approach to Helping*, Pacific Grove, CA: Brooks/Cole.

Erikson, E.H. (1980) *Identity and the Life Cycle*, London: W.W. Norton and Company.

Garner, R. (2010) '"Super head" makes failing school most improved in England', *Independent,* 14 January, https://www.independent.co.uk/news/education/education-news / super-head-makes-failing-school-most-improved-in-engalnd-1867259.html

Hearts and Minds (1995) [TV series], Channel 4.

Hope and Glory (1999–2000) [TV series], BBC.

Hope and Glory (2000) [TV Series], Series 2, Episode 1, BBC.

Leaton Grey, S. (2007) 'Teacher as technician: semi-professionalism after the 1988 Education Reform Act and its effect on conceptions of pupil identity', *Policy Futures in Education,* 5(2), pp.194–203.

McLaughlin, C. (1993) 'Counselling in a secondary setting – developing policy and practice', Bovair, K. and McLaughlin, C. (eds.) *Counselling in Schools: A Reader*, London: David Fulton Publishers, pp.36–51.

Pool, H. (2008) 'My memories of 1987, the last national teachers' strike', *The Guardian,* 24 April, https://www.theguardian.com/education/2008/apr/24/schools.uk

Proctor, B. (1993) 'An overview of counselling in Britain today', Bovair, K. and McLaughlin, C. (eds.) *Counselling in Schools A Reader*, London: David Fulton Publishers, pp.1–20.

Rampton, J. (1999) 'A class act: Lucy Gannon', *Independent,* 18 June, https://www.independent.co.uk/arts-entertainemnt/television-a-class-act-lucy-gannon-1101130.html

Robinson, K. (1999) *All Our Futures: Creativity, Culture and Education. Report of the National Advisory Committee on Creative and Cultural Education*, London: Department for Education and Employment/Department for Digital, Culture, Media, and Sport.

Sutcliffe, T. (1995) 'The prime of Mr McKenzie', *Independent*, 9 February.

Swann, M. (1985) *Education for All: Report of the Committee of Enquiry into the Education of Children from Ethnic Minority Groups*, London: HMSO, https://www.education-uk.org/documents/swann/swann1985.html

Sweeting, A. (1999) 'Lucy could do better', *The Guardian*, 23 June.

Upton, G. (1993) 'Putting problems in context – the family and the school', Bovair, K. and McLaughlin, C. (eds.) *Counselling in Schools: A Reader*, London: David Fulton Publishers, pp.81–96.

Wilby, P. (2009) 'Practising what he preaches', *The Guardian*, 7 April.

PART 3
Fragmentation

7

'EVERY CHILD MATTERS'

The 2000s' school as a holding and shaming environment

Teacher and student counsellor Nick Barwick's 2000 book, *Clinical Counselling in Schools*, views the 'whole school' environment through a therapeutic lens. Barwick argues that learning is an emotional experience; for him, the inner-city school is, in Winnicott's terms a 'holding environment', a place of intimacy, distance, confidentiality, transference and safety in relationships. Like earlier 'systemic' counsellors, Barwick is keen to emphasise that the school environment has an impact on the child and on the task of counselling in school; that learning itself can be understood therapeutically; that boundaries can be extended beyond the counsellor and student and that counselling in school can extend beyond the counselling room. The modality of the therapy is secondary to the context and the purpose of the counselling.

Counselling in Schools from 2002 (Bor et al., 2002) similarly explores the whole-school context of counselling, and notes what needs to be in place for a counselling service to work well in a school (good relationships between the counsellor and wider school staff, openness about the counselling process, record keeping and attention to legal and safeguarding concerns). In terms of the 'how', the introduction notes a diversity of practice but promotes a systemic and 'ecological' approach to children's difficulties rather than viewing problems as 'residing in the child' (p.4). The common thread of the counselling is Rogerian but there is an emphasis on 'solution-focused' practice which considers time limitations, context and the need to elicit 'competence, strength and personal resources' in the child and in the child's relationships (p.23). This all assumes, of course, the receptiveness of a school to the counsellor's involvement outside the room, which may be difficult to achieve in practice.

DOI: 10.4324/9781003715122-12

'Every Child Matters' (2003)

While the rhetoric of 'integration' has been present in guidance on school counselling since its inception and in work with children in general, occasionally shocking events give a reality to the idea. The horrific abuse and death of eight-year-old Victoria Climbié at the hands of her great aunt and her partner in the home they shared in London in 2000 gave a renewed urgency to the idea of 'information sharing' between children's services to safeguard children. The inquiry into Victoria's death and the subsequent Laming Report (Laming, 2003) was the spine of the New Labour administration's 2003 Green Paper, 'Every Child Matters' (Boateng, 2003). The Laming Report cited a catalogue of inaction in the many agencies with whom Victoria came into contact. Laming disputed that lack of resources was the cause of her neglect by services, citing rather 'organisational malaise', poor management, people simply not doing their jobs and senior people in 'strategic' roles not holding themselves to account. Of these witnesses, Laming is damning:

> Time and again it was dispiriting to listen to the 'buck passing' from those who attempted to justify their positions. For the proper safeguarding of children this must end. If ever such a tragedy happens again, I hope those in leadership posts will examine their responsibilities before looking more widely.
>
> (Laming, 2003, p.17)

'Every Child Matters' was the government's attempt to formulate a 'joined up' plan to safeguard and support all children from birth to age 19. The paper is prefaced with an emotive foreword from Prime Minister Tony Blair, noting that while for most parents 'our children are everything to us: our hopes, our ambitions, our future', some children, such as Victoria Climbié, are entrusted into the care of those who inflict unimaginable suffering. The government's response was to propose 'a range of measures to reform and improve children's care …requiring local authorities to bring together in one place under one person services for children' (Boateng, 2003, p.1). The introduction by Paul Boateng, the Chief Secretary to the Treasury, bluntly notes that children 'are entitled not just to the sentiment of adults but a strategy that safeguards them as children and realises their potential to the very best of their ability' (p.4). Child protection and safeguarding are characterised in preventative as well as reactive terms. Proposals include the establishment of Local Safeguarding Children Boards, the creation of a Minister for Children, Young People and Families (Margaret Hodge was appointed to this role) and the integration of the inspection of children's services. The paper proposed to build on New Labour's early foundations, particularly Sure Start Children's Centres, launched in 1999, which provided childcare and health services, family support and employment advice in one place.

A recent report from the Institute for Fiscal Studies has captured the short- and medium-term effects of Sure Start on children's outcomes (Carneiro et al., 2025).

It was found that children with access to a centre between birth and age four had improved educational outcomes, lasting at least until GCSEs. Hospitalisations for one-year-olds increased but fell by the time those children were 15 (suggesting better health advice for parents of some infants and a reduction in ill health throughout childhood thereafter). Socioeconomic improvements for children with access were less marked, the report found. Sure Start was phased out after 2010. The Sure Start Centre that was run from our local park is now a food bank for women who have experienced domestic abuse and homelessness and is run by a charity.

'Every Child Matters' foregrounds the developmental impact of wider early years' interventions and services for older children: additional speech and language therapy; extended school hours; family and parenting support for young children. Teenagers were offered carrots and sticks: they were provided with 'Connexions', a service to provide advice, guidance and 'personal development' for 13–19-year-olds (this fell foul of spending cuts in 2012); a teenage pregnancy strategy; new youth offending teams and youth justice boards; and measures to ensure that homeless families would not be housed in bed and breakfast accommodation. The Educational Maintenance Allowance would provide £30 a week for 16–19-year-olds from low-income families in full-time education. More investment in Child and Adolescent Mental Health Services (CAMHS) would increase capacity by 10% each year for three years. Multidisciplinary teams would be based in the community, in schools and family centres and 'high quality' mental health care would be commissioned (p.31).

Framed positively, 'Every Child Matters' launched a 'holding' environment for children and adolescents from birth to 19 throughout children's services, including schools. All those who encountered a child in a local authority service were accountable for that child's safety and wellbeing. At a more immediate level, this is the kind of supportive 'holding' environment described in the early 2000s counselling texts by Barwick and Bor et al, where counselling is integrated in the school, where problems do not reside in the child and are not boundaried by confidentiality.

Not long after the Laming Report and the Green Paper, however, further children died at the hands of their 'carers' and the government strategy was open to question. According to Senior Lecturer in Social Work, Liz Davies writing for *The Guardian*, the reforms 'led to many tried and tested systems being ditched' and:

> the government used the findings to justify a policy shift away from the proactive protection of a few children at high risk of harm to intense state surveillance of every child and family.
>
> (Davies, 2008)

With child protection registers swapped for 'at risk' designations, children were deemed not just at risk of harm from adults, but at risk of pregnancy, crime and 'anti-social behaviour'. In a similar shift, vulnerable families would, under the

Coalition, become 'troubled families' (Casey, 2014). In such an environment, holding and support have an underside of shaming and surveillance.

Shame

This underside is the focus of school stories from this decade, in which the secondary school, ostensibly a 'supportive' space, is also a place of shame, for adults and adolescents. Zoe Heller's novel *Notes on a Scandal* (Heller, 2003), Alan Bennett's play *The History Boys* (Bennett, 2004) and Jilly Cooper's novel *Wicked!* (2006) variously revel in, critique and lampoon 'safeguarding culture' and the shame it can evoke.

Gestalt theorists, following in the footsteps of German psychiatrist and psychoanalyst Fritz Perls (1969), emphasise the individual's experience in the immediate present and their way of perceiving and engaging with reality. Gestalt theory has articulated the origins and function of shame in child and adolescent development and uses the metaphor of the 'relational field' to denote the way the child's experience is co-created with the adults in their lives (Kaufman, 1989; Lee, 2007). The field has a 'ground' (the child's and adult's general way of being, temperaments, values and histories) and a figure (the primary need that shapes the child-adult relationship in the here and now, for example, the child's need to be held). When an adult is attuned to the child's expression of need, the child can 'regulate', and their emerging sense of self is supported. When the expression of need is missed or rejected repeatedly, the cycle of the child's experiencing is interrupted. Instead of the ebb and flow between the boundary of self and others, the child cuts off, becomes rigid (what therapists call a fixed gestalt) to make sense of and cope with the frustration of their need. When the demand of the adult or of an environment like a school exceeds the capacity of the child, or is made without offers of support, a similar 'interruption' occurs, and is experienced by the child as shame.

According to the Gestalt framework, shame is a part of the boundary between self and other and helps to regulate that boundary. It can be prosocial, supporting good boundaries in relationships, or inhibiting, as the child experiences self-disgust and the impossibility of connection. Adaptation to shame can be experienced as an internalised rejection or a denial of it, leading to an inflated projection of self into the world. At its etymological root, shame means 'covering oneself', so these elaborations describe the individual's response to feeling psychologically and socially 'uncovered'.

Notes on a Scandal

Shaming is the go-to tool of the old-school teacher, illustrated starkly in *Spare the Rod*, *Kes*, and interactions between *Grange Hill*'s Mr Bronson and any pupil he encounters. Shaming in these contexts is abused as a means of social control. In

Hearts and Minds, Drew is shamed by his colleagues and students for his use of a racial slur and in this context it is a form of social learning. Zoe Heller's 2003 novel *Notes on a Scandal* (which was made into a film starring Judi Dench and Cate Blanchett) foregrounds a school as site of shame [Heller, 2003; *Notes on a Scandal* (2006)], both its prosocial and controlling forms.

Heller, unlike many of the school story tellers, is a journalist with no background in teaching. She attended a London comprehensive school in the late 1970s and early 1980s. Her sister Lucy is the chief executive of the charity Ark, which is the parent organisation of the multi-academy trust Ark schools.

The narrative explores the uncovering of a 'relationship' between Bathsheba (Sheba) Hart, a pottery teacher at St George's, a North London comprehensive, and her 15-year-old pupil, Steven Connolly. It is a story about the breaking of a taboo and its consequences for the teacher (public shaming and punishment) and the student (temporary notoriety). The shame, however, is experienced more widely. The story is narrated by Barbara Covett, a history teacher at the school, who denies her own shame (her unrequited attraction to Bathsheba and a former colleague) and projects it on to others. It makes for a multi-layered narrative where we're reading the unreliable narrator Barbara while also reading the story she tells us.

Barbara's narrative opens in the aftermath of Sheba's 'relationship' with the schoolboy coming to light. Sheba has been charged and is on bail. Barbara initially casts herself as Sheba's confidante and protector. She encourages Sheba's candour about Steven Connolly, enjoying the 'insouciant frankness' which Barbara attributes to Sheba's upper-class upbringing. It is a kind of shamelessness which, Barbara notes, is not shared by most people who 'extract vows of discretion from you' before being honest, a promise not to expose or shame them. Barbara rails against the 'sanctimony' of the press in their reporting of the case, their 'hysterical prurience', 'titillated fury', while eliciting as much detail as possible from Sheba herself (p.5).

Barbara recounts Sheba's arrival at St George's, noting that she doesn't 'display' the 'usual new girl jitters' (p.18). She sets the scene of the staffroom, where some of the staff read 'the arts and media pages of the liberal newspapers mainly, or paperback editions of the lower sort of fiction' (p.12). When Sheba asks why the curtains are drawn, one of the old lags, Bill, quips 'it's so we can't look out at them. So they can smash each other up – do their raping and pillaging – and we're not required to intervene' (p.13). Barbara attributes this comment to the 'posturing cynicism about the pupils' displayed by many of St George's staff and from which Barbara distances herself. However, her account of the students is hardly a celebration of the comprehensive ideals. Because of its location, she writes, St George's is assumed to be one of those 'soft, safe comprehensives'. On the contrary, the 'cello-players get sent to St Botolph's Girls or King Henry's Boys'. St George's is 'the holding pen for Archway's pubescent proles' who must 'fidget and scrap' there until they 'embrace their fates as plumbers and shop assistants' (p.20).

Barbara has an equally damning view of former students who return to teach in St George's. They are 'people who have surmised that the world out there is a frightening place and who have responded by simply staying put' (p.16). As the longest standing member of staff, Barbara again reveals her own sense of inadequacy.

St George's staff raise their eyebrows at the fee-paying schools attended by Sheba's children, but Barbara has 'no quarrel with private education' (p.39). Her first job was at a fee-paying school in Dumfries, and she would have still been there if it had not been for some 'personal difficulties' with colleagues (p.39). The objections of her St George's colleagues to private schools are, in her view, 'simple-minded … up there with fur coats and fox hunting' (p.39). She is equally dismissive of the idealism of her younger colleagues about 'making a difference' (p.27), and the general shift towards 'inflated and grandiose' pedagogical ambitions, which, she claims, has coincided with a radical decline in the standards of basic literacy and numeracy (p.28). Barbara is not, in short, 'child-centred'.

Steven Connolly, reported in the media to be 'backward' or 'retarded', was one of what Barbara claims to be 'a good 25 per cent of St George's students… identified as having "literacy issues"' (p.27). While Sheba views Steven as brilliant and imaginative, written off by the school because of his dyslexia, Barbara claims he is distinctly average and that Sheba is blinded by her unfamiliarity with 'the working class', whom she sees both as a 'homogenous entity…tempery, florid-faced …addled by food additives and alcohol', a view which makes Connolly 'fascinatingly anomalous' (p.46). Although Barbara suspects something 'sexual' in Stephen's attitude towards Sheba when she first sees them together, she normalises it as part of the 'sexual undertow' of the secondary school:

> All those bodies pressed in on one another – bubbling with puberty and low-level adolescent fantasy – are bound to produce a certain *atmosphere*.
>
> (p.53)

Given this view of the school as a 'hormonal soup', Barbara isn't big on the idea of the school as part of a supportive, safe ecology. The head, Pabblem, had arrived from a school in Stoke Newington where he had created a drama department and an award-winning 'neighbourhood ecology project' and was 'very big on communication' (p.57). Barbara does her best to thwart Pabblem's initiatives, believing that beneath the cheery exterior lies a 'progressive bully', pedantic and controlling (p.58).

When Sheba and Richard's daughter Polly is revealed to be bullying younger children in her boarding school, her parents are summoned to meet the head and the counsellor, 'a nice, dim man' who tells them that Polly's behaviour indicates 'low self-worth' (p.135). When Barbara hears this verdict, she laughs out loud, fascinated as she is to 'hear bleeding hearts give their soppy rationalisations for delinquency' (p.137). Polly's bullying is not 'a behaviour', Barbara asserts, but 'a mark of her character' (p.136).

Barbara's narrative is framed by her own personal shame. The 'personal difficulties' with colleagues in Dumfries are echoed in the disintegration of her relationship with Jennifer Dodd, a former colleague at St George's. Barbara had regarded her as a close friend for over a year when 'with no warning' Jennifer said she wanted 'no further contact', referring only to Barbara being 'too intense' (pp.34–5). Eventually threatened with an injunction, Barbara was forced to leave her alone. Although there are few signs that Sheba is initially interested in Barbara's friendships, the latter is sure she discerns an 'intuited kinship', one which she eventually forces (p.18).

When Barbara first visits Sheba's home, she is struck by her 'absolute, bourgeois confidence in the rightness of her living room, her tatty gigantic furniture, her children's stray underwear' (p.98). She contrasts Sheba's lack of shame to her own 'terrible feeling of exposure' when Jennifer had visited her flat 'as if my dirty linen basket, rather than my unexceptionable sitting room, were on display' (p.98).

Barbara's eventual disclosure of Sheba's relationship with Connolly comes after a double rejection: first from Sheba and then from a young colleague, the Maths teacher Bangs. When he invites Barbara out she assumes their meeting is a date, but he is there only to seek advice on how to proceed with his own attraction to Sheba. Shamed again, and now primed for revenge, Barbara explains cryptically that Sheba is attracted to 'younger men' (p.193). The news eventually makes its way back to Sheba's husband and the head of St George's. With Sheba's infamy complete, Barbara can offer herself up as her carer and attempt to have the needs which she cannot express met by a woman who cannot meet them. In this story, surveillance neither protects the pupils nor penetrates the layers of shame which shroud the adults entrusted with their education.

The History Boys

State school, social class and shame also play out in Alan Bennett's *The History Boys*, first performed as a play in 2004 and adapted as a film in 2006 (Bennett, 2004; *The History Boys,* 2006). Set in a Sheffield grammar school in 1983 (Yorkshire held on to six grammar schools after the conversion of most state schools to comprehensives), *The History Boys* focuses on the '7th form', a group of students who, after receiving the necessary A-level grades, are prepared for the Oxbridge entrance exam. As Philip French reviewing the film for *The Guardian* notes, although it is set in 1983, there are no references to 'the Falkland's war, Sheffield's dying steel industry or the rise of the SDP… the picture is as much about Bennett's childhood and Blair's post-Thatcher world as about the Eighties' (French, 2006).

Bennett's introduction recalls his own experience of the Oxbridge entrance exam as a grammar school student in the 1950s. To explain the tensions in this experience, he references the work of another Leeds schoolboy, Richard Hoggart's *The Uses of Literacy*, in particular Hoggart's view of the 'scholarship boy' as:

> equipped for hurdle-jumping, so he merely thinks of getting on, but somehow not in the world's way ... He has left his class, at least in spirit, by being in certain ways unusual, and he is still unusual in another class, too tense and overwound.
>
> (Hoggart in Bennett, p.xxi)

The 'tense and overwound' scholarship boy, neither one class nor another but 'getting on', embodies a kind of social shame, represented in the play by Posner who is most vocal about his ambivalence about the Oxbridge 'hurdle-jumping'. While Bennett has a class-based critique of the Oxbridge entrance system, dominated as it was (and is) by privately educated students, he is also critical of Blairite education policy, which is also, in his eyes, neither one thing nor another. There is much, he writes, 'that is called education nowadays that is nothing of the sort and doesn't deserve subsidy, yet I still hold to the belief that a proper education should be free at the point of entry and the point of exit' (p.xx). For Bennett, public schools and top-up fees stand either side of a gate marked no entry to the working-class adolescent, even to those who manage to jump the hurdle.

The headteacher in the play is running at full speed with the idea of getting more boys over the hurdle. In conversation with the History teacher Mrs Lintott, who regards one 'centre of higher learning' as good as another, the head (who studied Geography at Hull) reveals he wants to push the students to Oxford or Cambridge. His investment in their success is a transparent ploy for his own and his school's advancement:

> I am thinking league tables. Open scholarships. Reports to the Governors. I want them to do themselves justice. I want them to do you justice. Factually tip-top as your boys always are, something more is required.
>
> (p.8)

The 'something more' is to be acquired by intensive tuition. The young men are to be taught by Hector (Sheffield graduate), the 'unorthodox' English teacher turned General Studies teacher who values knowledge for the sake of knowledge. 'I count examinations, even for Oxford and Cambridge, as the enemy of education. Which is not to say that I don't regard education as the enemy of education, too' (pp.46–7). Mrs Lintott (History, Durham), and good friend to Hector, is weary of the performative character of male historians and sees History as 'a commentary on the various and continuing incapabilities of men' (p.82). Irwin, a temporary teacher, apparently a graduate of Oxford, is drafted in by the headteacher and he approaches the exam strategically, as a game to be won. He encourages the boys to be bound neither by the truth nor authenticity of a point of view. 'History nowadays is not a matter of conviction. It's a performance. It's entertainment' (p.34).

While Hector offers them 'art', 'culture' and 'blurriness', Irwin provides 'education' (in its narrow sense) and 'focus' (p.36). The head reflects on the problem of Hector's teaching style, opining that 'it isn't that he doesn't produce results. He does. But they are unpredictable and unquantifiable and in the current educational climate that is no use' (p.65). That climate is, of course, both the 1980s and the Blairite years.

As Timms points out to Irwin: 'Mr Hector's stuff's not meant for the exam, sir. It's to make us more rounded human beings' (p.37). Hector's investment in the boys' 'roundedness' is also an investment in their youth and beauty. The play invites us to share the boys' tolerance for the predatory aspects of Hector's behaviour. In conversation with Irwin, Mrs Lintott nods to the layered aspects of Hector's identity. 'Hector is in fact a nickname. His name's Douglas, though the only person I've ever heard address him as such is his somewhat unexpected wife' (p.40). The boys seem to accept his attempts to fondle them on the back of his motorbike as a quirk of Hector's teaching style and a legacy of Hector being part of a generation in whom homosexuality was stigmatised. In an echo of Hector's 'shame', Posner confides to Irwin his attraction towards Dakin, and Irwin confides the same to Mrs Lintott.

When Hector is spotted by the Headmaster's wife 'fiddling' a 'boy on pillion', Hector is advised to retire (p.50). His response is typically idealistic, as he first denies then reframes the event through cultural history:

Hector:	Nothing happened.
Headmaster:	A hand on a boy's genitals at 50 miles an hour, and you call it nothing?
Hector:	The transmission of knowledge is in itself an erotic act. In the Renaissance…

(p.51)

The Headmaster loses patience with the emerging analogy and invokes the trope of 'deviant' art and artists to shut down Hector's defence:

> Fuck the Renaissance. And fuck literature and Plato and Michaelangelo and Oscar Wilde and all the other shrunken violets you people line up. This is a school and it isn't normal.
>
> (p.52)

Hector shakes off the Headmaster's words and his attempt to shame him. He shares an acknowledgement of unexpressed and unrequited desire in a conversation with Posner about Thomas Hardy and Philip Larkin's use of the compound adjective, created by the prefix 'un'. 'Un-kissed. Un-rejoicing. Un-confessed.

Un-embraced… Un-spent. Un-fingermarked' (p.54). These shamed, frozen and isolated states, Hector suggests, can be consoled by moments in reading:

> when you come across something – a thought, a feeling, a way of looking at things – which you had thought special and particular to you. Now here it is, set down by someone else.... And it is as if a hand has come out and taken yours.
>
> (p.54)

These shared thoughts, feelings and ways of looking at things offer 'holding' in place of shaming.

Although Hector ultimately dies on his motorbike, the play's last words affirm 'his kind of teaching'. 'Pass the parcel', Hector had said:

> That's sometimes all you can do.
> Take it, feel it and pass it on.
> Not for me, not for you, but for someone, somewhere, one day.
>
> (p.105)

In *The History Boys*, education shames but language holds.

Wicked! and *Ahead of the Class*

While *The History Boys* locates its disaffection with the utilitarianism of New Labour education policy in another historical moment, Jilly Cooper dives headlong into the details of education in the early 2000s. Set in her mythical county of Larkshire, *Wicked!* is a slapstick dramatisation of New Labour policies (Cooper, 2006). It is shot through with the particularities of public-private initiatives and New Labour's 'inclusive' policies.

The newly elected Tory MP Jupiter Belvedon of Larkminster is 'hotly tipped to take over the Tory party and oust Tony Blair' (p.19). Blairite policy is determining the local education scene. In January 2001 'central government decided to take the running of Larkshire's schools away from the local education authority'. The task was handed to a private company called S&C services, short, of course, for 'Support and Challenge' (p.19). Cooper captures the combination of the blandly pastoral and waspishly managerial that is the hallmark of 'post local authority' education services in which acronyms and slogans stand in place of meaning.

Larkminster boasts a range of secondary schools: Bagley Hall, its famous public school, the fortunes of which were turned around by the head, Hengist; two 'excellent' state schools, Searston Abbey and St James' and 'a perfectly frightful sink school', Larkminster Comprehensive, known as 'Larks' (p.19). Cooper is uninhibited in ventriloquising class-based slurs through her omniscient narrator (who at times uncannily echoes Heller's Barbara Covett) to sketch social types in caricature. The expansive cast of characters (12 pages long) sets the scene:

> Miss Basket, A menopausal misfit who teaches geography at Larks; Alex Bruce, Deputy Head of Bagley Hall, nicknamed Mr Fussy; Poppet Bruce, His dreadful wife, who traches RE. An acronymphomaniac, determined to impose total political correctness on Bagley Hall; Kylie Rose Peck, Sweet-natured Larks pupil... So eternally up the duff she'll soon qualify for a free tower block.

And so on. The caricatures are liberally distributed between the Larks and Bagley Hall communities, with Larks' 'Wolf Pack' (a group of Year Nines – Paris, Graffi, Pearl and Kylie Rose) rivalled by 'The Bagley Babes', including Amber Lloyd Foxe and Jade Stancombe.

The comprehensive, 'Larks', 'was situated on the edge of the town's black spot, the notorious Shakespeare Estate' (pp.19–20). An increase in violent crime was attributed to the estate and to Larks, which, sitting 'bottom of the league tables', was a candidate for closure (p.20). The Council, S&C and Westminster, however, were nervous of the potential uproar caused by a school closure after the resignation of the head, so an advert was placed in *The Times Educational Supplement* for his replacement. On a 'hot sunny day', Janna Curtis, Head of English at Redfords Comprehensive in West Yorkshire, 'caught the intercity from Leeds to Larkminster', though she would not do anything as 'elitist as travel first class' (p.20). On the train, Curtis has a look at the *Daily Mail* (despite her disapproval of 'right wing bastards' including S&C).

Janna is from a working-class family. Her mother was a single parent, abandoned by a violent, alcoholic husband. Her mother encouraged her to read and took her to the Bronte's house in Haworth, jump starting Janna's 'journey' into culture and tortured romance. Her mission to work at Larks is partly driven by social purpose and her need to escape from an affair with her current, married, head. In Cooper's Freudian universe, principle is always in some way driven by private, often sexual, interest and her stories play with the social shame when the latter is exposed.

After her interview by governors, local councillors and educationalists in a pub close to the school, Janna is appointed on the spot. Like Ian George in *Hope and Glory*, Janna befriends the site manager, Wally Bristow, who primes her for the task ahead. When Janna lays out her mission, 'Oh Wally, I've got to make every child feel they're the greatest and discover each one's special talents', Wally is quick to puncture it. 'Smokin', spittin', runnin' away, fightin', and urinatin' in phone boxes', intoned Wally. 'As we can't fill the places, we get all the dropouts that get sacked or rejected by other schools' (p.32). He paints a picture of truancy and vandalism, teenage pregnancies and anti-social behaviour – the 'issues' in the crosshairs of the 'Every Child Matters' agenda. Staff are 'demoralised...off sick from "stress" ... old dinosaurs hanging on for retirement, or commies who grumble at everything and threaten strike action if you keep them a minute late' (p.33). The scene is set for Janna's transformative powers, having been part of the team which revived her previous school Redfords from the ashes of special measures.

Cooper cites the story of Marie Stubbs, a 'super head' who was deployed to turn around a failing school, St George's Roman Catholic Secondary School in Maida Vale, as her inspiration for Janna's story. In 1995, the head of St George's had been murdered in front of his pupils by someone not associated with the school. The tragedy had shaken the community's foundations, and Stubbs, a recently retired head of a suburban London school, was contacted by the Director of Education for the Diocese to help arrest the school's downward fall.

In her memoir, *Ahead of the Class* (Stubbs, 2003), which was adapted for a film starring Julie Walters (2004), Stubbs objects to the 'super head concept', casting herself as 'a team player' (p.3). Stubbs' story is received, however, as a one-woman odyssey, a hero's journey. *The Independent* calls it a tale of 'triumph over adversity through determination and hard work' as she overcomes the hostility of a dispirited staff, disaffected pupils and dilapidated buildings (Cassidy, 2003). *The Sunday Times'* reviewer runs away with the simile of Stubbs sailing 'into this sorry mess like a pocket battleship', exploding the 'rancour and self-pity' of staff, relentlessly 'harrying' the children into uniform and good behaviour and attacking the school buildings 'to make them bright and welcoming' (Carey, 2003). By the end of her tenure, the school went from Ofsted special measures to 'a national example of good practice', success which Ofsted attributed to a 'strict positive regime with clear expectations, grounded on a strong set of values' (p.254).

As I suggested in Chapter 6, while the school stories of the post-war period foregrounded the efforts of 'the ordinary devoted teachers' to turn around the fortunes of their students, the turn of the millennium saw more of these stories of school transformation, spearheaded by exceptional headteachers. In schools, the 'Every Child Matters' agenda would depend upon the tenacity and vigilance of extraordinary leaders, modelled perhaps on Tony Blair himself – openly emotional, unbound by ideology and driven by 'moral purpose'.

Janna is not a Marie Stubbs, who foregrounds her story with an emphasis on her grandparental maturity and career experience. Part of Janna's 'journey' depends on her relative naivety and, as a Jilly Cooper heroine, her physical charms. Physical appearance is a marker of character in caricature and satire. Cooper's fictions are also comically erotic, so Janna's looks are suitably alluring: 'lots of dark freckles and wild, rippling dark red hair' (p.26).

When Janna browses the personal files of the Larks pupils, Wally Bristow is on hand to fill in the lurid details of the lives of the Year Nine 'Wolf Pack' with unsentimental bluntness. 'Feral Jackson. Comes into school to play football and start fights...mother's an addict...brother Joey was shot to death last year. Uncle Harley...is a mega pusher'. Paris Alvaston 'has been in different care homes since he was two...Goes AWOL ...searching for his mother'. Graffi 'was a thief...a good laugh' and graffiti artist. Pearl is 'trouble. Cuts herself' and Kylie Rose 'had one kid at twelve – wanted something to love' (pp.36–7). Janna, meanwhile, is struck by Feral's 'long dark eyelashes and…smile of utter innocence' and Paris's 'wonderful bone structure…watchful pale grey eyes of a merle collie' (pp.36–7). In her descriptions of these boys, Cooper invests in a long tradition of the 'noble savage', the exceptional primitive who throws shade on the 'civilised' culture around him. Janna's attachment to the boys, particularly Paris, goes beyond the maternal or the Platonic. Janna offers 'holding' in a literal sense. The transformative energy Janna brings is charged with something more libidinous though 'she is unaware of the havoc she is wreaking' on Paris (p.47). This observation echoes Barbara Covett's sense of the secondary school as a sexualised hormonal soup, with adolescent bodies prone to the gaze of wistful (or predatory) adults. Paris, the abandoned child, is, in Cooper's universe, redeemed by being an object of everyone's desire.

While in Heller's story this dynamic turns into a criminal investigation, the relationship between Janna and Paris is just one of many in the novel that are fuelled on shame-free erotic transference. The children and adults have the same desires and act on them with the same 'abandon'.

Within this 'comp romp', however, there is timely social and political satire, aimed to the left and right. Labour and Lib Dem councillors are in cahoots with the press. There are unscrupulous takeovers and mergers, and business comes before community. The independent school Bagley is also a 'transformed' school, reformed by the inspirational head, Hengist. But he seduces Jenna into a working and sexual relationship, knowing that collaboration with a local state school 'in need' justifies Bagley's charitable status and improves his chances as a Conservative political candidate.

Bagley pupils – Cosmo, Xav, Bianca, Jade, Dora – experience a different kind of neglect to the Larks' Wolf Pack, but are neglected, nevertheless. The schools, adults and children come together in performances and field trips and rebound as personal relationships implode. Paris Alvaston unites the schools in another way when he is transferred from Larks to Bagley. He is fostered by Bagley staff, Ian and Patience, though they are counselled by a downbeat social worker to keep their expectations low:

> I know you want to rescue a young life and Paris longs for a family…But your expectations are unrealistic. At an age when most adolescents are trying to escape from their parents…you're going against the grain and trying to form ties.
>
> (p.445)

The novel repeatedly veers into territory of child abuse, neglect and even murder but does not get absorbed in them. Such moments are set against a critique of 'over-vigilance' and political correctness, of interfering social workers and joy-sapping safeguards. There is an accusation of sexual abuse of Paris by a Bagley teacher, which is found to be untrue and reframed by Paris as a Platonic attachment. Poppet Bruce, Bagley Hall's RE teacher, is satirised for perpetually seeking out signs of damage and victimhood. She proposes the demolition of General Bagley's statue, and recommends children seek counselling with great frequency. Although through characters like Poppet it lampoons the 'Every Child Matters' ethos of surveillance, the novel ultimately affirms the Blairite vision for education, the merging of 'the best' of the private and public sectors. Janna is a recipient of a Times Educational Supplement award, 'the People's prize', for the teacher who the public believed had done the 'most heroic' job (p.931). In her acceptance speech, she thanks Bagley school and the now disgraced Hengist and makes a plea to her fellow state schoolteachers: 'We must stop demonising the independents as they demonise us. We've got to work together for all children' (p.933).

A review in *The Guardian* by Joanna Briscoe is troubled by the novel's unwieldy length and meandering plot but commends Cooper for 'bravely open[ing] herself up to potential ridicule as she does "common"' (Briscoe, 2006). Briscoe seems to credit Cooper with a Richard Hoggart-like perspective on working-class culture as she celebrates Cooper's 'valiant and convincing attempt to capture disaffected, deprived youth' (Briscoe, 2006). Briscoe, perhaps, has learned about 'disaffected youth' from the disciplinary language of 'Every Child Matters' and the newspapers which sold titillating stories about teenage pregnancies and ASBOs in the early 2000s. She mistakes working-class adolescence for its representation and commends Cooper for reproducing an already distorted image.

The therapeutic turn

Cooper's pastiche of the sentiments of 'Every Child Matters' anticipates a more academic rejection of 'safety surveillance' in Kathryn Ecclestone and Dennis Hayes' 2008 book, *The Dangerous Rise of Therapeutic Education*, reissued in 2019 (Ecclestone and Hayes, 2019). The introduction challenges the assumption that, in 2007, the UK faced 'an unprecedented epidemic of mental health problems, particularly in children and young people' (p.1):

> The goals and institutional arrangements of 'Every Child Matters' (ECM) formalise such concerns by requiring welfare and education agencies to ensure that, as part of being 'safe' and able to achieve educationally and socially, children's wellbeing is paramount.
>
> (p.1)

Ecclestone and Hayes claim that the creation in 2007 of the Department for Children, Schools and Families in place of the Department for Education and Skills '"erases" education as a social and political aspiration' and responds to 'popular concerns' with emotional problems by 'eliding welfare and educational goals and activities' (p.2). They cite the saturation of popular culture with 'therapy' and 'everyday explanations for behaviour...offered increasingly in terms of emotional fragility' (p.2). They claim that this unhelpful 'therapeutic turn' in which 'an eclectic mix of cognitive behaviour therapy, neuro-science, Freudian or Jungian analysis, transactional analysis or Rogerian counselling' pepper television and print media has its symbolic origin on 31 August 1997, the date of Princess Diana's death. While according to this narrative, Diana became the 'model victim and martyr' (p.10); the authors also claim that the veneration of victimhood and suffering were well-established by the time of her tragic death.

In this argument, the consequences of the 'therapeutic turn' for education policy involve a shift from addressing the effects of poverty to a vaguer emphasis on 'inclusion' to combat psychological harm, as though each is mutually exclusive. From 2007, the authors claim, government capitulated to the promotion of emotional literacy in schools: the 'therapeutic secondary school' now promotes 'soft skills' and 'relevance' at the expense of subject knowledge. An emphasis on 'learning', 'destigmatising mental health' by promoting emotional openness, mentoring and the PSHE curriculum are all vilified as an abandonment of 'humanist education' – the idea that everyone benefits from the acquisition of knowledge – for a 'humanitarian education' (pp.61–2). This shift beckons the erosion of 'subject disciplines' in favour of topics and processes 'that can only be engaging if they relate to the self' (p.63). The self at the centre of this education is a diminished subject, lacking in agency. The alternative proposal is a 'radical humanism', the 'making of scientific and social progress through reason' (p.162).

Much is made in the book of the novelty of this 'therapeutic turn' in the 1990s and early 2000s. My argument has shown that the 'progressive' case for educational reform since the Second World War is repeatedly made in terms of social justice *and* individual wellbeing and contested on the grounds of educational 'knowledge' and 'standards', as though the two are mutually exclusive. What is new at every turn is how 'wellbeing' is described, although the pedagogical aspects (relevance, learning, relational practice versus abstraction, teaching, direction) crop up cyclically.

While there is much to be said for the argument for 'radical humanism', what is more often offered in place of progressive ideas is 'common sense'. Common sense, a notion of uncontestable truth derived from strongly held opinion rather than truth arrived at by social and scientific consensus, is what has recently been invoked to counter so-called identity politics and what some see as the overemphasis on emotional wellbeing in schools. 'Common sense' has become the defence against the move towards increasingly bespoke 'learning journeys' in the state secondary school, a push back against the demands of identity and neurodivergence. It attaches itself to a defensive and regressive nationalism that risks leaking into education policy.

The following chapters explore the most recent structural changes in the state secondary sector, the formation of academy schools and the emergence of marginalised voices demanding 'inclusion'. In principle, the academy structure has the agility to respond to these voices but the pressures of accountability to the 'educational centre' take away the flexibility that academies could offer.

References

Ahead of the Class (2004) [Film] Shergold, A. dir., England: World Productions.

Barwick, N. (ed.) (2000) *Clinical Counselling in Schools*, London: Routledge.

Bennett, A. (2004) *The History Boys*, London: Faber and Faber.

Boateng, P. (2003) 'Every Child Matters', *Presented to Parliament by the Chief Secretary to the Treasury*, Crown Copyright, https://www.gov.uk/government/publications/every-child-matters

Bor, R., Ebner-Landy, J., Gill, S. and Brace, C. (2002) *Counselling in Schools*, London: Sage.

Briscoe, J. (2006) 'Larks with toffs and oiks!', *The Guardian*, 13 May.

Carey, J. (2003) 'Review: Education: *Ahead of the Class* by Marie Stubbs', *The Sunday Times*, 13 April.

Carneiro, P. et al. (2025) 'The short- and medium-term effects of Sure Start on Children's Outcomes', *Institute for Fiscal Studies Report*, 22 May, https://ifs.org.uk/publications/short-and-medium-term-impacts-sure-start-educational--outcomes

Casey, L. (2014) *Understanding Troubled Families, Department for Communities and Local Government*, July.

Cassidy, S. (2003) 'The triumph of traditional values', *The Independent*, 10 April.

Cooper, J. (2006) *Wicked!*, London: Corgi.

Davies, L. (2008) 'In the shadow of a tragedy', *The Guardian*, 28 January, https://www.theguardian.com/society/2008/jan/28/climbie.childprotection

Ecclestone, K. and Hayes, D. (2019) *The Dangerous Rise of Therapeutic Education*, Abingdon: Routledge.

French, P. (2006) '*The History Boys*, review', *The Guardian*, 15 October.

Heller, Z. (2003) *Notes on a Scandal*, London: Penguin.

Kaufman, G. (1989) *The Psychology of Shame: Theory and Treatment of Shame-Based Syndromes*, Princeton: Springer.

Laming, W.H. (2003) '"The Victoria Climbié with an e with acute accent Inquiry": report of an inquiry by Lord Laming', https://www.gov.uk/government/publications/the-victoria-climbie-inquiry-report-of-an-inquiry-by-lord-laming.

Lee, R.G. (2007) 'Shame and belonging in childhood: the intersection between relationship and neurobiological development in early years of life', *British Gestalt Journal*, 16(2), pp.38–45.

Notes on a Scandal (2006) [Film], Eyre, R., dir., London: Fox Searchlight Pictures.

Perls, F.S. (1969) *Gestalt Therapy Verbatim*, Lafayette, LA: Real People Press.

Stubbs, M. (2003) *Ahead of the Class*, London: John Murray.

The History Boys (2006) [Film] Hytner, R. dir., London, South and West Yorkshire: Fox Searchlight.

8

SPLITS AND MERGERS

The academy stories of the 2010s

In 2011 and 2015, another pair of nieces, sisters Emily and Helena, joined St Martin's Roman Catholic Comprehensive in Billingham, the school that I, one of my brothers and another three nieces had attended in previous decades. Their tenures coincided with the school's conversion to academy status and the arrival of smart phones. Emily describes herself as fairly shy at the start of Year Seven. She had loved primary school, but had mixed feelings about the new arrangement, especially after she started fancying boys and gravitated away from her primary school friends into a new group. History, English, RE and Form were winners for Emily, but she wasn't keen on Maths, and her Science teacher once described her as 'uncontrollable'. The school felt 'very Catholic', with Form mass once a month; confession on a Wednesday was a chance to get out of class. For the first few years it was easy to skip lessons, and she never did PE (upholding a family tradition). There were clashes with teachers about makeup and homework. Detentions followed as did threats from her parents to remove her from St Martin's. Change arrived when the school was taken into an academy trust from the beginning of Emily's Year Ten. A new regulation skirt and blazer initially horrified Emily but she warmed to the blazer as it had plenty of pockets in which to hide her most important accessory, her iPhone. Emily had had her phone since Year Eight (originally a Blackberry). Officially phones were meant to be handed in at the beginning of the school day but that rarely happened. By the time Emily left St Martin's, she had grown to like the place but doesn't remember having much guidance about what was to come next. University was never mentioned and transition days to Year 12

DOI: 10.4324/9781003715122-13

were to vocational colleges, not sixth forms. Emily did go on to university to study English and History and is now Internal Communication Specialist for an NHS Mental Health trust. Emily's favourite school stories: *St Trinian's* and Enid Blyton's *The Naughtiest Girl in School*.

Younger sister Helena joined in 2015, overlapping with Emily by a year. The school was rebuilt during her first year and had been rebranded as St Martin's Catholic Academy, with a feel very different to the school Emily had joined four years earlier. Helena had seen Emily have fun in her 'popular' group and wanted to do the same but found herself in a peer group who were largely well behaved and focused on validation from academic success. Teachers liked them so they got away with too much makeup and fake tan. She remembers that by Year Nine, male peers were smoking weed and using 'pills' but there was an increasing sense of the difference between the stricter culture at St Martin's and the other high schools nearby.

Helena had had a phone since Year Five and officially it wasn't allowed in high school, but the rules became laxer over her time there. She remembers posting selfies for likes on Instagram in Year Seven, a compulsion which she now describes as 'toxic'.

In March 2020, the country went into lockdown and Helena's year group had their GCSE examinations cancelled. She was 'gutted', though she did as well as she'd hoped in the teacher assessed version. She already had a prom dress, but no prom was organised. She remembers little online contact with school from March. Although she liked her sixth form college and excelled at A-level, the teaching provision during COVID was patchy and many friends struggled psychologically. Although she doesn't remember much talk of universities at school, she went on to study for a degree in Environmental Science and is currently on a Master's programme in 'Climate Change: environmental science and policy'. Helena's favourite school story: *Harry Potter*.

Integrating counselling

After a long period of decline in school-based counselling services, the first decade of the Millennium saw an increase in services, due in part to increased emphasis on the integration of children's services (after Laming), the Extended Schools Initiative which was part of the 2004 Children Act and other moves to improve children's and young people's services, including their delivery in schools. Most school-based counselling was coordinated by charities (such as the National Society for the Prevention of Cruelty to Children (NSPCC), Place2Be or Relate) or was provided by independent counsellors employed directly by schools.

In the House of Commons in 2002, MP for Guildford Sue Doughty asked Ivan Lewis, then Under-Secretary of State for Education and Skills, what measures were in place 'to improve counselling services available to young people in schools' (Hansard, 2002). The subsequent responses suggest that Lewis did not know but valiantly offered references to the roll out of 'Connexions', personal advisors and the establishment of a network of 3,000 learning mentors. Doughty answered her own question by noting that the NSPCC is 'responsible for much of the current provision' of school counselling. Pressed further by Doughty to 'ensure that every child in every school has access to the counselling services that will help them', Lewis agrees with the inference that school counselling matters but simply repeats, with added statistics, the information about 'Connexions' and learning mentors.

In a piece of research published in 2009, funded by the NSPCC, Claire Fox and Ian Butler reviewed the effectiveness of a school-based counselling service run by the charity: the NSPCC Schools Counselling Project (Fox and Butler, 2009). The findings were based on a small number of students (219) who filled out questionnaires at various points before, during and after school counselling. The analysis found that counselling was effective in reducing distress in the participants. The study notes that while school counselling provision had increased, it was still 'patchy', with 71% of schools offering some sort of counselling service, led by local demand rather than a universal offer. Provision seems to have stayed at this level since then. The study points out that while there have been evaluations of the effectiveness of counselling services for young people generally, specific studies of school-based counselling in the UK have been limited and that remaining resistance to counselling services in school is unlikely to be resolved while evidence for its efficacy is so limited. The paper is optimistic about the future growth of services due to the expectations of the 'Every Child Matters' agenda – an optimism that has yet to be realised.

Fox and Bulter's study involved 13 teams of NSPCC counsellors (of five to six counsellors or social workers per team), and each team worked with around ten schools between 2001 and 2003. Apart from the generally positive outcomes on the effectiveness of the counselling, the report also looked at the method of referral and found that more girls self-referred while boys were usually referred by teachers, suggesting perhaps that boys were attending counselling because they had been referred for 'behavioural' reasons while girls were identifying themselves as having emotional difficulties. Boys were also more likely to report school-related difficulties while girls more often presented with family or other relationship difficulties. In my own work with adolescents in and out of schools, girls far outnumber boys. Boys are more often referred to activity-based interventions and mentorship. When boys do arrive for counselling, however, their fears, embarrassments and griefs are just as vivid as those of the girls, and they don't need a football to disclose them, though the presence of a dog has sometimes helped.

In his 2014 book on integrating counselling into the whole school, school counsellor Nick Luxmoore notes that while, at the time of writing, there were several training courses available for those wanting to work therapeutically with children and young people, there was only one course for potential school counsellors (Luxmoore, 2014). Counselling young people and school counselling are different things, he stresses. Luxmoore's work makes a compelling case for counselling in the secondary school, and captures both its potential and its reality, based on his 26 years as a counsellor and more time as a teacher before that. He argues that instead of complaining about being undervalued, school counsellors need to make themselves valuable, be transparent about their work and not hide behind an invisibility cloak of confidentiality. He cites counsellors who cling to purist theoretical frameworks who never secure a second appointment from a teenager, and those who are 'problem vampires', 'pumped up on the adrenalin high of other people's distress' (p.69).

Splitting

Luxmoore tells a great story and vividly characterises the emotional and psychological landscape, the 'intrapsychic process' of the school. He explains and illustrates the 'splitting' that happens in schools (or any organisation). Splitting is a term that describes a primitive form of psychological defence, derived from Melanie Klein's work on infant development and the separation of the world into good and bad experiences (Klein, 1946). The good is idealised, the bad is reviled, and both are projected outwards (projective identification) before being taken in again (introjection) by the infant. As the infant develops, so does their capacity for ambivalence, the holding together of good and bad, which reduces the tendency to project.

Luxmoore teases out the various forms of splitting and projective identification that can occur in a school: between school and community, between staff (left and right wing, old and young, science and arts), between staff and students and between students. The school counsellor can be welcomed, in Kleinian terms, as 'a good object'. In narrative terms, the counsellor is 'a wizard with a magic wand' (p.19), a rescuer, a source of hope when all options have been exhausted. But they can rapidly become objects 'of envy and resentment' (p.29). From this position of envy and resentment, the counsellor is nothing special as *all* staff listen, empathise and understand the circumstances of a child's life. Only the counsellor has the luxury of one-to-one sessions, doesn't have to meet attainment targets or bear the brunt of classroom disruption and parental anger. Luxmoore holds his hands up to all charges. As a master of ambivalence, he acknowledges that it is this unique position that allows the counsellor to be what Winnicott called 'the container', the one who can bear the pain and distress until the one who experiences it can bear it themselves. Without 'the container', pain and distress run from one person to another like wildfire.

Luxmoore argues that the counsellor should not just be holding one-to-one sessions with students in private rooms, important though these are. He makes a case for counsellors to be visible on the corridors, in the canteen and in the staff room; to attend to the needs of students *and* staff and to 'develop cultures in which young people and staff feel more confident and valued than they would otherwise feel' (p.11); to be present for the school community's vulnerability *and* resourcefulness. So, the counsellor can listen to a teacher's frustration about an interaction with a student *and* watch an accomplished lesson; let a student cry about an issue in their family *and* see them laugh with their friend in the canteen. The counsellor is there to witness and reflect the multiplicity of school experience, not just to suck up the distress.

School counselling itself sits on one side of a 'split' in school culture. While the rise of school counselling in the early 2000s suggested a shift towards more 'inclusive' approaches to secondary education (and was part of the case for the prosecution for those who feared the 'victim culture' of therapeutic education), there was a simultaneous direction of travel towards 'school improvement', which was measured in terms of academic attainment.

Academies and free schools

As I argued in Chapter 7, the late 1990s and early 2000s phenomenon of the 'super head' was a response to shifting expectations of schools. Schools were expected to meet a range of children's needs after various pieces of legislation formally expanded the role of schools to keep all children 'safe' and 'included' in the mainstream setting. Local education authority resources were stretched and diminished. Examination targets and the Ofsted inspection reports made their work more transparent, which fuelled a culture of 'high stakes' accountability. With more responsibility and less external support, schools needed an almost magical response to engineer the much desired 'improvement'. Short of a supply of educational genii, charismatic, effective, sometimes ruthless 'super heads' were sent in to do transformative, headline grabbing work, however unsustainable that work would be.

The more 'sustainable' response of the New Labour government to this predicament was the 'academies' programme, which began with the Under Secretary of State for schools and learners, Andrew Adonis's City Academy scheme in 2002. City Academies were under the direct control of central government and were set up in areas of 'high deprivation'. The Building Schools for the Future initiative, launched in 2004, worked with authorities but was delivered by private providers. As Tim Brighouse and Mick Waters recall, there were political tensions and logistical difficulties in these early 'public/private' hybrids (Brighouse and Waters, 2021, pp.128–32) and ideological objectors dubbed them private raids on the public estate, a literal split with local authorities and local democracy.

Others took a more pragmatic approach, looking for the educational opportunities of the new arrangements. The academies programme was founded on the belief that structural change (funding and management) would improve the educational outcomes of the children in the newly branded organisations. Even those who were open to the principle were sceptical about the evidence that academisation itself would provide more for the children in the schools. As Kevan Collins, former director of education for Tower Hamlets, remembered in an interview with Brighouse and Waters:

> We came under a huge amount of pressure to put academies into Tower Hamlets. Our outlook was pragmatic. You bring the evidence that this structural change improves schools more quickly than we're improving and we will respond. They never did.
>
> (p.132)

Collins was also concerned that academisation put too much emphasis on schools in isolation. They would not be able to deliver 'bookended' care for children: the support that had to come from the local health sector (such as speech and language therapy) or from broader planning for the provision of jobs and skills for school leavers in the local community. Academies, he feared, would sever the link between schools and their 'local economy, local opportunities and local resources' (p.131).

Just as the new innovations of secondary moderns and comprehensives, super heads and parent governors provided great dramatic opportunity for the school story tellers, so 'the academy' became a by-word for private interest, undemocratic decision making and unscrupulous takeovers in the school stories of the New Labour era. The trope intensified after the Coalition government put its energy into the academy and free school programme, with the 2010 Academies Act landing on ministers' desks even before Larry the cat had moved into Downing Street (in February 2011).

Michael Gove was minister for education under the Coalition government from 2010 to 2014 and the pantomime villain of the sector for many years after his tenure. Gove picked up Adonis's academies idea and turbocharged it into a wide-ranging restructure of the sector. While Adonis had focused on injecting energy and funds into areas of deprivation with sponsored academies, Gove wanted to shake up the whole sector and to put clear water between schools and local authorities. All schools were to be 'free' to convert, and early adopters were incentivised with additional funds and a three-year reprieve from Ofsted inspections. Conversion meant direct funding from government, establishment of 'business' infrastructure at academy level (or Multiacademy trust – MAT – level), including internal financial services, HR functions and some autonomy on policy setting and pay scales. The National Curriculum was slashed, with academies 'free' to design and deliver their own curricula (although the new attainment measures would undermine any such 'freedom' this liberalising move implied). While these 'freedoms' were the carrot for already robust schools, others were under the threat of compulsory conversion and takeover by a MAT.

As Chair of Governors at a primary school, which was already in a 'federation' with another local primary (federations were a friendly, cooperative warm-up act to academies), I was front and centre of the conversion process when the then

Executive Head wanted to academise. The main carrot for this already strong primary was the ability to apply for funding for its ailing interwar building. Such funds would not be available from a stretched local authority or from central government funds for non-academy schools. Throughout the whole lengthy, time-consuming conversion process, which involved a lot of 'voluntary' hours from governors, I was mostly convinced of the business case but perplexed by the claims made for educational freedoms. 'Control our own destiny' was the mantra of the Executive Head, as he raised the spectre of the threat of a takeover by one of the emerging national trusts. The actual process felt more like an acceptance of the inevitable and an attempt to claw back some financial control in a system where everything else was hyper-centralised.

The so-called 'free schools' which were to be permitted under the act were unlike the urban free schools of the early 1970s, which sprang up to meet the needs of working-class and other children marginalised from or failing in the mainstream system. While Local Authorities were no longer allowed to build schools, existing MATs could apply to do so. Groups of parents, teachers and charities could also seek permission to establish a new school. The first free school to receive funding under the 2010 bill was the West London free school, established by journalist and controversialist, Toby Young. As a profile of Young in *Schools Week* in 2016 pointed out, Young had spent much of the early 2000s decrying the Labour government's education policies and 'work-shy' teachers (Phillips, 2016). As a father of four, Young was nervously contemplating the secondary education of his children, despite the capital's secondaries benefitting enormously from 'the London challenge', a school improvement programme launched by New Labour in 2002. Young claimed he could neither afford nor desired private schools for his children, having experienced the 'plutocratic' desires of the privately educated while working at *Vanity Fair* magazine. Young himself had been educated at a London comprehensive but what he seemed to want for his children was a grammar school. When an opportunity arose to set up a school in his neighbourhood, with a 'knowledge rich' curriculum, and which would accommodate his four children when they reached secondary school age, he set about rallying local interest. Young eventually became the CEO and, according to the profile, regretted his public criticisms of the state school system as he now realised the difficulties involved in changing the system.

Waterloo Road, *2006–15*

The drama of the New Labour and Coalition years in the education sector, from Blair's mantra of 'education, education, education', to Gove's invocation of 'the blob' as the enemy of progress, has provided the framework of several long-running secondary school stories and a new fault line in the fictional staff rooms. In 2006, the first season of *Waterloo Road*, about a comprehensive school in Rochdale, Greater Manchester, appeared on BBC 1 (*Waterloo Road*, 2006–15). It starts as *Hope and Glory* ended, on the school roof. While super head Ian George was on his school roof to calm down a distressed teacher, on Waterloo Road's rooftop the man mid breakdown, throwing paperwork into the playground, *is* the headteacher. This head was not feeling super.

The creator of *Waterloo Road*, Ann McManus, would, I suspect, be sympathetic to the argument that 'the therapeutic turn' of the 1990s undermined educational opportunity in state schools and nor would she be a champion of the academies programme. McManus had been a teacher in Glasgow, and as she told *The Guardian's* Peter Wilby in 2009, her first job, in 1984, was in a poor area with 'the highest instances of teenage pregnancy and single motherhood and God knows what else' (Wilby, 2009). The school was in a slump and compared unfavourably to McManus's own experience of secondary school in the late 1960s and 1970s. Even though she describes herself as 'disruptive' during her time at the Catholic comprehensive, and that the school 'lacked ambition for its pupils', she was shocked by the permissive attitude and the 'aching trendiness' of the school she later taught in. 'Children's rights' she says, 'should be confined to not being hit and being kept safe'. As a former member of the Communist Party and still 'very left wing', her views on education were 'like those of many communists...largely traditional', often more aligned to the Thatcherites of the staff room than to the soft left. However, it was the impact of Thatcherite cuts on education and the shifting professional status of teachers that saw her increasingly disillusioned. She found a way out of teaching as a writer.

The first iteration of *Waterloo Road*, ten series from 2006 to 2015, involves a revolving door of headteachers (seven, including the one on the roof). It is a school that would benefit from a large team of counsellors of the kind described above by Nick Luxmoore: to cultivate unity between the internal and external world of students and staff, the splits in the school staffroom and the split between the school and external authorities. Without those splits, of course, there would be no drama, so the scripts do not often call for the mediating presence of a school counsellor or any calm, reasonable adult.

The school's existence is under threat from the outset, with pressure first from the local education authority, then governors and then the encroaching peril of academy sponsorship or merger. Each head has their own 'hero's journey', threatened by assailants, illness, the appearance of past lives and present loves.

The series is an extended dramatisation of the tension between inclusion and standards, rendered in glorious melodramatic binary colours and echoed in personal relationships in the staffroom: Kim Campbell, art teacher and head of pastoral who champions relational approaches to student difficulties, is pitched against deputy head Andrew Treneman, private school import who promotes behaviourist approaches to discipline. (Reader, she marries him). Grantley Budgeon, old school disciplinarian, light on schemes of work, and as union rep, big on employment rights, who challenges every inexperienced idealist who makes an instant coffee in the staffroom. Steph Haydock, French teacher, colludes with the students' worst instincts in a bid for their approval and crosses anyone who upholds professional standards.

Most of the heads favour 'inclusion' and seek to get the 'powers that be' who repeatedly try to enforce higher academic standards, to understand the complex lives of their pupils. Jack Rimmer (Series One to Three) is a man 'from the inside' of Waterloo Road and has headship thrust upon him. He plays fast and loose with 'the system', uses his fists and risks his life to protect the school community. Having survived numerous physical assaults and attempted coups, he is eventually ousted in a rather banal fashion for financial impropriety when he misuses 'excellence in cities' funds, not for personal gain, but to give bursaries to academically able pupils of single-parent families, which he sees as a fast track to school improvement. His replacement Rachel Mason (Series Three to Five) advocates for vocational and skills-based study. She survives a fire, the bulldozing of the school by a former Chair of Governors, an attempt on her life by her former pimp and a takeover of the school by independent school head, Max Tyler. She eventually leaves after marrying the healthy schools coordinator. Her successor, Karen Fisher (Series Six to Seven) survives a personal vendetta from a member of the local education authority and is temporarily saved when the school community protests the attempt to oust her. Inexplicably she has been deposed anyway by the beginning of the next season; the school is now headed by Michael Byrne who, before his tenure begins, has survived a stabbing by a pupil (Series Seven to Eight). When, at the end of Series Seven, it is announced that the local authority is to shut Waterloo Road and distribute pupils in local schools, Michael comes up with a ruse to open a branch of Waterloo Road in Scotland, where Series Eight to Ten take place. (This bizarre plot twist coincides with the BBC's decision to extend its drama production further north than Greater Manchester.) After Michael prevents an attempt to turn Waterloo Road into a fee-paying school, he resigns. His successor, former English teacher Christine Mulgrew (Series Eight to Nine), struggles with alcohol addiction and the layers of deceit she creates to disguise it are finally uncovered when she crashes her car and is arrested. She steps down as head but later resumes her role as an English teacher. The final head of the first ten series is Vaughan Fitzgerald (Series Ten). Vaughan, who arrives at the school with his partner, new art teacher Allie, picks up the mantel of Waterloo Road heads before him, as community champion with a commitment to giving all pupils a chance. This stance is thrown into relief by his complex and distant relationship with the sons he left after his first marriage and brings him into conflict with the cynical deputy and former acting head, George Windsor.

In *Waterloo Road*'s early series, when McManus was still at the helm, threats of restructure, debates about status of the school as a comprehensive and what this stands for recur. Bringing these debates to life is the relationship between staff, and between staff and students. Permanently perplexed English teacher Tom Clarkson has the most inexplicably busy and complex love life, and an alarming fatality rate in his partners. 'Flirtatious' French teacher Steph Haydock would be at home in Jilly Cooper's *Wicked!* while all the heads have fraught relationships with present or former partners within the school. As in all serial television dramas, tragedy strikes with great regularity. In the first two series, a car accident kills a student, a teacher dies by suicide and another is stabbed and dies in the playground. The mortality rate remains high across all series and the school itself is nearly killed off or at least severely maimed several times: Luckily for Waterloo Road, as Rachel Mason, the head at the time of two near demolitions intones, 'this school is not just a building'. Characters role switches within the school: from pupil to school secretary, from 'troublesome parent' to stalwart of the school kitchen, from teenage tearaway to caretaker and eventually teacher. Teachers take on roles as informal foster parents and outsiders are allowed to integrate into the *Waterloo Road* cast and community. This is drama driven by heightened and unpredictable emotion. The school is not just populated by chronological adolescents but by emotionally adolescent adults, lurching from highs to lows, secretive but wanting to be seen.

The 'progressive' intent of the school is consistently tested by extreme acts of violence from within its community. The murder of Maxine Barlow (who is in the temporary care of French teacher, Steph) at the hands of fellow student Earl Kelly is just one beat in a regular rhythm of traumatic interludes. This storyline, about control and violence within a teenage relationship, is played out in the context of an exploration of teenage pregnancy, a theme of the 'Every Child Matters' agenda. The Netflix series *Adolescence*, which a decade and a half later addresses a similar outcome (the death of a girl at the hands of a male classmate), places the violence in the context of online misogyny and intergenerational trauma (*Adolescence*, 2025).

When Rachel Mason arrives at the murder scene, Steph blames the school's 'progressive' attitude for Earl's presence in the school and Maxine's death. Rachel blames herself and offers to resign (though is persuaded not to). Teacher/foster carer Steph and Maxine's best friend Janeece are both with Maxine when she dies. It is Janeece, a week after the tragedy, who approaches Steph with a desire to talk, acknowledging their need as witnesses to share their experience. Steph, who is drinking her way through her grief, brushes her away, defensively dismissing the value of talk and directs Janeece to the bereavement counsellor who has been drafted in support of the school in the aftermath of Maxine's murder. The tousle-haired counsellor, Charlotte, arrives at school on a motorbike, to be met with eye-rolling contempt by man of the common sense, Grantly Budgen who mutters 'trick cyclist' under his breath. Charlotte walks through the corridors of Waterloo Road dispensing emotional insight to pupils and staff. She is introduced to the audience on the last day of her tenure, a week after Maxine's death, and is thanked for putting the school back together again. As with everything in the *Waterloo Road* universe, this is fast work.

Waterloo Road brings extreme and rare occurrences from real life – including fatal violence perpetrated by students – and integrates them into the routine cycle of the school year. To some degree the dramatisation of otherwise apparently random acts of violence can bring narrative order and context and provide a fantasy of control in an arbitrary world. But *Waterloo Road* is a serial melodrama not a Shakespearean tragedy. Or comedy. It is an environment where change does not evolve, it is forced and sudden. The violence serves to move the plot and characters on so the cycle can begin again. It also, perhaps, gives space for the worst fears of the outcomes of comprehensive education to be realised. It feeds into the binary characterisation of the school (inclusion and permissiveness versus standards and safety). Violence, especially from pupils, temporarily tips the scales towards more restriction, only for another community champion to arrive as head for the case for inclusion to be made again.

By the end of the tenth series in 2015, Waterloo Road's playground may have been haunted by all the lost staff and students, but it had not succumbed to academisation. That battle was yet to come. In the next chapter I will revisit *Waterloo Road* in its second iteration and find that not only is another restructure underway but that the school has become 'trauma-informed' and that school counselling has achieved a new status.

Educating...

While *Waterloo Road* was representing the comprehensive school through the medium of serial drama with all the license that permits, Channel 4 commissioned a 'reality' series, set in a secondary school. *Educating Essex*, produced by TwoFour Productions and directed by David Clews, was screened across seven episodes from September 2011 (*Educating Essex*, 2011). I remember watching it with my partner and as it was the year before our eldest daughter was due to start secondary school, we were particularly attentive. As our last glimpses inside a comprehensive school were taken in those we attended, when discipline was instilled via force, the 'banta' between staff and students in this 2011 version was, to say the least, novel for both of us.

The series was filmed at what was the final year of Passmores Comprehensive, housed in its old, dilapidated building. The school converted to academy status and was relocated to a purpose-built building at the time *Educating Essex* was launched. While the story of its fictional counterpart Waterloo Road made much of its relationship with the local authority, possible takeovers and the pressure of maintaining educational standards in a complex setting, Passmore's story makes only passing reference to the educational context and no mention at all of its imminent restructure. Obviously, it would be politically difficult for an Ofsted Outstanding school to take potshots at the new Coalition government (although in their social and mainstream media commentary, the senior leaders Vic Goddard and Stephen Drew did not hold back).

Media reception of the opening episode was predictably divided. *The Telegraph* reeled at the 'bad language' used by teachers and students alike and disapproved of senior staff's childish pranks (*The Telegraph*, 2011). They wheeled out the spokesperson for the 'campaign for real education' to wonder if this school is outstanding, what's a bad one like? Sam Wollaston from *The Guardian,* on the other hand, is particularly taken with Deputy Head Mr Drew (Wollaston, 2011). He celebrates the 'unedited' quality of *Educating*, while noting the blurring of fact and fictional tropes: that 'one minute it's *Waterloo Road* (presumably when it's dealing with "issues") the next it's *Dead Poet's Society*' (when Drew is revelling in his role as History teacher and his relationship with his Year 11 class).

The narrative arc of this series, and to some degree of the four that follow in Yorkshire, London's East End, Cardiff and Greater Manchester, is the 'journey' towards five A*–C grades at GCSE (including Maths and English) for the Year 11 cohort. As staff repeatedly intone to their miscreant charges, these grades are the magic keys that open the door to 'the next stage'. This sounds as compelling as drying paint, but that 'journey' is brought to life vividly and movingly under Clews' direction.

Despite being dubbed 'fly on the wall' due to its use of 65 fixed head cameras located around the school building, the documentary is, in Bill Nichols' terms, 'participatory' (Nichols, 2024). Director David Clews, speaking off camera, introduces each episode, provides connecting narrative to introduce new 'characters' or key events and, with other members of the production team, conducts interviews with staff and pupils. Although these usually appear as monologues, the presence of the 'maker' is transparent.

Clews has won plaudits for other work, especially 2012's *The Family*, which used the same fixed rig, multiple camera technique with voiceover and evident collaboration with the production team to provide insight into the daily lives of British families. In an interview with the 'star' of *Educating*'s second series, Matthew Burton, Clews emphasised that his approach to the schools would not be 'expose' (unlike Panorama's *Best Days?*). Clews seems to like adolescents, but he likes teachers too and is not intent on creating a 'split' in the narrative between staff and students, or school and audience.

The adult stars of *Educating Essex* are its avuncular, physically imposing Head Vic Goddard and his more diminutive, eccentric and slightly bumptious Deputy, Stephen Drew. Goddard insists that no child will be left behind and that at all possible costs, no child will be excluded. Stephen Drew deals with rule enforcement and can be seen confiscating hoodies, fastening top buttons and removing coats. He is also a History teacher, where he switches persona from 'evil overlord' to 'quite fun…a legend'. Drew harks back to a time when 'the boundaries between adults and young people' were more secure and notes mournfully that many of the latter 'don't understand the word no'. But Goddard and Drew are committed to using exclusion as a last resort and creating a 'no fail organisation'. They reflect on how they might be perceived by viewers, including then education secretary Michael Gove, as 'spineless' and admit to how their broadly restorative approach to discipline can leave them powerless. 'Once they decide they don't care', Drew reflects 'you're stuffed'.

Each episode focuses on an individual or small group of students: those who pose behavioural challenges; those with friendship difficulties and those from disrupted family lives whose issues show up at school. The emotional pull of this series is towards Year 11 students Vinni and Ryan. Vinni arrived at Passmores in Year Seven, 'bright, sporty' and with his family intact. A cherubic primary school boy, Vinni had even appeared in adverts, and he was every inch the poster boy for Passmores. The breakup of his parents hit Vinni hard. His behaviour disintegrates, his previously buoyant relationships with teachers, especially his PE teacher and Head of Year Miss Conway, become strained. An argument with his mum ends so badly that he is placed into residential care, an event which moves Mr Goddard to tears. (If this had been a storyline from *Waterloo Road*, Vinni would have been placed in the temporary foster care of Miss Conway. But this is real life and there are no such quick solutions.) There is palpable hope that Vinni's story will provide the transformative 'moment' in the school year and the series, but his attendance and behaviour carry on in free fall. He isn't at school for shirt signing day nor the tearjerking final assembly, though his Year Seven face is projected in the photo montage on a white screen on the assembly hall stage. He is not allowed to attend prom (though he does arrive on his bike to watch the spectacle of sharp suits, big dresses and even bigger limousines), and at the grand finale of GCSE results day, he seems almost surprised when the reality of his presumably underwhelming results is revealed to him. The voiceover reassures us that Vinni accumulates good enough grades to move on to a plumbing course and that he was being reconciled with his family by the end of the series.

While much goodwill, many contact hours and evident concern are directed towards Vinni from staff up to and including Vic Goddard, I re-watched the series in discomfort as the then 15-year-old boy dramatically exits classrooms, turns his back, paces around the corridors, runs from the premises and asks to be placed in care. I wanted to ask of those kind, concerned and experienced adults, 'who is working with him and to what end?' The mantra of the staff is, understandably, about getting him to the safety of five GCSEs, A*–C, including Maths and English, to secure a future he has evidently lost faith in. Repeatedly, staff remind him that he is making 'poor choices', that he is not making the most of his potential. It is their job to do so, just as it is the social worker's job to find him a place of relative safety to live in. Goddard reflects on the increasing involvement that schools have in the lives of the families in their community and that in multi-disciplinary meetings it is the school who takes the lead. Schools are excellent problem-solving organisations who spend many hours with their charges. As this series reflects, they are also, despite the wealth and policies and protocols, necessarily places of improvisation, of adapting to circumstance, which is why they are so energising and exhausting to spend time in. When I imagined the role of a counsellor for a child like Vinni, it would be someone who would stop the reasoning and problem solving, while probably going on the move around the building with him. While counselling may not have been the gateway to his GCSEs (at this stage), a counsellor may have been the only person not already invested in a particular destination for Vinni, not bound to help him to his five A*–Cs nor even reconciliation with his mum. A counsellor could listen to his fury, or at least witness it, without feeling bound to tell him to make a 'better choice'. The end point of his 'school journey' may have been the same. But by spending time with someone who could tolerate his internal world as it was, because there was nothing at stake for them in witnessing it, Vinni may not been so split or have carried with him the baggage of shame that he evidently did this time round.

It is not easy to work therapeutically with a boy like Vinni, who would simultaneously charm and reject his counsellor as he does his teachers. But a counsellor who can withstand that attempt to split the outside world into those who leave and those who stay might give everyone else in school a chance to get him where they need him to be.

Ryan, another Year-11 boy, describes himself as having been variously diagnosed as 'autistic' and having 'Aspergers' (a diagnosis that is no longer offered and would now be called autistic spectrum disorder, or ASD). Ryan provides Series One with its tearjerking catharsis with his final assembly speech. He does not undergo a transformation. Ryan leaves as he arrives: cheerful, curious and warm. We watch as a support worker instructs him on looking after himself in the outside world and gain a little insight into his vulnerability. But he has a good relationship with his supportive mum, regards the school as a family and adores his headteacher. He is successful in his GCSEs. As this series reminds us with respect to many students, the split is in the world around him not in Ryan. Ryan is perfectly fine as he is.

Series Two, *Educating Yorkshire*, produces the iconic moment of transformation that the series seems to set us up to expect. Musharaf Asghar (Mushy) nearly left Thornhill Community Academy in his first year. He had had a stammer since the age of five and it got worse when he started high school. He was bullied. Thanks to the support of the pastoral team, Mrs Marsden and Mrs Crowther, he stayed, made friends and even made it to the heights of Year 11 prefect (though he temporarily lost this status for a Facebook misdemeanour). We meet him as he is preparing for his GCSE English exam, which includes an oral presentation. Mushy's magical agent is English teacher, Mr Burton. It is Mr Burton, not Mr Drew, who dreams of Dead Poets' Society levels of inspiration. He stands on desks, jokes with his class and looks by turns as if he might explode with the pressure of getting these kids to the right side of the C/D border and with the pleasure of getting them to experience the creative joy of language.

In an interview with a producer, Mushy describes, via his laptop screen, the split between his internal voice and the sounds he fails to make. His English grade is hanging in the balance. He has evidently had access to speech therapy as Mr Burton phones his therapist to ask for advice. But the arc of this narrative is the revelation of Mr Burton's improvised technique, derived from a film about a stammering monarch, *The King's Speech*, and the technique that freed his voice. In a one-to-one session, Mr Burton produces his mobile phone and asks Mushy to listen to some of the teacher's 'awful' music while reading Margaret Atwood's poem, 'The Moment'. The words, at first faltering, start to come in a staccato but steady rhythm. It is television magic and a 'teaching moment' that is built on trust, a teacher who is trying things out to enlighten the pupil in front of him and an outcome with benefits which go beyond the required C grade (though Mushy does achieve that). In the final assembly, Mushy is ushered to the front of the hall by the wonderfully lachrymose Mrs Marsden (a woman who I'd want to be on my children's side). She holds her breath while Mushy dons his headphones. At first, Mushy struggles to get the sounds out but as his words of reflection and thanks emerge with increasing fluency, Mrs Marsden bursts into tears. Year 11 collapse in an emotionally exhausted heap along with the television audience.

In *Educating the East End* (2014) the 'star teacher' of Frederick Bremer School in Walthamstow is a School Direct trainee English teacher Mr Bispham. We watch as he falls foul of perceived indiscretions with two students, Tawny and Acacia. He accidentally discloses that Tawny is auditioning for a place at the Brits school, and encourages a class to discuss the impact of terminal illness in the presence of Acacia who is scared that her mum is about to die. Both 'ruptures' are repaired, the first more easily than the second. The head, Mrs Smith, observes the fallout from the incident with Acacia. Speaking to camera, she says that while Acacia is desperately worried about her mum, she doesn't want to speak to a counsellor, to 'go deep', but needs a 'pragmatic' person to help her navigate her academic life and allow her to make the odd phone call. Mr Bispham's panic when he realises why Acacia is crying and Mrs Smith's empathic but bustling resolution to get her some practical help is symptomatic of the way distress is 'managed' in busy environments like secondary schools. In the urgency to help, staff can try to find 'solutions' before really allowing students to feel much at all. Resilience does not arise from burying difficult emotions but from having them heard and 'contained'. When distress is felt in the presence of another who can bear it, it becomes more tolerable for the sufferer. Such an experience is rarer than we might think.

All seasons of the *Educating* series emphasise the revolving door of school life, where year groups, or 'cohorts' go on 'journeys' (heroic or otherwise), experience change and move on. Vic Goddard reflects on his capacity to attach and detach from a year group as they enter and eventually leave his care: 'okay, bye – next!'. The momentum of school life is towards the moment that the student leaves. The momentum of my work is towards the ending, although there are less defined pathways towards it and the ending is defined, in Rogerian terms, by internal not external loci of evaluation. Though teachers do not have the same role as counsellors, it is crucial in schools that not every interaction is framed through the end point of attainment and that there are adults who can bear and encourage the expression of distress when adolescents cannot bear it themselves.

Ackley Bridge

Channel 4's *Ackley Bridge* was launched in 2017 (*Ackley Bridge*, 2017–22). It was created by Ayub Khan-Din, Kevin Erlis and Malcom Campbell, whose previous credits had included the play *East is East* (1996) about a dual-heritage, working-class family in Salford and *Shameless* (2011–21), a comedy series about a chaotic white working-class family living on the fictional Chatsworth Estate in Manchester. *Ackley Bridge* was welcomed as Channel 4's return to dramatic form, although *The Telegraph* dubbed it '*Grange Hill* with a mobile phone and a northern accent' (Hogan, 2017). Primary headteacher Chris Dyson, writing for the *TES Magazine*, was disappointed that the opening episodes would not inspire a future generation of teachers and did not represent the reality of schools as he knew them (Dyson, 2017). The demand for school stories to hold an accurate mirror to the sector does not diminish.

The first three series of *Ackley Bridge* were centred around the friendship of Missy Booth and Nasreen Paracha, two 17-year-old girls, born on the same day and living next to each other in a Yorkshire mill town, twins in all but DNA. It was filmed in Halifax and other Yorkshire locations. Several episodes make use of 'breaking the fourth wall' conventions to disrupt the serial drama convention of realism, as Nas and Missy speak directly to the camera and other characters appear in freeze-frame as the girls move around them. Such devices diminished as the series went on. The last two series moved into an earlier time slot and were pitched at younger audiences.

We join Missy and Nas one evening as they sit on a sofa on top of a skip in an alleyway between rows of terraced houses and look down on the town. The alleyway is a recurrent feature in representations of lives in working-class housing, as in stories like *Billy Elliot*, which features Billy running, skipping and dancing away from the heaviness of his grieving household down the back alleys of his north-eastern mining town, or in BBC's recent *What It's Like for a Girl*, with Byron changing his clothing and escaping through the alley of his Nottinghamshire home from his father's bigotry. It is the urban equivalent of the Shakespearean woods, a place of play and transformation with occasional intrusions from reality. The skip in the alley is where Missy and Nas dream and collude away from others in their shared lives.

Missy lives with her nan Julie and younger sister Hayley, while her mum Simone, who struggles with addiction, comes and goes; Nas lives next door with her mum Kaneez, granny, sister Razia and brother Saleem. Her father Iqbal lives a dual life, ostensibly spending time in Pakistan while he has a second family in Bradford. We join the school as the Head Mrs Carter is rehearsing her speech to the new cohort of the merged academy Ackley Bridge College, formed from a school for the Muslim population and another for the white working-class community. These communities, Mrs Carter says, have been segregated and split, and promises that the new academy will bring them together.

The first series belies the idea of the split communities in the long-lasting 'organic' relationship between the Booths and the Parachas but demonstrates the pitfalls of enforced community in an organisational setting, the new academy school. The academy has a sponsor, Sadiq Nawaz, the affluent owner of a local mattress company whose children, twins Alya and Riz, are also to attend Ackley Bridge. In Jilly Cooper style, the merger has already been secured by a brief affair between the head (who is married to PE teacher Steve Bell) and the sponsor. When Nawaz's business founders and he can no longer afford to sponsor the school, the management of Ackley Bridge is taken over by the Valley Trust. The school acquires new pupils but more problematic staff who the Trust was struggling to manage. Instead of community harmony, more splits emerge.

In the classroom, there are tensions in Year 11 about whose school Ackley Bridge is. The tensions are mainly stirred by 'troubled' Jordan Wilson, who lives with his older brother Corey and bullying dad Kevin. Jordan is also the father of a baby with his ex-girlfriend Candice, a member of a far-right family. Jordan is deliberately provocative and hangs a set of spoof 'school rules', offensive to the Muslim students, in the school precinct. He uses the school's tannoy to make a speech about the superficiality of the merger and the hopelessness of life in Ackley Bridge. Jordan knows how to expose the tensions that the school wants to brush over. He is a boy bullied by his father who trusts no one, provokes and escalates and refuses containment.

A discussion about Jordan between Head Mandy, Steve and the school sponsor Sadiq reveals the new lines of authority in the academy, when the sponsor calls for the boy's exclusion. As in *Waterloo Road*, the issue of who oversees the school and who is in charge in the classrooms is a recurrent theme.

English teacher Emma Keane is a younger version of *Waterloo Road*'s Steph Haydock and is liberal to the point of collusive. She arrives for the first day of term in a taxi, fresh from her summer holiday and sporting flipflops. When she draws up a contract with her English class, she agrees with her students that texts that do not speak to their reality will be binned. Head Mandy, who observes the lesson, rails at this misplaced liberalism, and wants Emma to hit the students with 'facts': that one in three in the town fails GCSE English and that studying the prescribed curriculum is their key to escape. Noone mentions that somewhere between these poles of literature as a mirror to one's own identity and a utilitarian passport to academic success is literature as imaginative engagement with difference, with history, with subjectivity and the transformative power of language.

The engaging centre of this academy drama is the relationship between Missy and Nasreen. Missy has spent her life caretaking her family and consequently underperforms academically and must retake Year 11. Best friend Nas is an academic highflier with her sights set on a course in medicine at Oxford University. Alya, the socially powerful daughter of the school sponsor, freezes Missy out, and encourages Nas to reject her, which, temporarily, she does as she tries to conform with Alya's group. Tensions between Missy and Nas frequently erupt into conflict, as Nas pulls away from Ackley Bridge and Missy fears being left behind. But there are parts of both girls which keep them together. Missy is a dreamer, 'mystic Missy' who champions Nas's dreams when she loses faith in them (epitomised in a fantasy sequence flash mob in Oxford when Missy sings 'Tomorrow' from the musical *Annie* with a chorus of passers-by, to entice Nas back to her University interview). Nas's 'journey' towards Oxford reworks the working-class 'scholarship story', in which the leaver in Hoggart's words is 'uprooted and anxious' and the left behind are unchanging (Hoggart, 1957). In her own words, Nas is a working-class, northern 'brown lesbian', multiply marginalised, clever and ambitious. Nas fears Missy changing as much as Missy worries about losing Nas. As her mum Kaneez points out to Nas, 'you want your life to change but no one else's. You want our lives to stay the same'. But hers and Missy's story reveals that the emotional loss of change is not one-directional, that the 'left behind' change as much as the leaver.

In a plotline that has echoes of *Waterloo Road*, tragedy strikes. Missy and Nas sit on the sofa on the skip and reconcile from a fight about holding one another back. Nas commits to go to Oxford and Missy decides she will join the fairground as 'mystic Missy'. Sadly, what Missy doesn't see coming is a speeding car which knocks both girls to the ground. Subsequent episodes play with audience expectations about the girls' survival. After initial relief that they both emerge with only concussion and broken bones, we see Missy 'wake up' at home to find her nan in the living room. As her nan had died in the first series, it becomes clear that Missy too is dead. Nas finds her lifeless body in bed and turns her grief into a furious search for vengeance on the driver. The series allows the impact of Missy's death, the grief of her family and friends and the repercussions of an Asian driver being responsible for the death of a white working-class girl to play out in several ways and racial tensions resurface in the school and the community.

Missy and Nas's status as friends whose relationship transcends boundaries is echoed in the scene settings following Missy's death. The school attempts reconciliation by walking the warring parties through a snow-covered forest, the archetypal transitional place in storytelling. Missy's funeral procession begins in the dreamers' alleyway, and the send-off ends with a nighttime lantern release from the out-of-bounds school playground.

For the rest of the third series, Nas's grief undercuts her ambition and her enthusiasm for Oxford waxes and wanes. An imagined conversation with Missy (on the sofa on the skip in the alley) restores her hope and we see Nas integrate Missy's faith in the future. When her friend Naveed, who wants to go to drama school and become a comedian, performs a dark and uncomfortable comedy routine confronting the difficult issues of Pakistani heritage, Nas reminds him that what their Pakistani community also have in common is 'ambition'. Leaving Ackley Bridge, she comes to understand, is an extension rather than a betrayal of the values of their immigrant families. Kaneez illustrates this after Nasreen misses the required grade for her medical course. She secretly drives to Oxford to make a case for her daughter's acceptance, and, miraculously, succeeds.

Before Nas sets off for her new life, she scatters Missy's ashes on the moors, starting a new life for both. On the way to the train station, Nas and Kaneez pass the skip, which is finally being removed from the alleyway, having served its purpose for the dreaming girls who have both moved on. At the station, Kaneez gives Nas water and snacks and her permission not to look back. As Kaneez walks away, she raises her hand in goodbye and does not look back either. Kaneez is the container for her daughter's fears and, in Missy's absence, is also the holder of her dreams.

These stories show us school life going on alongside and sometimes despite structural change. Academy status is not spoken of in *Educating…* but is treated with suspicion if not derision in *Waterloo Road* and *Ackley Bridge* as a sticking plaster over deeper splits. The following chapter foregrounds those splits, and the voices which demand recognition of their identity, their history and in some cases the damage wrought by the education system on its charges.

References

Ackley Bridge (2017–2022) [TV Series], Channel 4.

Adolescence (2025) [TV Series], Netflix.

Brighouse, T. and Waters, M. (2021) *About Our Schools: Improving on Previous Best*, Carmarthen: Crown House Publishing.

Dyson, C. (2017) '"Under-prepared and not ready to inspire": a headteacher's review of Channel 4 TV show *Ackley Bridge*', *TES Magazine.*

Educating Essex (2011) [TV Series], Channel 4, TwoFour.

Educating the East End (2014) [TV Series], Channel 4, TwoFour.

Educating Yorkshire (2013) [TV Series], Channel 4, TwoFour.

Fox, C.L. and Butler, I. (2009) 'Evaluating the effectiveness of a school-based counselling service in the UK', *British Journal of Guidance Counselling*, 37(2), pp.95–106.

Hansard (2002) 'School counselling services', *Volume 384, debated on Thursday,* 25 April.

Hogan, M. (2017) 'Ackley Bridge episode one has promise but is yet to make the grade', *The Telegraph*, 7 June.

Hoggart, R. (1957) *The Uses of Literacy*, Harmondsworth: Penguin.

Klein, M. (1946) 'Notes on some Schizoid mechanisms', *The International Journal of Psychoanalysis*, 27, pp.99–110.

Luxmoore, N. (2014) *School Counsellors Working with Young People and Staff: A Whole School Approach*, London: Jessica Kingsley Publishers.

Nichols, B. (2024) *Introduction to Documentary*, 4th edn., Bloomington: Indiana University Press.

Phillips, N. (2016) 'Profile: Toby Young, founder and CEO, West London free school', *Schools Week*, 6 May.

The Telegraph (2011) 'Educating Essex: teachers call students 'scumbags' at outstanding school', 23 September.

Waterloo Road (2006–15) [TV Series], BBC.

Wilby, P. (2009) 'Melodrama class', *The Guardian*, 3 March.

Wollaston, S. (2011) 'TV review: *Educating Essex*', *The Guardian*, 22 September.

9

INDIVIDUATION, TRAUMA AND IDENTITY

Stories of resistance and school utopias

Andy arrived in teaching via his talent for Maths and a PGCE. The latter gave him the skill to deliver the former but didn't provide much information about the teenage recipients of his newfound ability. In 2002 he was appointed as Deputy Head to a South Manchester School, in an area where affluence and poverty are just streets apart. The school was a mixed comprehensive but was attended mainly by boys and had a lukewarm reputation in the community. The school had a rebuild, a rebrand and appointed another Deputy to develop an arts curriculum (a ruse to attract more girls) and which led to the school's designation as a specialist school for the Performing Arts. The designation and the money that went with it no longer stand, but its legacy is there in the ongoing arts-rich curriculum, including the offer of music, dance and drama to GCSE, long after many state secondary schools have cut arts subjects from their curricula. The school is now a high performing part of a multiacademy trust with Andy at the helm. It is also, he says, the most challenging school in the trust, not because of the breadth of ethnicities and cultures of its students but because of the growing gulf between the most affluent and the poorest students.

Andy is wary of school counsellors, frustrated by the traditional model of one-to-one confidentiality, which means they are unaccountable on measures for attainment, attendance and behaviour. For Andy, change comes from the curriculum. He has weathered the huge tome that was New Labour's National Curriculum and the slashed Gove version, which ostensibly offered schools more freedoms but was accompanied by outcome measures which

DOI: 10.4324/9781003715122-14

undermined any real choice. In Andy's account, 2010 was the pinnacle of the inclusive curriculum, when students in the school he then led, could choose from 46 subjects via 'pathways' that suited different aptitudes. His hopes for the current administration's curriculum review are the opportunity to rebuild some of that variety, a curriculum that is vocational and knowledge-rich with assessment methods to suit a range of students.

Andy doesn't like stories about secondary schools as they don't represent things as they are. Though he does have a soft spot for *Teachers*, as the donkey walking the corridor sums up how he feels about working in schools. Anything can and does happen.

Where does the school counselling tradition and frameworks about adolescent development fit into schools like the one Andy describes? The schools which succeed by the measures on which they're asked to succeed but which are still faced with young people whose challenges are describable but not quantifiable? Andy was eloquent on the difficulty of supporting children and their families in a city which has lost many of its partnerships and where the social infrastructure has gone online. His frustration with the demands on secondary schools to stand in for reduced services spills over into his wish that solutions and support would be found in the early and primary years. For instance, he suggests that the problems with attendance in some areas of the city could be solved by more work with families whose children are moving between multiple schools at primary level and find it hard to settle into one secondary school.

It is easy to come away from such a conversation with an experienced and dedicated educator feeling that an interest in the inner lives of teenagers is an esoteric luxury, irrelevant to the lessons in 'survival' that Andy mentions are a priority in relation to pupils and trainee teachers. It's how I often felt in governors' meetings when the scale of the tasks of secondary schools was laid bare and I had the audacity to ask for more. I recognise and empathise with the slightly weary blankness that descends upon school leaders when well meaning outsiders talk of 'wellbeing' initiatives, sensory rooms and time out passes. The students I talk to and who are the beneficiaries of such measures express that weariness too, aware as they are that supportive 'interventions' do not take away the pressures of an attainment-focused system.

Wellbeing and the trauma-informed school

Financial restriction and the large populations of some secondary schools means that the direction is towards 'whole school' measures rather than services dedicated to a smaller number of students. Books like those by Clare Erasmus, in which she uses her long experience in secondary schools to provide a do-it-yourself 'whole school' approach to staff and student wellbeing, or Jenny Hulme on anti-bullying initiatives are pragmatic guides to such approaches (Erasmus, 2019; Hulme, 2015).

Safe spaces, mentors, assembly power-points, student voice, focus groups and mindfulness apps are wonderful things if they are the responsibility of someone in the school, preferably someone senior, who is invested in them. All too often they fall short because they are too fleeting to reach the depths of individual difficulty and too onerous for staff with multiple responsibilities to manage.

One of the problems with 'wellbeing' initiatives is the looseness of the term and their potential to lose momentum when other more pressing and tangible demands (Maths and English Grade 4) appear. Wellbeing activity becomes a sort of ill-defined soup, into which go things as diverse as bake sales and trauma therapy. The term 'trauma-informed' is at risk of being the sort of thing that schools believe they are, to the extent that they know that some students have difficult life experiences and that they are affected by them. But how much further than that does being trauma-informed go?

The work of psychologist and psychotherapist Margot Sunderland, who co-directs the organisation 'Trauma Informed Schools UK', Lisa Cherry, Director of 'Trauma Informed Consultancy Services' and Betsy de Thierry, Director of 'Trauma Recovery Global', is aimed at helping organisations to understand that being 'trauma-informed' goes deeper than spotting trauma. They have each produced resources and training for schools who want to become trauma responsive as well as trauma-informed. A trauma-responsive culture starts with what Dan Hughes coined as PACE (playfulness, acceptance, curiosity and empathy), a way of being in relationships throughout the school as well as in a behaviour or safeguarding policy. Schools need to have the capacity to recognise when a student needs more intensive work either within or outside of school (Hughes, 2007).

Trauma is not, of course, a new term but it has taken on a new level of familiarity, which risks it being misunderstood. Freud and his contemporaries developed ideas of 'hysterical trauma', a response to sexual abuse which was unrepresentable in language. In this model, a period of latency, where the trauma would lay dormant, would be followed by an event which triggered the memory of the original traumatising event. Freud talks of defences including dissociation, splitting and repetition compulsion, which still inform psychological approaches to trauma, as does the understanding that traumatic memory lacks narrative coherence. It is hard if not impossible to tell the story of trauma.

As Bessel Van der Kolk has told us, the modern understanding of trauma emerged in 1980, when a group of Vietnam veterans and the psychoanalysts who had been treating them for a variety of symptoms since their return from service, successfully lobbied the American Psychiatric Association to create a new diagnosis: PTSD, Post Traumatic Stress Disorder (Van der Kolk, 2015). PTSD was defined in the *Diagnostic and Statistical Manual of Mental Disorders* in 1980 as arising from 'a psychologically distressing event outside the range of usual human experience' accompanied by 'intense fear, terror, and helplessness' (American Psychiatric Association, 1980). From this point, there was funding for new research and attempts to find novel treatments. The advent of brain imaging tools in the 1990s allowed a deeper understanding of the impact of trauma on the brain: researchers saw activation in the limbic system, particularly the brain's alarm system, the amygdala, the triggering of 'stress hormones and nerve impulses to drive up blood pressure, heart rate and oxygen intake' and a decrease in the Broca's area, one of the brain's speech centres, which explains why trauma takes away linguistic expression (van der Kolk, pp.42–3). Trauma-focused therapy like Eye Movement, Desensitisation and Reprocessing (EMDR), which uses bi-lateral stimulation to mimic the process of REM sleep, and polyvagal approaches, which focus on toning the vagus nerve and nervous system, work by letting the body know that the danger of the traumatic event is passed (Porges, 2011; Shapiro, 2018).

Trauma-informed therapies for children often focus on developmental trauma: ruptures to the 'normal' processes of development, traumatic events or the absence of nurturing relationships that put children into a defensive state. A trauma-informed *and* -responsive environment therefore must pay attention to and relieve a traumatised body. Spend a day in a secondary school to understand how antithetical such environments are to the ideals of trauma recovery.

If we allow the term 'trauma' to become as hollow as 'wellbeing', we risk losing our attention to the humanity of the young people we work with. When Andy talks of teaching students and trainees to 'survive' in the school environment, he is invoking the language of trauma and acknowledging the helplessness of schools to alleviate the distress that some students and staff bring to schools. This goes well beyond the 'stress' induced by a high stakes examination system. Gordon Brown has recently highlighted the levels of poverty in which increasing numbers of children and adolescents live, a number which has grown since the austerity years of the Coalition and Conservative governments. These conditions are, by anybody's assessment, traumatising and make success in school both essential and difficult to achieve for such students (Brown, 2025).

'The school system' still colludes in the long history of trauma by its direct (legislated) or indirect reproduction of cultural norms which marginalise or stigmatise ways of being and pathologise aspects of development. School stories have long dramatised this history of trauma through proscriptions on sexualised, gendered and racialised bodies. In recent years, many school stories – *Blue Jean, Butterfly*, *Small Axe* 'Education' and *Adolescence* for instance – have told the stories of those proscriptions and their consequences.

Clause 28 and RSE 2026

I have argued that adolescent 'development' receives scant attention in secondary school policy, but it does make an appearance in England in Personal, Social, Health and Economic (PSHE) education and the recently mandated, and more recently reviewed, Relationships and Sex Education (RSE) curriculum (Df E, 2025). PSHE has been shadowing secondary schools since the 1990s but only RSE is statutory and only since 2020. The 'driver' for the delivery of PSHE (the thing that makes schools engage with it) is the Office for Standards in Education Framework, in which matters of development are bracketed loosely under 'behaviour and attitudes' and 'personal development'. Behaviour must be good; attitudes must be positive. Personal development must involve 'character' (formation?), 'resilience', citizenship and the adoption of British values, which includes respect for the protected characteristics named in the 2010 Equalities Act. The recent review of the Relationship and Sex advice was in part prompted by arguments about the safety of children in the context of what they are taught about 'gender'. A consultation generated a range of opinions, including a document by the right-wing think tank, Policy Exchange. In a document called *Asleep at the Wheel*, the authors cite the dangers of schools 'disregarding' safeguarding guidance by teaching (and implicitly 'promoting') the 'contested idea of gender identity' (Policy Exchange, 2023). For Policy Exchange, biological sex is scientifically real and binary while gender identity is a dangerous, relativist, cultural myth. The recent reassertion of the Equalities Act, that 'woman' is defined by biological sex and the subsequent guidance for single-sex organisations have heightened what has been a fractious debate. The 2025 iteration of the RSE guidance (Df E, 2025), to be implemented from September 2026, asserts that pupils should be taught 'that people have legal rights by virtue of their biological sex which are different from the rights of those of the opposite sex with the protected characteristic of gender reassignment' (p.26). Pupils are to be taught that people 'with the protected characteristic of gender reassignment' should be treated with respect and dignity, but schools should 'not teach as fact that all people have a gender identity' (p.36).

The guidance is a reassertion of a preexisting legal position, and it marks a shift from the practice of schools informally supporting 'social transition' or at least complicates it. A period of expansion of ideas about gender that seemed to emerge into popular culture in the 2010s (alongside the 'body positivity' movement which celebrated and promoted the representation of all body abilities, shapes and sizes) has constricted again (along with the return of body ideals of thinness, underpinned by weight loss drugs).

Ideas about sex, gender and sexuality and the relationship between mind and body during adolescence are as culturally and historically defined as ideas about teenagers' suitability for economic activity or their right to vote. Because we can 'see' bodies, we assume we can read them, but they are in many ways as opaque as the minds we concede it takes time and attention to understand. The invocation of biological fixity is rarely used to support increasing freedom. For instance, the 1963 Newsom Report, which sought to collapse the distinction between the 'academic' and 'vocational' content in the secondary modern curriculum and pave the way for comprehensive schooling, was quite content to assert that industrial skills were for boys and that housecraft was for girls, as the latter 'know that whether they marry early or not, they are likely to find themselves running a home' (CACE, 1963, p.135). What appears natural here is culturally prescribed.

Developmental theory includes a variety of ways to understand the 'emergence' of the sexual and the gendered self: from the ideas of the 'natural' stress and conflicts and identity crises of adolescent sexuality in the work of Freud, Blos and Erikson (which are sometimes referred to as 'essentialist' theories) to the 'social constructivist' theories which emphasise the linguistic and culturally variable expressions of adolescent development, including sexual and gendered development (Moore and Rosenthal, 2006). On sex and gender, the work of Judith Butler, for instance, is a social constructivist intervention into the debate (Butler, 1990, 1993, 2024).

Blue Jean

A number of school-based dramas, made between 2018 and 2023, foreground adolescent sex, sexuality and gender identity as both vulnerable aspects of development, to be protected, boundaried and safeguarded (a view that is perhaps essentialist in its foundations) and, from a more constructivist position, as unfolding, fluid parts of the developing self, to be celebrated and nurtured. There have been many moments when potential 'harms' to children's development as sexual and gendered beings have led to state intervention, framed in terms of moral wellbeing. One such moment came in 1988, to which I referred in Chapter 5, when the Conservative government imposed a ruling on local education authorities, known as Clause 28, which prohibited the 'promotion' of homosexuality in schools. This legislation is the backdrop for the 2022 film *Blue Jean*, the directorial debut of its writer and producer Georgia Oakley (*Blue Jean*, 2022). In a BFI interview, Oakley talks about her conversations with lesbian teachers and their experiences of Clause 28 (BF I, 2023). She wanted to explore internalised homophobia and 'performative selves', the shifts in our expression of self in different settings and relationships.

The film is set in Tyneside in 1988 (a location chosen because of Oakley's familiarity with the place and because it was not, in the 1980s, a place of widespread queer community). The action is punctuated by radio and television reports of Conservative political commentary about the legislation and about the protests against it. We watch as Jean Newman, a popular PE teacher in a comprehensive school, grows more anxious with each report. Jean is in a relationship with Viv. While Viv refuses to be 'closeted' by the political climate, Jean is anxiously private about their relationship. She keeps it from her family and her colleagues at school and becomes increasingly fearful as conversations in the staffroom start to echo the moral panic about gay teachers in schools.

When a new girl, 15-year-old Lois, joins the school, Jean spots her sporting prowess and encourages her to join the netball team, which provokes the ire of star player Siobhan. Jean sees Lois in a gay bar that she frequents with Viv and their friends and fears that Lois will disclose her sexuality at school. As the political commentary becomes more shrill, Jean becomes more anxious and ashamed, now internalising a fear of being seen as a sexual predator. When Siobhan confects a story about Lois 'attacking' her in the school showers, Jean colludes with Siobhan's story and Lois is suspended from school. Viv argues that it is Jean's responsibility to be open with Lois, with her family and with the school, and not to repeat the damage that was wrought upon them by a homophobic society. Jean introduces Lois to the circle of friends she shares with Viv who tell her about the 'bog fund', a pot of money available to 'every poor lesbian in the Northeast'. Jean is emboldened by Lois, who doesn't carry the shame of the older woman, and is able to 'come out' to her family. She is last seen arriving at school with a sense of purpose that isn't revealed at the story's end.

Butterfly

Jean's story is both a dramatisation of a moment in history (a moment of which the writer and director Oakley admits she hadn't been aware, despite being at school while the legislation was in place) and an intervention in the early 2020s debate around safeguarding and sex and relationship advice in schools. The Policy Exchange document that informs the recent updates bemoans the acceptance of social transitioning, the self-determination of pronouns, forenames and codes of dress which may not be consistent with the gender assigned at birth. In a sign of how quickly social attitudes and cultural norms shift, it was only in 2017 that ITV broadcast a well-received three-part dramatisation of an 11-year-old child's transition story, *Butterfly* (*Butterfly*, 2017). The child's secondary school features as a crucial part of the process; it is the place where she faces taunts and acceptance from peers, where staff liaise with her family about the practicalities of social transition, adopting new pronouns, a new name and a new mode of dress. (It also happens to have been filmed in the school my own children attended.)

In 1996, the drama's creator Tony Marchant had written *Different for Girls*, a film about a transgender woman; he made other films about neurodivergence and adoption. *Butterfly* is the story of 11-year-old Max, assigned male at birth but wanting to live as a girl, Maxine. Marchant sought advice from the trans charity 'Mermaids' (which is also represented in an episode of *Butterfly*) and the individuals and families who used their service, to create a story which captured the potential fallout for a family with different perspectives on transition. In an interview with *The Huffpost*, Marchant said he wanted to counter some of the aggressive 'hysteria' about trans people coming from radical feminism and the right, which he saw as reminiscent of the discourse around Clause 28 (Marchant, 2018).

Maxine's parents Vicky and Stephen are separated and relate differently to Maxine's gender expression. Vicky is scared but supportive, Stephen is scared and hostile. While Vicky is increasingly attentive to Maxine's needs, Stephen vows to 'fix' his child by returning to the family home, which only exacerbates the tensions. When Maxine starts high school, dressed in a 'boy's' uniform, she wets herself rather than use the male toilets and is subjected to homophobic bullying. With the encouragement of her older sister, Maxine adopts a girls' uniform and, with guidance from Mermaids, conversations ensue between her parents and the broadly supportive school head about the implications of social and biological transition: 'it's not like getting a different coloured pencil case or playing netball' she warns Maxine. The place of the school in Maxine's narrative is a benign if uncertain interlocutor between the parents and the questioning world. Maxine is initially jeered at by school peers, but is befriended by Molly, a girl with an eating disorder. Molly encourages Maxine to show the scars of her self-harm as she reveals hers. The scars are the all-too-common signs of adolescents trying to soothe their internal distress by inflicting physical pain upon their bodies (Inckle, 2017).

As Maxine's revulsion from her changing body intensifies and her desperation to match her physical being to her felt sense of gender increases, the family are referred to a gender clinic. Their hope for puberty blockers is swapped for a reality of psychological intervention and encouragement to Maxine to 'change the way you think'. Psychological services are represented as processes of assessment rather than therapy for Maxine and her family. Eventually, Vicky engages the support of an American clinic which offers the puberty blocking treatment (medication which suppresses the release of the hormones which promote biological changes in puberty), which is initially denied to Maxine in the UK. The final episode plays out the various competing 'safeguarding' concerns surrounding Maxine, as her voice recedes from her story and the adults who are trying in various ways to protect her go to war. The denouement, however, sees her parents united in their consent for Maxine to receive puberty blockers in the UK. The supply of puberty blockers to children and young people under the age of 18 was indefinitely banned by the UK government in December 2024, after the Cass Review of April that year recommended puberty blockers be subject to further medical trials (Cass, 2024).

The critical reception of *Butterfly* was largely positive, welcoming its sympathetic representation of gender dysphoria and the attitudes of Maxine's family, school and peers towards her transition, though the drama's perceived didacticism, its representation of Maxine's suicide attempt and its apparent denigration of 'masculine men' provoked the ire of some commentators (Mangan, 2018; Pearson, 2018; Stanley, 2018).

Sex Education and *Heartstopper*

Butterfly addresses adolescent gender dysphoria and the familial and social response in the tradition of realist narrative, specific in time and recognisable in place. *Sex Education,* a Channel 4 school drama which was created by Laurie Nunn and ran for four series from 2019 to 2023, adopted a form which led to a confused initial reception (*Sex Education*, 2019–23). *The Independent's* review of the opening series wants to place it in the social realist tradition associated with state school stories and balks at its simultaneous contemporaneity and its 'retro' look, including its use of 'brick' phones (Power, 2019). *Sex Education* was filmed in Wales but its location in the story is vague, the characters have a range of English accents and the 'look' of the schools (Moordale High in Series One to Three and, in the final series, Cavendish Sixth Form) draws more on an American or Australian high school tradition than an English one. *GQ Magazine* noted it evoked 'a kind of pop cultural no-man's-land, where characters with English accents wear varsity jackets and hang outside yellow lockers, without uniforms, in between classes', an 'aesthetic' which is more comic book than American (Pometsey, 2020). Nor are the stories grounded in contemporary education policy: Moordale is apparently a state school but its closure at the end of Series Three comes about because of the withdrawal of financial investors. Reality only intrudes when Jean Milford, the sex therapist mother of the protagonist Otis, is found to be talking to the students about matters beyond the prescribed sex and relationship curriculum and is removed from her role as temporary school counsellor.

The four series of *Sex Education* can be seen an alternative to the official sex education curriculum. It seeks to represent young people back to themselves as sexual beings and 'promote' pleasurable, consensual relationships and self-expression. The narrative device holding together the plethora of sexual experiences is the sex therapy clinic set up by Otis and Maeve in a disused school toilet. Originally a ruse by Otis to use his mother Jean's expertise to impress Maeve, the clinic becomes a source of guidance and acceptance from within the adolescent peer group.

Despite its overall 'positivity', sex is not unproblematic in *Sex Education.* There are plotlines about consent and assault, desire is at times unrequited, and relationships end messily. The series critiques the social pressure to 'lose your virginity'. However, one form of consensual expression of sexuality or gender is not privileged over another. Cal Bowman is non-binary and takes testosterone to transition, a process which is represented as complex, but which is supported by family and peers. When Series Four shifts from Moordale to Cavendish College, a progressive utopia of a sixth form, a trans couple, Roman and Abbi, join the preexisting cohort of Otis, Eric, Aimee and Maeve as central characters.

Second individuation and sexual development

Otis's adolescent story is quite conventional and can be read as a sexual bildungsroman, fulfilled through a process of 'individuation'. Individuation underpins much theory of adolescent development but was a term used particularly by Austrian American paediatric psychiatrist and psychoanalyst, Margaret Mahler (Mahler, 1963). Mahler describes a stage of infant self-focus and oblivion to the external world. This develops into a symbiosis with the mother, who is a source of need but is not yet external to the infant psyche, before a formative sense of separation from the mother and a sense of self emerges. While Mahler's work is on the infant process, she and others recognise that individuation is replayed throughout life. Jung, for instance, describes individuation as 'the process by which a person becomes a psychological "in-dividual," that is, a separate, indivisible unity or "whole"'; this is a life-long process (Jung, 2014, p.275). Bowen, to whose work I referred in Chapter 5, explores individuation in the context of family systems, and the dynamics in which it fails.

Peter Blos focused on what he called the 'second individuation process of adolescence' (Blos, 1967). Like Erikson and others writing about adolescence in the mid- to late twentieth century, the figure of the 'delinquent' underpins many of Blos's observations as he tries to delineate the psychic processes at work which distinguish between 'adaptive' (healthy, 'normal') development and adolescent pathology. Using terms drawn from object relations theory, Blos described the 'regressions' to the infantile process which are necessary for adolescent development. The behaviours which earlier twentieth-century psychology saw as 'defenses' (aggression, moodiness, procrastination, withdrawal) were reclaimed by Blos as necessary regressions to infantile individuation, a revisiting of the stage in which child and mother are at first merged then ambivalently separated. The task of adolescence is to work through this process again, to separate from the infantile love objects (the idealised mother and father) and to find new 'stage appropriate' objects in a peer group. An example of the 'normal' regression of adolescence for Blos is the obsessive interest in idols of contemporary culture, emblazoned in posters on bedroom walls, which for Blos are the updated, idealised parent figures of infancy. A more pathological version is the adolescent who cuts off from the family, drops out of school or turns against all authority in favour of peer relationships. According to Blos, such an adolescent is simply replacing childhood dependencies rather than maturing through them and is set up for a life of arrested development. In such theory, disruptions to the process of separation-individuation inhibit the development of a strong sense of self and the capacity to internalise a sense of others, which leads to difficulties in adult social relationships and intimate ones. We now think of such disruptions as 'developmental traumas'.

Sexual development is implied in the separation-individuation process, but sexuality in such theory is more often referred to in its 'pathological', problematic version. Blos, for instance, considers 'promiscuity' a consequence of an avoidance of the healthy process of separation from parents and family (p.167). It is unclear what would count as 'adaptive' sexual behaviour. As we saw in *Blue Jean*, sexual development may follow a psychological process but its expression, the definition of what is healthy or pathological, is socially, culturally and politically prescribed and what is 'normal' in one context is unhealthy in another.

Otis's 'problem' in *Sex Education* is that, unlike most of his peers, he is 'still' a virgin, and the pressure to 'lose' his virginity is represented as just as restrictive as a prohibition on sex acts between adolescents. To have sex, Otis must repress, but not cut off, his dependency on his mother Jean. Instead of separating from his mother, Otis imitates her and draws on her authority as a sex therapist to dispense advice to his literally fumbling peers. While Otis holds on to his idealised mother (by copying her professional role), he finds it hard to access an idealised father at all. Otis is disturbed by a memory from early childhood of his estranged father (also a therapist) having sex with a client. For Otis, therapists do not make ideal parents or real ones.

Otis and Maeve circle each other for four series before they have sex. Maeve is abandoned by her father who never appears in the story, and by her mother who is ruled by, and eventually dies because of her addiction. It is difficult to separate and individuate when there are no parents to separate from. Enmeshed and abandoned, Otis and Maeve struggle to find each other until they work through their 'infantile regressions'.

Sex Education is a story of developing bodies and selves, but it also foregrounds the linguistic aspect of adolescent development and the power of literature to promote that growth (what Blos refers to as the symbolic expressions of mature individuation as opposed to the preverbal acting out of enmeshment). Maeve's English Literature teacher offers literary guidance and encourages her to apply for a scholarship for a writing programme in the US, where the authenticity of her writing voice is challenged. Her little sister Elsie's foster carer takes Maeve in and offers her a comfortable bed and books. Maeve is often seen with a copy of George Eliot's *Middlemarch*, the story of a young woman who sublimates sexual desire into intellectual ideas. Maeve's task is to integrate mother figures and novels, sexual and intellectual expression. To some degree, she does this when she supports her friend Aimee after a sexual assault. Maeve takes Aimee to the police (forgoing her own birthday celebrations) and stays with her until Aimee finds the language to describe what happened to her. To support her recovery, Maeve gives Aimee a copy of Emily Nagoski's *Come As You Are*, a book which debunks myths about female sexuality and explores 'the biological, psychological and social processes underlying sexual behaviour' (Nagoski, 2015, p.3). *Sex Education* is in some ways a dramatised manual for Nagoski's book, as each episode explores a different aspect of sexual behaviour in the context of relationships, family, 'cultural' expectations and bodily differences.

Netflix's *Heartstopper*, based on a series of graphic novels by Alice May Oseman, is aimed at a younger audience than *Sex Education* (*Heartstopper*, 2022-; Oseman, 2019–26). It focuses on the relationship between two grammar schoolboys, Charlie and Nick, and plays on well-worn high school tropes about 'odd couples' (one creative and clever, one popular and sporty) to tell a sweet and romantic story while exploring developmental 'issues'. Charlie is subjected to homophobic bullying and struggles with an eating disorder while Nick negotiates a relationship with a distant and preoccupied father and a homophobic older brother. Their friendship circle includes Elle, whose transgender status is only referenced by her transfer from the boys' grammar to a nearby all girls' school. Like *Sex Education, Heartstopper* is a utopian fantasy of school communities which ostracise and eventually reform the bullies and bring the marginalised and oppressed to the centre.

Blue Jean, *Butterfly*, *Sex Education* and *Heartstopper* variously depict the secondary school as prescriptive and oppressive or benign and pragmatic in its contribution to adolescent sexual and gender development. Each story is alert to the social and cultural, as well as individual and familial, process of individuation, which allows a self to emerge with an integrated sense of gender and sexuality. As organisations which convey direct and indirect messages about normative development, secondary schools *are* part of this process rather than its passive observers.

#MeToo and *Adolescence*

Secondary schools can also, of course, be sites of abuse focused on sexuality, gender and sex, and misogynistic abuse has been called out in recent years. The #MeToo movement, which was started in 2006 by American activist Tarana Burke to empower young women to speak out against sexual violence in high schools, became a viral online movement from 2017 onwards, after the powerful film producer Harvey Weinstein was outed as a sexual predator and rapist. In 2020, a UK-based online campaign, 'Everyone's Invited', was launched by Soma Sara, to encourage survivors of sexual assault, harassment and violence in schools to testify. A list of the schools and colleges where alleged assaults, acts of coercion, shaming and rape took place was compiled and circulated online. The rape and murder in London of Sarah Everard at the hands of a police officer during the 2021 lockdown intensified the movement and called into question the culpability of the sex education curriculum with the perceived misogyny in girls' day-to-day experience. The 2025 Netflix drama *Adolescence*, created by Jack Thorne and Stephen Graham, intervenes in this setting (*Adolescence*, 2025). It draws attention to the normalisation of misogyny in the online 'manosphere', perpetrated by influencer Andrew Tate and his acolytes, and imagines an extreme act of violence as its outcome.

The drama begins with the dawn arrest at the hands of armed police of 13-year-old Jamie in the home he shares with his parents and older sister. A sweet-faced 'everyboy' with a talent for art, Jamie's bedroom is adorned with space motifs; he wets himself when he is ordered at gunpoint to leave his bed. What seems to be a terrible mistake unfolds over four episodes as a more terrible reality. A police interview reveals that Jamie has been arrested on suspicion of the murder of his classmate Katie, in a knife assault which was captured on CCTV, but which Jamie denies. As the investigation moves to the school both children attended, another student, Adam, the son of DI Luke Bascombe, reveals to his father a culture of online misogyny and bullying. When Bascombe registers the gulf between his and his son's understanding of online communication, the officer resolves to spend time with his own adolescent boy, having seen first-hand the consequence of losing a child to other authority figures.

But this drama is not just about the generational gulf in the online world. Mrs. Fenumore, a teacher at Jamie's school, who shows the investigating officers round, is well meaning but ineffectual, and other teachers are represented as having given up any authority they had in the face of student indifference. The school is, in Bascombe's words, 'a fucking holding pen'.

An interview with Jamie conducted by a psychologist probes the teenager's attitudes towards women and his relationship with his father, Eddie, which prompts a sudden and angry outburst from Jamie, as he simultaneously defends his dad and recalls the shame of not meeting his expectations. The final episode switches back to the family home, several months after Jamie's arrest. We watch in discomfort as his mother and sister try, unsuccessfully, to create a celebratory atmosphere for Eddie's birthday. As the women tread on eggshells around a man who veers between genial good humour and explosive rage, he discloses the story of his own father's physical violence and his attempt to be a different kind of father.

The one-shot technique used to film *Adolescence* brings us into the emotional intensity of the fallout of the central event. It also keeps us within the only perspective that is available within the single shot (there are no flashbacks or simultaneous scenes of exposition to provide more information). We learn about Jamie at the same pace that his family and the professionals he meets during the investigation do and have the same blind spots. His grief-stricken parents recall that when Jamie came home from school and shut himself in his bedroom with his computer, they thought he was safe, shielded from the potential dangers of life outside.

Adolescence garnered much praise but also much commentary on the 'realism' or otherwise of the police, teacher and psychologist representation. *The Guardian* wrote 'rarely has state secondary school been so vividly portrayed...It's *Grange Hill* with Smartphones and security lanyards' (Hogan, 2025). (This comparison is used frequently of reviews of state school stories. I don't think it's accurate.) Like much of the commentary about *Adolescence*, Hogan sees the story as 'a cautionary tale about getting teenagers off screens and engaging with real life again', the dangers of the online 'manosphere' and a reminder that 'human contact and family time might save them'. But the drama reveals multiple contexts in which to read Jamie's crime, including multigenerational male violence within the home. The initial rush of the Labour government to respond to *Adolescence* was to consider a ban on mobile phones in schools, rather than promote better 'cyber literacy' and to tackle the broader context of misogyny, violence against women and knife crime perpetrated by and on young men and boys in 'real life'.

Black Lives Matter and *Small Axe*

To be socialised in an environment where misogyny is unchallenged or where one's sexual and gender identity is seen as aberrant is traumatising. While 2020 brought a howl of outrage about the place of secondary schools in this process, it was also the year in which racialised trauma was highlighted, not just as a topic for the History curriculum but as a lived experience for racially marginalised students. In May 2020, the murder of Black American George Floyd under the knee of white police officer Derek Chevin, which was filmed and circulated globally, sparked protests which coalesced under the Black Lives Matter banner. Black Lives Matter is a 'call to action', a movement which had begun in the US in 2013 in response to police brutality, vigilantism and legal injustice against the Black community and which was built on decades of activism for racial justice. George Floyd's death, during the COVID-19 pandemic, which disproportionately affected the lives of racialised minorities, sparked demands for reform in the education sector: to 'decolonise' Eurocentric curricula, foreground Black history and address the underrepresentation of black teachers and school leaders and the disproportionate number of black students excluded from schools.

Film-maker Steve McQueen's response to this moment came in five beautiful films shown on the BBC in 2020. *Small Axe* (2020a) confronts the racism of London from the 1960s to the 1980s and the resistance that racism met from Afro-Caribbean communities. The final film is *Education*, which dramatises the scandal of secondary schools in the 1970s which placed large numbers of Black children in schools for the 'educationally subnormal' (*Small Axe*, 2020b).

Like *Adolescence, Education* introduces us to a sweet-faced boy with a talent for art. Twelve-year-old Kingsley Smith is also interested in space, with ambitions to be like Neil Armstrong. When he tells his friend that he wants to be an astronaut, the comeback is immediate 'You can't have a Black man in space'. This is the early 1970s. Kingsley lives with his shift-worker parents and his older sister Stephanie, an aspiring fashion designer, in a semi-detached house in North London. In his classroom, Kingsley struggles to read aloud and is verbally abused by his teacher. His mother is called to a meeting with the headteacher, who claims that Kingsley's 'disruptive' behaviour and his poor score in a recent IQ test means there is no place for him in the school. As a 'second chance', Kingsley is to be placed in a 'special school'. Kingsley's parents are too tired and too focused on getting through to put up a fight.

The 'special' school offers little in terms of an education or even adult supervision. A visit from psychologist Hazel Lewis (under cover as a journalist), who had been a teacher in British Guiana, brings a fresh gaze on the school. On Hazel's prompting, campaigner Lydia Thomas visits Mrs Smith and introduces her to the work of Bernard Coard, whose book had recently been published by New Beacon Books, the first Black publishing house in the UK (Coard, 1971). Coard had uncovered the systemic targeting of Afro-Caribbean children in mainstream schools, based on claims that academic standards were being eroded by their presence. This was a view fuelled by a local authority report by headteacher Alfred Doulton, which claimed that Afro-Caribbean children had low IQs (based on IQ tests that were culturally skewed). *Education* dramatises a meeting of activists and parents in which Thomas reveals that children are being moved to schools for the 'educationally subnormal', because they are seen as 'too loud, too slow, too lively'; not only are Afro-Caribbean children being removed from mainstream schools on spurious grounds but also many of those who remain achieve little. Thomas invites Mrs. Smith and the other parents to send their children to Saturday schools, the voluntary network of Black supplementary schools run outside of the mainstream system, and to write to the newly appointed secretary of state for education: Margaret Thatcher.

In an interview with *The Guardian*, writer and director Steve McQueen draws a parallel between Kingsley's and his own experience of schooling in the early 1970s (Okolosie, 2020). McQueen was dyslexic but was written off as 'stupid'. He draws a further parallel between the practice of sending Black children to ESN schools on the grounds of disruptive behaviour and low intelligence and the disproportionate number of exclusions of children, especially boys, of Afro-Caribbean heritage from mainstream schools in the contemporary system. The article notes that after a period from 2006 to 2012 when permanent exclusions almost halved, the 2019 Timpson Review warned that numbers were rising again. More recent figures from the DfE show that total numbers of exclusions have risen considerably since the pandemic, though the data on student demographics is held at school level.

Kingsley's story is of the trauma inflicted by local education authorities, schools and individual teachers upon a cohort of students whose parents had been sold a dream of educational opportunity in 'the motherland'. It also tells a story of the agency and resistance of a community and the subsequent recovery of an individual child. Too often, individual children are expected to recover independently. Some models of therapy are premised on this idea; that children are or can be helped to be 'resilient' by drawing on internal resources. But a trauma inflicted institutionally upon a community cannot be overcome by individual resilience or strength of character alone.

Rocks

A review by Robbie Collins in *The Telegraph* of Sarah Gavron's 2019 film *Rocks* (the nickname of the 15-year-old protagonist Shola) foregrounds and celebrates the 'energy and resilience' of the 'hardy young female inhabitants' of East London (Collin, 2021). In what he calls a 'melting pot aesthetic' arising from the friendship of a group of girls whose parents and grandparents hail from Nigeria, Somalia and Poland, Collins waxes lyrical about the representation of their 'youthful potential…its extraordinary ability to flower in even the most unpromising soil'. While the girls' friendships are indeed the heart of the film, Gavron pays more attention to that unpromising soil than Collins wants to see. Shola's 'resilience' is born from early adult responsibility, caring for her little brother Emmanuel when her mum is not well enough or when she is at work. When her mum leaves, Shola is desperate to stay with Emmanuel and uses her premature maturity to evade social services. This is not resilience, it's survival.

School scenes revel in the hilarity of the girls' conversations and the rhythms of their speech, against which adult 'schoolese' rings hollow. Some teachers forlornly police the girls' uniforms and try to direct them along subject and career 'pathways' while others meet the girls' energy and laughter. As the weight of her mother's absence and responsibility for Emmanuel grows, Shola is more distracted and withdrawn. Only her best friend Sumaya tries to draw her back.

When the electricity in their flat is cut off, little Emmanuel uses a child's magical thinking and his light sabre to shock the light switch back to life and muses he could do a charity run to raise money for them to live on. The disconnection between Shola's reality and the requirements of the school environment grows and spills over into a riotous food fight in food technology. When Shola spots social services at the door of their flat, she finds temporary refuge in Sumaya's home; time spent with an extensive and happy family only makes Shola feel more isolated and pushes her towards new girl Roche, whose life is less stable than Sumaya's. Shola and Emmanuel move from place to place, first in flight from social services and then from Roche, from whom Shola stole money. Little Emmanuel's advice to his sister to 'stop thinking about all your worries' echoes the 'positive mindset' mantras of resilience culture and is about as effective as the light sabre on the defunct switch.

When Emmanuel and Shola are eventually separated and moved into foster care, Shola howls in despair. While her little brother is 'placed' in Hastings, Shola goes to a family nearby in a house adorned in African art and who offer her curried goat. Shola politely declines. Her return to school and her friends is momentarily stilted but she soon accepts an offer of cake from Sumaya, and the relationships resume with laughter and no reflection. The girls gather money to get Shola the train fare to Hastings to find Emmanuel and nervously jump the ticket barrier to go with her. As the girls stand against the fence of Emmanuel's new primary school, watching him play amongst a group of white peers, Shola relinquishes him to his new life. Not because she wants to but because she must. Again, that's not resilience; it's survival.

The story is produced and narrated according to the conventions of social realism: it is shot in the locations in which the story is set and most of the actors are non-professionals from the same area. As Collins notes, the style also grows from documentary. There is no 'booable villain' but rather a system in which the lives of Shola and Emmanuel are small and precarious. The arc of the story – Shola's lack of a parent, her attempt to keep life together for her little brother, the fall out with her friends, the arrival of social services and separation from Emmanuel, the reconciliation with friends and her acceptance of Emmanuel's new life once she sees him 'happy' – heads towards the unhappy ending of the social realist tradition. Shola's family are not magically reunited, although as they peer through the fence of Emmanuel's new primary school, the friendship of two teenage girls, Shola and Sumaya, offers a glimpse of a future.

The return of *Waterloo Road*

After a six-year gap, *Waterloo Road* was revived in 2021, with the return of art teacher and wellbeing champion, Kim Campbell, now as the headteacher (*Waterloo*

Road, 2021–). The school has another incarnation, back in Greater Manchester and it is, in fact, another school completely: William Beswick High. The first episode opens with a playground protest against the name of the newly opened school, Beswick being a nineteenth-century slave owner. Brandishing 'Black Lives Matter' placards, the students demand the name be changed. This opening draws criticism from tabloid, broadsheet and online media for its 'woke' agenda, an epithet which was rolled out again as criticism when a storyline about a transgender student in Series 15 aired in 2025 (Deacon, 2025). Such criticism overlooks the relationship between *Waterloo Road* and issues which have contemporary currency since its inception.

The series is conscious of the way the issues are now received. The old split between strict behaviourism and relational approaches in schools is recast in terms of the so-called 'culture wars'. For instance, in the opening storyline, Black Deputy Head Linden wants to squash the protest and advocate for a 'behaviour unit' to deal with miscreants while Kim recognises the students' need to be heard. By the end of the first episode, everyone's wishes are granted: the LA agrees to a name change for the school and it just so happens that the name Waterloo Road is available. In a concession to Linden, Kim makes it clear to the students that the school is a hierarchy not a democracy and agrees with Linden that they need to fast track an onsite behaviour unit.

Other approaches to challenging behaviour are flagged up throughout the series. Former pupil Chlo returns, now married to former bad boy and heartthrob Dante and mother to their two children. In the opening episode, Chlo is on her way to school to offer her 'animal therapy' services to the head but falls foul of the curse of Waterloo Road. She is hit by a car that is caught up in the protest and subsequently dies of her injury. Animal therapy is off the agenda, but other forms of therapy are now routinely mentioned as means of support.

When Kelly Jo is diagnosed with ADHD, there are promises of an Education and Health Care Plan (EHCP) and a referral for Cognitive Behavioural Therapy. EHCPs were introduced in 2014 in the Families and Children Act. They replaced 'statements' for children with special educational needs and involved families and students in the planning for educational provision, although they are currently being reviewed as demand is outstripping available resources.

The way that Kelly Jo's story is narrated could not be further from the representation of Karla Bentham in Series Three. Karla's story begins when she transfers into Waterloo Road and her 'prior history' is not disclosed to staff. This prior history is her Asperger's diagnosis and her need for medication, the absence of which leads to a violent outburst, provoked by dinosaur disciplinarian Grantley Budgeon. Her story eventually dispels the stigma that marks its beginning, but the language used about Karla's neurodivergence and the fear which the disclosure of her diagnosis engenders is an insight into the very different cultural norms of 2007.

Kelly Jo's story goes beyond her struggles with ADHD and picks up the narrative thread about race and cultural identity. Her interest is sparked in the range of cultures in the school, and she initiates a debate in her History lesson about the British Empire. The History teacher warns against being led by 'sloganeering' but leads the lesson to 1948 and the arrival of the Empire Windrush. The school proposes a 'culture day' and Kelly Jo launches a podcast where she proposes to explore her own racial identity. There are tensions underlying this celebration. Coral (the school cynic) wants to rid new starter Amy of the 'naive belief you can help them all' and that 'investing in kids like Kelly Jo is a high-risk strategy' while Linden argues that 'Black children need continuous sustained support'. Inclusion and strict behavioural standards are still at odds in the newly minted Waterloo Road.

In Series 15, the new head Dame Stella Drake arrives at Waterloo Road having been shamed out of another post for making critical comments about parents. After the death of a student at the hands of the son of the previous head (do keep up), the school is now 'trauma-informed'. It has a wellbeing area, and students are seen queuing for a slot with the school counsellor. This 'trend' is quickly dismissed by the new head who believes that the students are manipulating the tragedy. We eventually understand Stella's resistance to school counselling as something more than a belief in innate resilience. We learn that her daughter has episodes of mental illness so severe that she is hospitalised and Dame Stella is dismissive of the heightened rhetoric around 'the worried well'. However, when Stella is attacked by an irate parent and struggles to come into work, she is advised to seek therapy, which she reluctantly does. As though I had written this episode myself, the therapist turns out to be former Waterloo Road head, Jack Rimmer, who retrained after his own traumatic experiences at the school. So convinced is Stella by the value of Jack's work and his insights as a former head, that she invites him to return to his old stomping ground as school counsellor.

In Series 16, counsellor Jack duly arrives. He still looks like a headteacher but spends quite a lot of time in the staffroom looking for someone to support. His arrival has coincided with a dictate from the academy trust that, in a bid to recruit more students, the school should not have any religious practice. The former prayer room is handed over to Jack as his counselling room. The ruling causes outrage amongst Christian students who question the school's 'inclusive' credentials and deface a recently painted rainbow walkway, a sign of the school's allyship with its LGBTQ+ community. A more peaceful protest, a sit-in in the former prayer room by one of the Christian students, encourages Jack to take the matter to the head. Religious practice is duly back on the cards, and the Head Stella decides instead that increasing arts subjects could encourage recruitment.

While Jack largely hovers meaningfully when he spots imminent or unexpressed distress, he looks more comfortable in his former role of crisis management. Opportunities arise with a fatality, the death of the headteacher's granddaughter, Hope. When Hope eats a cake laden with dairy rather than its vegan alternative, she succumbs to a severe allergic response. While this plot development follows the tradition of the *Waterloo Road* rapid-fire tragic arc, where a character is barely established before we're invited to mourn their loss, the representation of her grandmother/headteacher Stella's grief is raw and painful. Jack hovers, inviting her to share but she angrily shuts down. The plight of another student, Dwayne, however, seems to provoke a shift in Stella. Dwayne, a sensitive 15-year-old, has had a difficult adolescence, due to his mum's alcoholism. The pressures of teenage development – sexual attraction, exam performance, self-image, uncertainty in friendship – ramp up until he experiences a psychotic break and internal critical voices prompt a separation between Dwayne's subjective experience and his external reality. In flight from staff who are trying to help him he escapes through a tile in the school ceiling and crawls through the ventilation space, an inverted school underworld. Eventually he falls back through the ceiling into the reality of a classroom. Hovering Jack has tried and failed to reassure him, but Stella is able to reach the frightened and disoriented boy and get him the help he needs. A rapid hospital assessment, the promise of Child and Adolescent Mental Health Services (CAMHS) support and appropriate medication see Dwayne back in school and well again before the end of the series. If only.

Stella is on a 'journey' from rigid, defensive and role-bound towards allowing her emotional and rational selves to integrate, partly due to the services of Jack who is often seen by her side. Jack, meanwhile, is on another trajectory. His role as a counsellor becomes more blurred (in narrative terms, counselling sessions do not move at the normal speed of *Waterloo Road*) as he gradually steps into staff mentorship and then management when he resumes a leadership role, this time as Deputy Head. However, he faces a two-headed nemesis: Machiavellian Media Studies teacher Darius and the addiction to alcohol which had numbed his traumatic experiences at Waterloo Road the first-time round. Darius manipulates Jack into drinking again and Jack's tenure as both counsellor and Deputy Head ends as quickly as they began. He leaves the school with a sorry box of belongings and Darius, the expert in narrative spin, talks himself into the Deputy Headship.

Steve

The helplessness and vulnerability of the adults who support 'troubled' adolescents is often the focus of *Waterloo Road* and is the theme of the film *Steve* (2025), set in 1996 (at the end of the long Conservative administration) at an experimental boarding school. The school offers holistic care to boys excluded from mainstream schools and, in some cases, estranged from their own families. The film is adapted from Max Porter's expressionist novel *Shy*, which represents the fragmented subjectivity of the eponymous 17-year-old resident of the school, inspired by Porter's experience of leading storytelling and creative writing workshops in prisons. The film re-centres the narrative around a day in the life of the school headteacher, Steve, played by Cillian Murphy. Some years earlier, Steve survived a traffic accident in which a young girl died, and which left him in constant physical and emotional pain; he self-medicates with alcohol and prescription drugs. Steve is committed to the care, education and rehabilitation of his students, putting everyone at the top of his to-do list but never quite gets to any of them. Things slip away as crisis piles on top of crisis. At times, the film gives this escalating calamity a comic frame, especially when a film crew embed themselves in the school to make a short feature for a local news programme: 'indulgent waste of taxpayers' money or worthwhile experiment in adolescent care? You decide!'. The boys play up to the cameras; the production team intrude into the boys' rooms and are generally voyeuristic; a local Tory MP arrives to glad hand in front of the cameras only to be shot down and insulted by a not very grateful Shy. Amid the chaos, the Trust that runs the school announces that the building is to be sold and the school is to be closed within months. After one tragedy – the attempted suicide of Shy – is averted, the film lurches ambiguously towards a less certain ending for Steve. Beneath a voiceover, one of Steve's tape-recorded briefings, which gives a new member of the team an engaging overview of each boy's character and potential, Steve ascends a ladder to the attic of his home, whiskey bottle in hand. While he speaks of wanting to give each boy something to hope for, Steve seems to have run out of hope for himself. Through Steve, the film represents the helplessness of working with volatile young people at the bottom of everyone's list and the fury and despair when even the crumbs of 'an offer' are taken away. Steve's fragmenting consciousness is a synecdoche of a disappearing welfare state, a long way from the avuncular optimism and ordinary devotion in the stories of post-war teachers.

References

Adolescence (2025) [TV Series], Netflix.

American Psychiatric Association. (1980) *Diagnostic and Statistical Manual of Mental Disorders*, 3rd edn., Washington, DC: American Psychiatric Publishing.

Bf I. (2023) *Blue Jean: Georgia Oakley on creating a 'conversation with the present' about Section 28*, https://www.bfi.org.uk/interviews/blue-jean-georgia-oakley-section-28

Blos, P. (1967) 'The second individuation process of adolescence', *The Psychoanalytical Study of the Child*, 22(1), pp.162–86.

Blue Jean (2022) [Film] *Oakley*, G. dir., Harrow: Kleio Films.

Brown, G. (2025) 'Nothing prepared me for the child poverty I see in Britain. November's budget can and must halt its inexorable rise', *The Guardian*, 15 September.

Butler, J. (1990) *Gender Trouble*, New York, London: Routledge.

Butler, J. (1993) *Bodies that Matter*, New York, London: Routledge.

Butler, J. (2024) *Who's Afraid of Gender?* London: Allen Lane.

Butterfly (2017) [TV Series], ITV.

CACE (1963) The Newsom Report, *Half Our Future: A Report of the Central Advisory Council for Education*, London: HMSO.

Cass, H. (2024) *Cass Independent Review: Final Report*, https://cass.independent-review.uk/hom/publications/final-report/

Coard, B. (1971) *How the West Indian Child is Made Educationally Sub-Normal in the British School System*, London: New Beacon Books.

Collins, R. (2021) '*Rocks* review: A wildly charming celebration of teen potential', *The Telegraph*, 11 April.

Deacon, M. (2025) 'This trans drama is the most excruciating thing the BBC has ever made', *The Telegraph*, 15 February.

DfE (2025) *Relationships and Sex Education (RSE) and Health Education*, https://www.giv.uk/governemnt/publictions/relationships-education-relationsips-and-sex-education-rse-and-health-education

Erasmus, C. (2019) *The Mental Health and Wellbeing Handbook for Schools: Transforming Mental Health Support on a Budget*, London: Jessica Kingsley Publishers.

Heartstopper (2022-) [TV Series], Netflix.

Hogan, M. (2025) '"Unnervingly on-the-nose": Why *Adolescence* is such powerful TV that it could save lives', *The Guardian*, 17 March.

Hughes, D.A. (2007) *Attachment-Focused Family Therapy*, New York: W.W. Norton and Co.

Hulme, J. (2015) *How to Create Kind Schools: 12 Extraordinary Projects Making Schools Happier and Helping Every Child Fit In*, London: Jessica Kingsley Publishers.

Inckle, K. (2017) *Safe with Self-Injury: A Practical Guide to Understanding, Responding and Harm-Reduction*, Monmouth: PCCS Books.

Jung, C.G. (2014) *The Archetypes and the Collective Unconscious*, 2nd edn., Hove: Routledge.

Mahler, M. (1963) 'Thoughts about development and individuation', *The Psychoanalytic Study of the Child*, 18(1), pp.307–24.

Mangan, L. (2018) '*Butterfly* review – An important, truthful drama about a transgender child', *The Guardian*, 14 October.

Marchant, T. (2018) '*Butterfly* writer Tony Marchant on changing attitudes to transgender children and the importance of trans representation on screen', *Huffpost*, 14 October.

Moore, S. and Rosenthal, D. (2006) *Sexuality in Adolescence: Current Trends*, Hove: Routledge.

Nagoski, E. (2015) *Come as You Are: The Surprising New Science That Will Transform Your Sex Life*, London: Scribe.

Okolosie, L. (2020) 'Discrimination at school: Is a Black British history lesson repeating itself?', *The Guardian*, 15 November.

Oseman, A. (2019–2026) *Heartstopper*, Vols. 1–6, London: Hachette Children's Group.

Pearson, A. (2018) 'The tyranny of the transgender minority has got to be stopped', *The Telegraph*, 17 October.

Policy Exchange (2023) *Asleep at the Wheel: An Examination of Gender and Safeguarding in Schools*, https://policyexchange.org.uk/publiction/asleep-at-the-wheel

Pometsey, O. (2020) '*Sex Education*'s creators: "It's more like a comic book world than an American one"' *British GQ*, 17 January.

Porges, S.W. (2011) *The Polyvagal Theory: Neurophysiological Foundations of Emotions, Attachment, Communication, Self-Regulation*, New York: Norton.

Power, W. (2019) '*Sex Education* review: Gillian Anderson's Netflix comedy is eager to please but tonally confused', *The Independent*, 11 January.

Sex Education (2019–23) [TV Series], Netflix.

Shapiro, F. (2018) *Eye Movement, Desensitization and Reprocessing (EMDR) Therapy*, 3rd edn., New York, London: The Guilford Press.

Small Axe (2020a) [TV Series], BBC.

Small Axe (2020b) [TV Series], Episode 5, 'Education', BBC.

Stanley, T. (2018) 'Who would choose to be a man in our straitjacketing, anti-masculine society?' *The Telegraph*, 16 October.

Steve (2025) [Film] *Mielants*, T. dir., Bath: Big Thing Films.

Van der Kolk, B. (2015) *The Body Keeps the Score*, London: Penguin.

Waterloo Road (2021-) [TV Series], BBC.

AFTERWORD

The COVID reset that didn't begin

The merry-go-round of inclusion and standards

The education system since the Second World War has been subject to constant policy change, which has seen the structure of secondary schooling, its oversight, curricula and assessment shift at least once a decade. Our assumptions about the subjects of state secondary education – adolescents – are more resistant to change. 'Adolescence' has expanded as a category since the pre-war all-through elementary schools and grammars were reimagined as secondary moderns, grammars and, for a short while, technical schools. Adolescence was once a descriptor for the leisured or educated youth of the upper and middle classes, whose inner worlds became the subject of 'coming of age' novels, memoirs and, in the nineteenth century, psychological texts. The mid-twentieth century saw young working-class people become available for the same scrutiny. In school for longer than their predecessors, post-war working-class adolescents were now subject to the same psychological observation and pedagogical theorising as their middle-class peers. Extended schooling created the possibility for many young people of being valued beyond the worth of their labouring or reproductive bodies. It offered hope that their minds too could contribute to the recovery and future wealth of the post-war nation.

Progressive pedagogy has sought ways to draw out the 'natural interests' (skills) of adolescents while more traditional approaches have sought to feed them knowledge. Those who respond to neither approach have been pathologised as 'delinquents', psychologically troubled and social trouble. The stories we have told about those adolescents and the schools which have educated them are rarely celebratory or even optimistic. While the development of the welfare state seemed to offer the promise of all adolescents having a period to develop their minds and bodies, attempts to equalise the opportunities to do so have prompted the best dramas and the most dispiriting cultural commentary. Comprehensive schools, now mostly organised as academies outside local authority control, have been vilified since their arrival. The absence of a selective gateway means that comprehensives can be imagined as boundaryless, shapeless things, always about to collapse.

The presence of a wider cohort of adolescents and especially the spectre of them being taught in one building provoked a debate about the nature of education in the 1970s. Was schooling for the transmission of knowledge, reason, a common humanity, the cultivation of skills or the creation of a fair society? Every wave of 'inclusion' (focused first on class, then race, cognitive and physical ability, sexuality and gender, and most recently neurodivergence) has been met with cries about lowering educational standards and the creation of a culture of victimhood. The response of the political centre to such outcry is an intensified attention to academic outcomes. The drive to close the achievement gap as the sign of progress in our schools has narrowed the kind of 'mind' the education system values.

Anxious and feral

The start of a new academic year prompts a wave of stories about the 'state' of our schools which illustrate our cultural amnesia, as they rehash decades old fears and fantasies about our state-educated 'youth' with updated historical details. For instance, on the day before the start of academic year 25/26, *The Sunday Times* published two school-related articles, one about an epidemic of anxiety amongst 16- and 17-year-olds, particularly in girls, and another on the days of schooling lost to disruptive behaviour, implicitly largely involving boys (Eccles, 2025;Wheeler, 2025). The first piece was based on a poll of 1,100 16- and 17-year-olds, conducted by the organisation 'More in Common'. Thirty-three percent of girls 'said they suffered from anxiety' and had missed school because of it. They worried most about school in general and exams, feared for their future financial security and reflected on the impact of the pandemic, most believing that the closure of schools had adversely affected them. Their exposure to social media and online pornography also concerned them. Ten percent of respondents said that they would confide in an AI chatbot if they had a personal problem, compared to 8% who would confide in a known adult or friend. For some, the online world is both the source and the salve of their 'anxiety'.

The education secretary Bridget Phillipson responded to these findings by citing her 'mission' to 'build a resilient new generation with the grit and wherewithal to cope with life's ups and downs' and to give access to 'in-school and college mental health support' (unspecified). Phillipson is cited in the headline of the second *Times* article about days missed to a 'behaviour crisis', as identified in a survey of 5,000 teachers (Eccles, 2025). Half of the respondents reported calm and orderly classrooms, but others complained of low-level disruption and verbal and physical abuse. 'Social media use' and 'poor socialisation skills after the COVID-19 lockdown' are identified as causes, as well as the tendency of some parents to challenge schools' attempts at discipline. The cure, according to Phillipson, is to be a joint effort by parents and schools to 'get children in class and ready to learn'. Behaviour and attendance hubs (groups of schools working together) are to be launched to share good practice and, ominously, a 'crack down' on bad behaviour is promised in the next education white paper.

So, in one article social media leaves young people anxious, in the next it turns them feral; in the first, lockdowns left them socially unsure and hesitant and in the second, they were 'unsocialised' and abusive. Victims or perpetrators? The possibility that all these effects could be felt in one young person, that what makes one withdraw and one act out, is the same thing, is not suggested. The comments section under the article about behaviour was like a portal back to 1973, invoking absence of discipline, standards and an emphasis on 'inclusion' as the source of 'the crisis' and a return of 'reform schools' as the antidote.

We have collectively forgotten the promises about system reform which were made during the height of the pandemic, when even *The Telegraph* was predicting fundamental changes in education, 'from the ways we assess schools to class sizes to exams' (Pozniak, 2020). While problems emerging from the pandemic are recognised, the promises of a response seem to have evaporated, reduced to badly handled 'catch up' tutoring or the now promised 'crack down' on poor behaviour. Where is the understanding of or even curiosity about the impact on development of the lockdowns, an impact that was felt unevenly depending on the circumstances of a child's or adolescent's home life? And, for the benefit of the education minister, resilience is not injectable. It is the outcome of a process, of experiences in which need is met by resources (social, emotional and economic).

Lockdown stories

Our three children collided with the lockdowns at different ages and stages of their education. The eldest, our daughter Sadie, was two-thirds of her way through an art foundation course at a nearby university. Alfie was in his first year of A-level study at sixth form college. Iris was in Year Nine at our local high school. We have a house large enough for everyone to have their own room and both adults could work from home. We all contracted the virus at different points. We all queued enthusiastically for the vaccine. We are believers in a 'social contract' and had a strong sense that people more vulnerable than us needed to be protected, so we followed 'the rules', even when they became labyrinthine and absurd. This is how our children remember that time now.

> Iris had just celebrated her 14th birthday in March 2020 when the country was locked down. She had already been sent home from school for two weeks in what was called a 'reset' with an expectation that school would reopen after the Easter break. When that didn't happen, the school sent out existing PowerPoints from lessons before launching interactive Teams teaching. 'I hated it all...I completed work for a full lesson in about 15 minutes. I remember crying,

giving myself a hard time for not doing it properly then finding out my friends hadn't done it at all. Socially it was weird – I remember meeting a friend when we were allowed to and being worried she'd think I was weird if I was following the rules too closely and worried we'd be told off for meeting at all. When we went back to school in Year 10 we would stay all day in one class, and the teachers would come to us. We had to go to the toilet with a teacher. We had more freedom when we were in Year Seven. If you came into contact with someone who had COVID you had to stay at home for 10 days – what was worse was everyone would know who you'd spent time with outside school. The atmosphere at school was awful. It felt like a family that was fighting. We'd have 'debates' in form at the end of the day when we'd all already had enough. It turned into a boys vs girls thing. I remember after Sarah Everard was murdered, and the girls were saying 'how do we know who's safe?' and the boys weren't taking it seriously. The Deputy Head spoke to the girls and told us not to respond to the boys 'emotionally' as they were less mature than us. We were promised assemblies and proper conversations, but they never happened. Year 11 was better, but the school still felt divided into the rule followers and the ones who didn't bother. We got to do modified GCSE exams, and they were fine. There didn't seem to be a hangover from COVID when we started sixth form, but I don't know. We all play it down now like it never happened'. Iris is now in her first year at drama school. Her favourite school stories: *Wolfblood* and *Summer Heights High* (though, as a Gen Z, she worries that the latter is 'problematic').

Alfie was in Year 12, his first year at sixth form college, and was on the way to the gym when he was told that classes were cancelled a few days before we went into lockdown. The college sent videos and PowerPoints of lessons. 'I did some work but spent most of my time on PlayStation with my friends, lifting weights and occasionally going on a bike ride. College reopened in June, but I don't remember much. I went back to my swimming club in the summer. When college started in September I was sent home almost straight away for 14 days because someone I sat next to tested positive. I was in and out a lot. In January 2021 I remember I was with the family in the living room when the announcement came that A-levels were cancelled again. I stopped myself from crying. The previous year had been a mess for A-level students, and I just felt like there was no future. I just went to bed. When we had online Teams lessons, I'd log on, switch off my camera and go back to sleep. Things got better at the end of February when they announced how they would assess the A-levels – no algorithm. We would do in class assessments. I worked a lot for these, and we finished mid-May.

My first memory of face-to-face socialising was April 2021 in someone's garden. Because I went to a Scottish university in the autumn the restrictions were stricter. I remember everyone going wild at first because they hadn't really been out before. We had to show COVID ids at clubs. There was very little in-person teaching. After Christmas I had an injury so couldn't swim with my club. I was in my room a lot and felt rubbish. I came home to do my exams online. I failed a couple of exams, and my average grade was low, but I did well in the resits. Lockdown, moving away, online university and a relationship break-up meant I wasn't feeling good for quite a while. Things have got a lot better now though'. Alfie is in the fifth and final year of a master's degree in aeronautical engineering. His favourite school stories are *The Inbetweeners* and *Harry Potter*.

Sadie was part way through an arts foundation course when she was told to clear her things from the studio. As a fashion student she was meant to be learning how to put together garments for a final exhibition in the summer. 'Instead, I wrapped my little sister in newspaper and did a fashion shoot in the garden'. Lockdown was 'sort of exciting at first but some of my best friends were travelling and that was worrying. Two of them got stuck in India for ages. I had my university place already but was a bit worried about whether we'd be allowed to go. I wasn't so scared about COVID – selfishly I was more frustrated about not being able to go out. I remember there were complicated rules once we were allowed to see our friends. There's loads of photos of us on walks in masks. And I think we drank a lot. I'd been furloughed from my job as a kitchen porter but started again for a bit in the summer before I went to university.

'There were five of us in our university flat and luckily we got on really well. Freshers' events were 'sit-down' things. Me and my friend went to one in the first week and got a text from someone we'd met afterwards saying she'd tested positive. All of us in the flat got it then, which caused a bit of tension. We were all quite ill with fevers. I lost my sense of taste and smell. I don't remember being frightened. It just felt like we'd all been silly. I don't remember how we got food – we didn't get any deliveries from the university. After we recovered we started cooking together and looking after ourselves. We got really close. People were fined for having parties – one person got fined £10,000. It took ages to sort it out. She really struggled.

'We were hardly allowed into uni in the first year. When I had to go in to do a presentation I was so stressed I couldn't speak! I was meant to be getting all the basic skills like pattern cutting and working with the sewing machines – we had online tutorials, but it was really hard to do the practical stuff like that from the flat. I never really caught up. Socially I was fine but for ages I was fearful that I didn't have the right skills for the course and felt stupid. I did a placement in industry in my third year and that really helped me to learn, and I did well in my final year. I still avoided making garments though. I now work as a fashion designer and am still scared of making actual things. The whole thing taught me that showing your face and being with other people is really important in learning skills, getting known and getting work. I couldn't do that for the first two years of the course and started to avoid it but overcame it in my placement year and got a job quite quickly after my degree'. Sadie's now working as a fashion designer. Her favourite school stories are *High School Musical* and *Harry Potter.*

Thankfully, these are not stories of trauma. Each of them is an intensified version of something they were about to encounter in their adolescence: 14/15-year-old Iris's heightened social anxiety, indignation at loss of independence and sense of personal and social injustice; 16/17-year-old Alfie's collapse into hopelessness around his academic life, compensated for by constant online connection with friends; 18/19-year-old Sadie's wistfulness for her lost social life, navigating illness for the first time with friends instead of family, fear of failure on her course exacerbated by avoidance of risk. They all 'caught up'. How much do we know about what others lost during those strange months and years? The COVID enquiry has recently begun to explore the effect of school closures on children and adolescents, the lack of planning and impact assessment, and the dreadful consequences for many children (Weale, 2025). But five years have elapsed since the rupture was made and for many there has been no repair.

Breathe, feel, think

The dramatic and literary world have not yet dwelt on the COVID period in England's state secondary schools, presumably because so few children and adolescents were in there, but there are many stories to tell. The second series of *Educating Yorkshire*, returning over a decade after its first outing, does refer to the experience of the pandemic and its possible impact on some of its pupils (Educating Yorkshire, 2025). Year 8 Amy with her anxious vigilance around friendships and worry for her Nan who has cancer, whose fears spill out into physical and verbal tics; distractable and angry Scott, who is redeemed by his talent for rugby; multiply bereaved and restless Jacob, who walks himself into trouble; self-conscious Lewis who is painfully aware of the jibes the world is waiting to offer him. The school seems well-resourced with kind and attentive teachers, staff dedicated to pastoral support who have the time to talk, all led by the now promoted teacher hero of the first series (who helped Year 11 student Mushy to find his voice), Head teacher Mr. Burton.

Just like in the first series, however, the impulse of the extremely likeable staff is to 'fix' and cajole. Students barely articulate an emotion before it is normalised, rationalised and acted upon from an adult perspective, as the engaging Year Eight 'Student Manger', a pastoral head of year, readily admits. The pupils' behaviour is categorised as either special educational need – which would warrant support – or a 'poor choice', which earns a consequence. What would happen if these uncomfortable bodies, tears and confusion were met with something slower, a physical breathing space and emotional empathy before planning and decision making begins? As I noted in Chapter 1, the 'neurodevelopmental' model offered by Dan Seigel is a simple and practical way to respond to anyone in distress (Siegel, 2013). Work from brainstem to limbic system to frontal cortex: breathe and move; engage emotionally; plan rationally.

Former Head of Ofsted, Baroness Spielman, has resurrected the spectre of the 1970s and the 1990s of schools becoming dangerously therapeutic in their focus. She asserts that there is a risk, post-pandemic, that schools descend into a negative spiral in search of difficult emotions. For Spielman, pupils need to be engrossed in academic learning and extra-curricular activity, not engaged in 'cosy chats with a therapist' (Eccles and Lintern, 2025).

Speilman here derides the humanistic talk therapy used in schools but which evidence, found by a team led by Mick Cooper, suggests does help to reduce the kind of psychological distress (around self-esteem, self-awareness and relationships) which can escalate into more intractable symptoms of anxiety and depression (Cooper et al., 2021). Cooper asks for more research to be conducted into the effectiveness of other kinds of interventions which are more directive, able to alleviate greater levels of difficulty and which are integrated with other aspects of school life and services: the kinds of integrated therapies that have been argued for since the 1960s, as I have recalled in this book. That is the kind of evidence needed to counteract voices of 'common sense' and patrician robustness like Speilman's, who calls for a good run around the playground to overcome what she calls the 'lumps and bumps' of adolescence. If only that happy ending was so easily achieved for all adolescents without rewriting the whole state school story.

Since their arrival in English state secondary schools in the late 1960s, school counsellors have swum against the stream of education policy. Currently, school counselling is part of 'whole school' approaches, which ideally should mean that the counsellor is part of a system around the child. At its worst, this means watered down 'wellbeing messages' being delivered to the 'whole school' without any counselling professional being employed by the school. While the repeated refrain from 'the educational centre', of whichever political colour, is to improve academic standards, counsellors and others appointed to supporting roles in secondary schools find children and adolescents who are not by anyone's measure 'improved' by their school experience. Adolescents seem to be intransigently marginal to the way in which 'schooling' is conceived, the way the school day is shaped, and especially the way in which school buildings are designed. This may be why school stories for younger audiences in which adolescents are the focus, where adults are secondary and the curriculum is irrelevant are so popular and why stories aimed at an older audience, about the flawed humanity of the adults in charge, persist.

The story which has not been written (yet) is of the children who, in increasing numbers, are absenting themselves from school altogether. The DfE has coined a term for their malaise: emotionally based school avoidance. I have worked with several teenagers who have this designation. The 'emotion' is generated by a combination of the post-pandemic shift in the contract between families and state schools about attendance and students who are increasingly being identified as, or identifying as, beyond the scope of mainstream education. Schools and politicians are rewriting policies on attendance, flailing between threat and support, coercion and seduction. 'Bespoke' plans are formulated for students who cannot or will not tolerate the norms of state secondary school life, but schools are not well enough resourced to fulfil them. This is a long way from 'universal offer' of the 1944 Education Act and is, perhaps, a tipping point in our understanding of education for all. It's not *To Sir, With Love* but we don't yet know what it is.

Favourite school stories

As a final note, I want to comment on the 'favourite school stories' shared by members of my English state-educated family. I invited them to name one or two stories of any genre, time period, nationality or media. Stories of wizard schools, American and Australian high schools, private day and boarding schools and a school for werewolves win out over the largely realist stories that represent 'our schools' and that I've focused on here. It seems we like to dream a little with our after-state school snacks. Education ministers, please take note.

References

Cooper, M.et al (2021) 'Humanistic counselling plus pastoral care as usual versus pastoral care as usual for the treatment of psychological distress in adolescents in UK state schools (EHOS); a randomised controlled trial', *The Lancet: Child & Adolescent Health*, 5(3), pp.178–89.

Eccles, L. (2025) 'Bridget Phillipson: Pupils lose 45 days a year to behaviour crisis', *The Sunday Times*, 31 August.

Eccles, L. and Lintern, S. (2025) 'You're not therapists, schools told in warning of "negative spiral"', *The Sunday Times*, September 28.

Educating Yorkshire (2025) [TV Series], Channel 4, TwoFour.

Pozniak, H. (2020) 'How Covid-19 has fundamentally changed education, and what the future holds', *The Telegraph*, 31 August.

Siegel, D. (2013) *Brainstorm: The Power and Purpose of the Teenage Brain.* London: Scribe.

Weale, S. (2025) 'Covid school closures in UK damaged "very fabric of childhood"', *The Guardian*, 29 September.

Wheeler, C. (2025) 'Age of anxiety: poll reveals teen views on stress, social media and school', *The Sunday Times*, 31 August.

INDEX

For Product Safety Concerns and Information please contact our EU representative GPSR@taylorandfrancis.com Taylor & Francis Verlag GmbH, Kaufingerstraße 24, 80331 München, Germany